WEBSTER'S
SPANISH-ENGLISH
ENGLISH-SPANISH
DICTIONARY

A Quick and Easy Language Reference
for Home, School & Travel

English & Spanish Abbreviations

New, Revised & Expanded Edition

Clear, Easy to Read Typeface

COMPREHENSIVE BILINGUAL DICTIONARY

"The Webster Dictionary is not associated with, or published by, the original publishers of Webster's Dictionary or their successors."

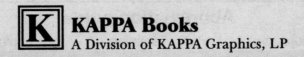

KAPPA Books
A Division of KAPPA Graphics, LP

Visit us at www.kappapublishing.com/kappabooks

English
to
Spanish
Section

Abbreviation guide

adj	adjective	*f*	feminine	*pl*	plural	
adv	adverb	*int*	interjection	*prep*	preposition	
art	article	*m*	masculine	*pro*	pronoun	
conj	conjunction	*n*	noun	*v*	verb	

A

a, art, un, una
abacus, n m, ábaco
abandon, v, abandonar, desamparar
abandoned, adj, abandonado
abandonment, n m, abandonamiento, abandono, desamparo
abbreviate, v, abreviar
abbreviation, n f, abreviación
abdicate, v, abdicar
abhorrence, n, aborrecimiento
ability, n f, habilidad
ably, adv, hábilmente
abnormal, adj, anormal
abolish, v, abolir
abolition, n f, abolición
abominable, adj, abominable
abominate, v, abominar
abound, v, abundar
about, prep, acerca
above, adv, encima
abridge, v, compendiar
abroad, adv, afuera
abrogate, v, abrogar
abrogation, n f, abrogación, casación
absolute, adj, absoluto
absolutely, adv, absolutamente
absolve, v, absolver
absorb, v, absorber
abstain, v, abstenerse
abstinence, n, abstinencia
abstract, v, abstraer
absurd, adj, absurdo
absurdity, n m, absurdo, despropósito
abundance, n f, abundancia
abundance, n m, henchimiento
abundant, adj, abundante
abuse, n m, abuso, maltrato
abuse, v, abusar, maltratar
abyss, n m, abismo
academy, n f, academia
accede, v, acceder

accelerate, v, acelerar
accent, n m, acento
accentuate, v, acentuar
accept, v, aceptar
acceptable, adj, aceptable
acceptance, adj, aceptación
acceptation, n f, acepción
acceptor, n m, aceptador
access, n m, acceso
accessory, adj, accesorio
accessory, n m, accesorio
accident, n m, accidente, lance
acclaim, v, aclamar
acclamation, n f, aclamación
acclimatize, v, aclimatar
accommodate, v, acomodar
accommodation, n m, acomodamiento, acomodo
accompany, v, acompañar
accomplice, n m, cómplice
according to, prep, según
account, n f, cuenta
accredited, adj, acreditado
accumulate, v, acumular
accumulation, n f, acumulación
accumulator, n m, acumulador
accusation, n f, delación
accuse, v, acusar, delatar, inculpar
accuser, n m, delatante, delator
accustom, v, acostumbrar
acetate, n m, acetato
acid, adj, ácido
acid, n m, ácido
acknowledgement, n m, acuse
acorn, n f, bellota
acquainted, adj, sabedor
acquiescence, n f, aquiescencia
acquire, v, adquirir
acquirer, n m, adquiridor
acquisition, n f, adquisición
act, n f, acta
act, n m, acto
act, v, actuar
action, n f, acción, facción, fechoría
active, adj, activo
activity, n f, actividad

actor, n m, actor, cómico
actress, n f, actriz
actual, adj, actual
actuality, n f, actualidad
actually, adv, actualmente
actuation, n f, actuación
acute, adj, lince
acuteness, n f, agudeza
adaptable, adj, inadaptable
adaptation, n f, adaptación
add, v, añadir
addition, n f, adición, añadidura
additional, adj, adiciónal
address, n f, dirección
adept, n m, adepto
adequate, adj, adecuado
adhere, v, adherir, apegar
adjacent, adj, adyacente
adjust, v, ajustar
administer, v, administrar
administration, n f, administración
administrative, adj, administrativo
administrator, n m, administrador
admirable, adj, admirable
admiral, n m, almirante
admiralty, n, almirantazgo
admiration, n f, admiración
admire, v, admirar
admissible, adj, admisible
admission, n f, admisión
admit, v, acoger, admitir
adobe, n f, tapia
adolescent, n m, mancebo
adopt, v, adoptar
adoption, n f, adopción
adored, adj, adorado
adorn, v, adornar, agraciar, ornamentar
adorning, n m, adorno
adult, adj, adulto
adulterate, v, adulterar
adulteration, n f, adulteración
advance, n f, alza
advance, n m, adelanto, anticipo
advance, v, adelantar, despuntar
advantage, n f, ventaja

advantageous, adj, adventajoso
adventure, n f, aventura
adversary, n m, adversario
adverse, adj, adverso
advice, n f, advertencia, amonestación
advise, v, aconsejar, amonestar
advocate, v, abogar
aeration, n f, aeración
aerial, adj, aéreo
aeronautics, n f, aeronáutica
affability, n f, afabilidad
affable, adj, afable, apacible
affect, v, afectar, aficiónar
affectation, n f, afectación
affection, n f, afección, afición
affection, n m, cariño
affectionate, adj, afecto, cariñoso
affirm, v, afirmar
affirmative, adj, afirmativo
afflict, v, afligir, desconsolar
affliction, n f, aflicción
affliction, n m, ahogo, desconsuelo
affluence, n f, afluencia
affront, n f, afrenta
affront, v, afrentar
aforesaid, adj, antedicho
after, prep, tras
afternoon nap, n f, siesta
afternoon, n f, tarde
afterwards, adv, después
agate, n f, ágata
age, n f, edad
agency, n f, agencia
agenda, n f, agenda
agent, n m, agente
aggravate, v, agravar
aggregate, n m, agregado
aggregate, v, agregar
agile, adj, ágil
agitate, v, agitar
agitated, adj, agitado
agitation, n f, agitación
agreeable, adj, agradable
agreement, n f, iguala
agreement, n m, acuerdo, ajuste

agricultural, adj, agrícola
agriculture, n f, agricultura
agriculturist, n m, agrícola, agricultor
aim, n f, mira
aim, v, apuntar
air, n m, aire
airplane, n m, aeroplano
airship, n m, aeróstato
airy, adj, airoso
alabaster, n m, alabastro
alarm clock, n m, despertador
alarm, n f, alarma
alarm, v, alarmar
alarming, adj, alarmante
alcohol, n m, alcohol
alert, adj, alerta
alias, adv, alias
alibi, n f, coartada
alienable, adj, enajenable
alienate, v, enajenar
alienation, n m, desapropio
alienation, n, desapropiación, enajenación
alight, v, apear
all, adv, todo
allegation, n f, alegación
allegation, n m, alegato
allege, v, alegar
alleviation, n m, alivio
alliance, n f, alianza
alligator, n m, caimán
allot, v, adjudicar
allowance, n m, abono
allowance, n, bonificación
allude, v, aludir
allusion, n f, alusión
almanac, n m, almanaque
almost, adv, casi
aloe, n m, aloe
alone, adj, solo
alpaca, n f, alpaca
alphabet, n m, abecedario, alfabeto
alphabetical, adj, alfabético
already, adv, ya
also, adj, también
alter, v, alterar

alteration, n f, alteración
alternate, adj, alternativo
alternate, v, alternar
alternative, n f, alternativa
although, adv, aunque
altitude, n f, altitud
aluminum, n m, aluminio
always, adv, siempre
amateur, n m, aficionado
amazed, adj, absorto
amazement, n m, embeleso
Amazon, n f, Amazona
Amazon, n m, Amazonas
ambassador, n m, embajador
amber, n m, ámbar
ambiguity, n f, ambigüedad
ambiguous, adj, ambiguo
ambition, n f, ambición
ambitious, adj, ambicioso
ambush, n f, emboscada
ambush, v, emboscar
amen, n m, amén
amendable, adj, enmendable
America, n, América
American, adj, americano
amicable, adj, amigable
amicably, adv, amistosamente
amity, n f, amistad
amount, n f, monta
amount, n m, importe, monto
ample, adj, amplio
amplify, v, ampliar, amplificar
amuse, v, divertir, embebecer, recrear
anarchy, n f, anarquia
ancestors, n mpl, antepasados
anchor, n f, ancla
anchor, v, anclar
anchorage, n m, ancladero
anchoring ground, n f, agarradero
anchoring, n m, anclaje
ancient, adj, vetusto
ancient, adv, marras
anciently, adv, antiguamente
and, conj, e, y
anecdote, n f, anécdota

anger, n f, cólera, saña
anger, n m, berrinche, enojo
anger, v, encolerizar
angle, n m, ángulo, recodo
angry, adj, colérico, enojadizo
anguish, n f, angustia, zozobra
animal bell, n m, cascabel
animal, n m, animal
animate, v, animar, encorajar
animated, adj, animado
animation, n, animación
animosity, n, aminosidad
annex, v, anexar
annexed, adj, anejo
annihilate, v, aniquilar
anniversary, n m, aniversario
annotation, n f, anotación
annotation, n m, apunte
announce, v, anunciar
announcement, n m, anuncio
annoy, v, fastidiar
annual, adj, añal, anual
annually, adv, anualmente
annuity, n f, anualidad
annul, v, anular
anoint, v, untar
anonymous, adj, anónimo
another, adj, otro
answer, n f, contestación
answer, v, contestar
antagonist, n f, antagonista
antecedent, n m, antecedente
antechamber, n f, antecámara, antesala
anteport, n f, antepuerto
anticipate the date, v, antefechar
anticipate, v, anticipar, prever
anticipated, adj, adelantado
anticipation, n f, anticipación
antidote, n m, antídoto
antipodes, n mpl, antípodas
antiquated, adj, anticuado, antiguo
antiquity, n f, antigüedad
antithesis, n f, antítesis
anvil, n f, bigornia
anvil, n m, yunque

anxiety, n f, ansia, ansiedad
anxiety, n m, afán
anxious, adj, anheloso, ansioso
apart, adv, aparte
apathetic, adj, apático
apathy, n f, apatía
aperitive, adj, aperitivo
apex, n m, apice
apogee, n m, apogeo
apology, n f, apología
apostle, n m, apóstol
apostrophe, n f, apóstrofe
apothecary, n m, farmacéutico
apparatus, n m, aparato
apparent, adj, aparente
apparition, n f, aparición
appeal, n f, apelación
appeal, v, apelar, interpelar, aparecer
appearance, n f, apariencia
appearance, n m, talante
appease, v, apaciguar
appellant, n m, apelante
appendix, n m, apéndice
appetite, n f, apetencia, gana
appetite, n m, apetito
applaud, v, aplaudir
applause, n m, aplauso
apple tree, n m, manzano
apple, n f, manzana
apple, n m, pomo
applicable, adj, aplicable
application, n f, aplicación
apply, v, aplicar
appoint, v, apalabrar
appointment, n f, cita
appraise, v, evaluar, tasar, valorar
appraisement, n f, tasación
appraisement, n m, aprecio
appraiser, n m, apreciador, tasador
appreciate, v, apreciar
appreciation, n f, apreciación
apprehend, v, aprehender
apprehension, n f, aprehensión, aprensión
apprehensive, adj, aprehensivo,

receloso
apprentice, n m, aprendiz
approach, v, acercar
approbation, n m, beneplácito
appropriate, adj, apropiado
appropriate, v, apropiar
appropriation, n f, apropiación
approval, n f, aprobación
approve, v, aprobar , approximate
approximate, adj, aproximado
approximate, v, aproxirnar
approximation, n f, aproximación
apricot, n m, albaricoque
April, n m, abril
apron, n m, delantal
apt, adj, apto
aptitude, n f, aptitud, idoneidad
aptly, adv, aptamente
aqueduct, n m, acueducto
arabesque, n m, arabesco
arbitrarily, adv, arbitrariamente
arbitrariness, n f, arbitrariedad
arbitrary, adj, arbitrario
arbitrate, v, arbitrar
arbitration, n f, arbitración
arbitration, n m, arbitraje
arbitrator, n m, arbitrador
arbitrator, n m, árbitro,
  compromisario
arbor, n m, emparrado
arc, n m, arco
archduke, n m, archiduque
archdukedom, n m, archiducado
archer, n m, ballestero
archipelago, n m, archipielago
archives, n m, archivo
argue, v, opinar
arithmetic, n f, aritmética
arm sling, n m, cabestrillo
arm, n m, brazo
armchair, n m, sillon
armor, v, blindar
army, n m, ejército
around, adv, alrededor
arrange, v, arreglar
arrival, n f, venida

arrive, v, llegar
arrived, adj, venido
arrow, n f, saeta
arrowroot, n f, maranta
art, n mf, arte
artichoke, n f, alcachofa
article, n m, artículo
artificial, adj, postizo
as, prep, como
asbestos, n m, amianto
ash colored, adj, ceniciento
ashes, n f, ceniza
ask, v, pedir, preguntar
aspect, n f, facha
aspect, n m, viso
ass, n m, borrico
assault, v, agredir
assay (minerals), v, quilatar
assay, n m, ensayo
assay, v, ensayar
assembly, n f, tertulia
assess a tax, v, amillarar
assiduous, adj, hacendoso
assist, v, acudir
associate, v, mancomunar
association, n t, mancomunidad
assure, v, cerciorar
astonish, v, embelesar
Atlantic, n f, Atlántico
attachment, n m, apego
attack, n f, acometida, embestida
attack, v, acometer, embestir
attempt, n f, tentativa
attempt, v, tentar
attention, n f, atención
attenuate, v, adelgazar
attitude, n f, actitud
attorney, n m, mandatario
attraction, n m, aliciente
attractive, adj, llamativo
auction, n f, almoneda, venduta
auctioneer, n m, vendutero
audacious, adj, descompuesto
auger, n f, barrena
auger, n m, barreno
augment, v, engrandecer

August, n m, agosto
aunt, n f, tía
authentic, adj, fehaciente
author, n m, autor
authorize, v, facultar
automobile, n m, automóvil
autumn, n m, otoño
autumnal, adj, otoñal
avalanche, n m, alud
avenge, v, vengar
avenue, n f, avenida
avoid, v, evitar
avoidable, adj, evitable
awful (fearful), adj, pavoroso
awkwardness, n f, desmaña
awning, n m, entoldado
ax, n f, segur, hacha
axis, n m, eje
Aztec, n m, azteca

B

bachelor degree, n m, bachiller
back, n f, zaga
back, n m, dorso
backpack, n f, mochila
bacon, n m, tocino
bad, adj, malo
badge, n f, insignia
badly, adv, mal, malamente
badness, n f, maldad
bag, n f, churla, saca
bag, n m, fardel, zurrón
bag, n mf, talego
baggage, n m, bagaje; equipaje
bailiff, n m, esbirro
baize, n f, bayeta
baize, n m, bayetón
baker, n m, panadero, tahonero
bakery, n f, tahona
balance, n m, alcance, balance
balance, v, abalanzar, balancear
balcony, n m, balcón
bald, adj, calvo
baldness, n f, calvicie
bale, n m, fardo

ball, n f, bala, bola
ball, n m, baile, sarao
ballad, n f, cantinela
balmy, adj, balsámico
balsam, n m, balsarno
balustrade, n f, balaustrada
bamboo, n m, bambú
band, n f, banda, faja
band, n m, zuncho
bandage, n f, fajuela, venda
bandage, v, vendar
bandit, n m, bandido
banker, n m, banquero
banking, adj, bancario
bankruptcy, n f, bancarrota
bankruptcy, n m, quebrado
banner, n f, bandera
banquet, n m, banquete
baptism, n m, bautismo
baptize, v, bautizar
bar, n f, barra, barrilla
barbarity, n f, barbaridad
barbarous, adj, bárbaro
barber, n m, barbero
bare, adj, desprovisto
barefoot, adj, descalzo
bargain, v, regatear
bargaining, n m, regateo
barge, n f, barcaza
bark, v, ladrar
barking, n m, ladrido
barley, n f, cebada
barometer, n m, barometro
barrel, n m, barril, tonel
barrier, n f, barrera, valla
barter, n f, barata
barter, n m, cambalache
barter, v, baratar
barterer, n m, baratista
bartering, adj, cambiante
base, adj, nefando
base, v, basar
basin, n f, jofaina
basin, n m, bacín
basis, n f, base
basket maker, n m, canastero

basket, n f, banasta, canasta
basket, n m, canasto, cesto
baste, v, embastar
bastion, n m, baluarte, bastión
bath, n f, bañera
bath, n m, bañe
bathe, v, bañarse
bathing place, n m, bañadero
bathing, adj, balneario
batiste, n f, batista
battalion, n m, batallón
battery, n f, batería
battle, n f, batalla, pelea
battle, v, batallar
bay, adj, bayo
bay, n f, bahía
bayonet, n f, bayoneta
bazaar, n m, bazar
be, v, estar
beach, n f, playa
beacon, n f, valiza
beadle, n m, bedel
beak, n m, pico
beam of wood, n m, madera
beam, n f, viga
beam, n m, bao
bean, n f, haba
bear, n m, oso
beard, n f, barba
bearer, n m, dador
beast, n f, bestia
beat (as a heart), v, latir
beat, v, batir, majar
beaten, adj, batido
beautiful, adj, bello, hermoso
beautify, v, hermosear
beauty, n f, beldad, belleza, hermosura
beauty, n m, primor
because, conj, porque
become, v, hacerse
bed, n m, catre, lecho
bedroom, n f, alcoba
bedroom, n m, dormitorio
bee hive, n f, colmena
bee, n f, abeja

beer, n f, cerveza
beet, n f, acelga
before, adv, ante
before, prep, antes
beforehand, adv, antemano
begin, v, comenzar, incoar, principiar
beginning, adj, incipiente
beginning, n f, comienzo, principio
behave, v, comportarse
behavior, n f, comportamiento
behead, v, degollar, descabezar
beheaded, adj descabezado
behind, adj, trasero
behind, adv, detras
being, n m, ser
believe, v, creer
bell shaped, adj, campanudo
bell, n f, campana
bell sound, n f, campanada
belladonna, n f, belladama
belligerent, adj, beligerante
belly, n f, barriga
belly, n m, vientre
belong, v, pertenecer
beloved, adj, amado, querido
below, prep, debajo
belt, n m, cincho, cinto, cinturon
bench, n f, bancaza
bench, n m, banco
bend, n f, comba
bend, v, bornear, combar
benefactor, n m, bienhechor
beneficial, adj, beneficioso
beneficiary, n m, beneficiario
benefit, n m, beneficio
benefit, v, beneficiar
benevolence, n f, benevolencia
benevolent, adj, benevolo
benign, adj, benigno
bent, adj, corvo
benzine, n f, bencina
bequeath, v, legar
berry, n f, baya
berth, n m, camarote
best, adj, óptimo

bet, n f, apuesta
bet, v, apostar
between, prep, entre
bevel, v, achaflanar
bewitch, v, hechizar
beyond, adv, allende
Bible, n f, biblia
bicarbonate, n m, bicarbonate
bicycle, n f, bicicleta
bicycle, n m, velocipedo
bier, n m, féretro
bill of exchange, n m, cambial
bind, v, vincular
binding, n f, encuadernación
binocular, adj, binocular
binoculars, n m, binóculo
biography, n f, biografía
biped, n m, bípedo
biplane, n m, biplano
bird, n f, pájaro
bird, n m, pájara
birth, n m, nacimiento
birthday, n m, cumpleaños, natal
biscuit, n m, bizcocho
bishop, n m, obispo
bits, n mpl, añicos
bitter, adj, amargo
bitterness, n f, amargura
black, adj, negro
blackberry, n f, zarzamora
blackbird, n f, merla
blackbird, n m, mirlo
blackboard, n f, pizarra
blacken, v, denegrecer, denigrar, ennegrecer
bladder, n f, vejiga
blamable, adj, delatable
blame, v, culpar
blaspheme, v, blasfemar
blaspheming, n f, blasfemia
blazon, v, blasonar
bleach, v, blanquear
bleacher, n f, blanqueador
bleaching, n m, blanqueo
bleed, v, sangrar
blemish, n f, mancilla

blemish, v, mancillar
blessed, adj, bendito
blind, adj, ciego, obcecado
blind, n m, blindaje
blind, v, obcecar
blindly, adv, cegarrita, ciegamente
blindness, n f, ceguera
block, n m, bloque, calzo, zoquete
blockade, n m, bloqueo
blockade, v, bloquear
blockhead, n m, zopenco
blond, adj, rubio
blood, n f, sangre
bloodhound, n m, sabueso
blot, n m, borrón
blotted, adj, borroso
blouse, n f, blusa
blow, n m, golpe
blow, v, ventear
blue, adj, azul
blunt, v, embotar
bluntness, n f, embotamiento
boar, n m, verraco
board a ship, v, abordar
board, n f, tabla
board, n m, bordo, tablero
boarding a ship, n m, abordaje
boast, n f, chufa
boast, v, jactarse, ufanarse
boasting, n f, jactancia
boat load, n f, barcada
boat, n f, barca
boat, n m, barco, bote
boatman, n m, barquero
bobbin, n f, bobina
boil, v, hervir
boiled, adj, cocido
boiling, adj, hirviente
bold, adj, denodado, descarado
boldly, adv, denodadamente, descaradamente
boldness, n f, osadía
bolt, n m, cerrojo
bombard, v, bombardear
bombardment, n m, bombardeo
bone, n f, canilla

bonfire, n f, hoguera
bonnet shop, n f, bonetería
bonnet, n f, capota
bonnet, n m, bonete
book, n m, libro
bookkeeping, n f, teneduría
borax, n m, bórax, borraj
border, adj, cenefa
border, n m, borde
border, v, orlar
bore, n m, taladro
bore, v, barrenar, taladrar
bosom, n m, seno
botanic, adj, botánico
botch, v, chapucear
both, adj, ambos
both, pro, entrambos
bottle, n f, botella
bottle, v, embotellar
bottom, n m, fondo
bound, adj, ligado
boundary, n f, meta
bovine, adj, vacuno
bow, n m, lazo
bowl, n m, cuenco
box, v, encajonar
boy, n m, chico, muchacho, niño
braggart, n m, jaque
brain, n m, cerebro
brake, n f, retranca
bramble, n f, zarza
bran, n m, salvado
branch off, v, bifurcarse
branch, n f, bifurcación, rama
branch, n m, bifurcamiento, ramo
brand, v, tildar
brandish, v, blandir
brandy, n m, aguardiente
brass, n m, latón
brave man, n m, valiente
brave, adj, animoso
bravery, n f, guapeza
Brazil, n f, Brasil
bread roll, n m, panecillo
bread, n m, pan
break, v, quebrantar, quebrar,

romper
breaker, n m, quebrantador
breakfast, n m, almuerzo, desayuno
breakfast, v, almorzar, desayunarse
breast, n m, pecho
breath, n m, aliento, halite
breathe, v, alentar, respirar
breathing, respiración
breeches, n mpl, calzón
brewery, n f, cervecería
bribe, v, cohechar
bribery, n m, cohecho
brick, n m, ladrillo
brickwork, n f, enladrillado
bridle, v, embridar, enfrenar
brief, adj, lacónico
brig, n m, bergantín
bright reddish color, adj, bermejo
brine, n f, salmuera
bring, v, aportar, traer
bristly, adj, cerdoso
brittle, adj, deleznable, quebradizo,
   vidrioso
broad, adj, ancho
broiled steak, n f, carbonada
broken, adj, cascado, quebrado, rota
broker, n m, cambista, prendero
broth, n m, caldo
brother, n m, hermano
brotherhood, n f, hermandad
brown, adj, bazo, castaño
bruise, n m, magullamiento
bruise, v, magullar
brush, n m, cepillo
bubble out, v, borbollar
bubbling, n m, borbollón
bucket, n m, balde, pozal
buckle, n f, hebilla
buffet, n f, bofetada
buffet, n m, aparador
bug, n f, chinche
build, v, construir
bulb, n f, bombilla
bulk, n m, tomo
bulky, adj, abultado
bull, n m, toro

bullfight, n f, corrida de toros
bully, n m, fanfarrón
bump, n f, calabazada
bundle, n m, envoltorio, fajo, manojo
burden, n m, cargo
burden, v, gravar
Burgundy, n f, borgoña
burial, n m, mortuorio
burn, n f, quemadura
burn, v, abrasar, arder, quemar
burning, adj, ardiendo
burr, n f, bardana
bury, v, enterrar
bush, n f, mata
business, n m, negocio, oficio
busybody, n f, entremetido
but, conj, sino, mas, pero
butcher, n m, carnicero
butler, n m, bodeguero
butter, n f, manteca, mantequilla
butterfly, n f, mariposa
buttock, n f, nalga
button, v, abotonar, abrochar
buttress, n m, machón
buy, v, comprar
buyer, n m, tomador
buzz, v, zurriar

C

cabbage, n f, berza, col
cabin, n f, cabaña
cabinet, n m, gabinete
cable, n f, amarra
cable, n m, cable, calabrote
cable, v, cablear, cablegrafiar
cablegram, cablegrama
cackle, n m, cacareo
cackle, v, cacarear
cactus, n m, cacto
caddy, n f, caja para té
cadence, n f, cadencia
cadet, n m, cadete
caffeine, n f, cafeína
cage, n f, jaula
cage, v, enjaular

cajole, v, embromar
cake, n f, pastilla, torta
caked, adj, aplastado
calamine, n f, calamina
calamitous, adj, calamitoso
calamity, n f, calamidad
calash, n f, calesa
calculate, v, calcular
calculating, adj, astuto
calculation, n f, calculación
calculation, n m, cálculo
calculator, n m, calculador
caldron, n f, caldera
calendar, n m, calendario
calf leather, becerrillo
calf, n m, ternero
calibre, n m, calibre
calico, n m, calicó
caligraphy, n f, caligrafía
calk, v, calafatear
calker, n m, calafate
calking, n m, calafateo
call out, v, evocar
call upon, v, visitar
call, n f, llamada
call, v, llamar
calling, n f, profesión
calm, adj, sereno
calm, n f, calma
calm, v, tranquilizar
calumnious, adj, calumnioso
calvary, n m, calvario
camel, n m, camello
cameo, n m, camafeo
camera, n f, cámara
camp, n m, campo
campaign, n f, campaña
can, n f, lata
can, n m, jarro
canal, n f, acequia
canary, n m, canario
cancel, v, cancelar
cancellation, cancelación
cancer, n m, cáncer
cancerous, adj, canceroso
candid, adj, cándido

candidate, v, candidato
candies, n mpl, dulces
candle, n f, candela, vela
candlestick, n m, candelabro, candelero, cirial
candor, n m, candor
candy store, n f, confitería
candy, n m, caramelo
cane, n f, bengala, rejilla
cane, n m, bastón
canine tooth, n m, colmillo
canine, adj, canino
cannibal, n f, caníbal
cannon, n m, cañón
canoe, n f, almadia, canoa
canopy, n m, dosel
cant, n m, caló
canteen, n f, cantina
canvas, n m, cañamazo
cap, n f, boina, gorra
cap, n m, birrete, casquillo
capable, adj, capaz
capacity, n f, capacidad
cape, n f, capa
capital, adj, capital
capital, n f, capital, mayúscula
capital, n m, capitel
capitalist, n m, capitalista
capitalize, v, capitalizar
capitol, n m, capitolio
capitulate, v, capitular
capitulation, n f, capitulación
capon, n m, capón
caprice, n m, capricho
capricious, adj, caprichoso
capsule, n f, cápsula
captain, n m, capitán
captivate, v, captar, encantar
captive, n m, cautivo
capture, n f, toma
capture, n m, apresamiento
capture, v, captura, cautivar
car, n m, vagón
carat (gemology), n m, quilate
caravan, n f, caravana
caravel, n f, carabela

caraway seed, n f, alcaravea
carbine, n f, carabina
carbon, n m, carbón
carbonate, n m, carbonate
carbonic, adj, carbónico
carburetor, n m, carburador
card (wool), n f, carda
card board, n f, cartulina
card maker, n m, cardero
card trick, n f, baza
card, n f, carta, tarjeta
cardboard, n m, cartón
cardinal, n m, cardenal, cardinal
care, n m, cuidado
career, n f, carrera
careful, adj, cuidadoso
carefully, adv, cuidadosamente
careless, adj, descuidado, parado
carelessly, adv, descuidadamente
carelessness, n m, desaliño, descuido
caress, n f, caricia
cargo, n f, carga
cargo, n m, cargamento, carguío
caricature, n f, caricatura
carmelite, n f, mi, carmelita
carmine, n m, carmín
carnage, n f, carnicería
carnation, n m, clavel
carnival, n m, carnaval
carnivorous, adj, carnívoro
carp, n f, carpa
carpenter, n f, carpintero
carpentry, n f, carpintería
carpet maker, n m, alfombrero
carpet, n f, alfombra
carriage, n f, carro
carriage, n m, acarreo, carruaje, coche
carrier, n m, acarreador, arriero, trajinero
carrot, n f, zanahoria
carry, v, llevar, portar, traunar
cart, n f, carreta
cartage, n m, camionaje
carter, n m, carretero

cartridge box, n f, cartuchera
cartridge, n m, cartucho
carving block (for meat), n m, tajadero
carving knfe (for meat), n f, tajadera
cascade, n f, cascada
case, n f, caja
cash, n m, dinero
cashier, n m, cajero
cashmere, n f, cachemira
casino, n m, casino
cask, n f, barriquita
casket, n f, cajita
casque, n m, casquete
cassia, n f, cañafístula
cast, n f, tirada
cast, n m, vaciado
cast, v, tiro
castanet, n f, castañeta, castañuela
caste, n f, casta
Castilian, adj, castellano
castle, n m, alcázar, castillo
castor, n m, castor
casual, adj, casual, venturero
casually, adv, casualmente
casualty, n f, casualidad
cat, n m, gato
cataclysm, n f, cataclismo
catacombs, n fpl, catacumbas
catalog, n m, catálogo
catapult, n f, catapulta
cataract, n f, catarata
catastrophe, n f, catástrote
catch, v, coger
catching, n f, cogida
catechism, n m, catecisrno
catechize, v, catequizar
categorical, adj, categórico
category, n f, categoría
caterpillar, n f, oruga
cathedral, n f, catedral
cathode, n m, polo negativo
catholic, adj, católico
cattle, n m, ganado
cauliflower, n m, coliflor
cause, n f, causa

cause, v, causar, irrogar
causeway, n f, calzada
causing, adj, causante
caustic, adj, cáustico
cauterize, v, cauterizar
caution, n f, cautela
caution, n m, recato
cautious, adj, cauto
cautiously, adv, cautamente
cave, n f, cueva
cavern, n f, caverna, gruta
cavity, n f, cavidad
cease, v, cesar, vacar
cedar, n m, cedro
cede, v, ceder
ceiling, n m, techo
celebrate, v, celebrar
celebrated, adj, afamado, célebre
celebration, n f, celebración
celery, n m, apio
celestial, adj, celeste
cell, n f, celda
cellar, n f, cava
Celt, n m, Celta
cement, n m, ceento, cimento
cemetery, n m, cementerio
censure, n f, censura
censure, v, censurar, motejar, tachar
census, n m, censo
cent, n m, centavo, ciento
center, n m, centro
centime, n m, céntimo
central, adj, central, céntrico
centrifugal, adj, centrífugo
century, n f, centuria
century, n m, siglo
ceramic, adj, cerámico
cereal, adj, cereal
cereals, n mpl, cereales
ceremony, n f, ceremonia
certain, adj, cierto
certainly, ciertamente
certainty, n f, certeza
certificate, n f, certificación
certificate, n m, certificado

certified, adj, certificado
certify, v, certificar
cessation, n f, anulación, cesación
cession, n f, cesión
chafing dish, n f, chofeta
chagrin, n f, pesadumbre
chain stitch, n f, cageneta
chain, n f, cadena, urdimbre
chain, v, encadenar
chair, n f, silla
chalice, n m, cáliz
chalk, n f, greda, tiza
chalk, n m, yeso
challenge, n m, desafío, reto
challenge, v, recusar, retar
chamber, n f, cámara
chameleon, n m, camaleón
chamois, n f, gamuza
champagne, n f, champaña
champion, n m, campeón
championship, n m, campeonato
chance, n f, ventura
chance, n m, acaso, acierto
chancellor, n m, canciller
change, n f, mudanza
change, n m, cambiamiento
change, v, cambiar
changeless, adj, constante
channel, n m, canal
channel, n m, desaguadero, desaguador
channel, v, acanalar
chant, n m, canto
chant, v, cantar
chaos, n m, caos
chapel, n f, capilla
chapter, n m, capítulo
char, v, carbonizar
character, n f, calaña
character, n m, caracter
characteristic, adj, caracteristico
characteristic, n f, caracteristica
characteristic, n m, caracteristico
charcoal maker, n m, carbonero
charcoal, n m, carbón de leña
charge, n f, reconvención

charge, n m, acusación, adeudo, encargo
charge, v, reconvenir
charitable, adj, caritativo
charity, n f, caridad
charlatan, n m, charlatan
charm, n m, encanto
charming, adj, encantador
chase, n f, caña, caza
chasm, n f, abertura
chastise, v, castigar
chastity, n f, castidad
chat, n f, charla
chat, v, charlar
chattels, n mpl, enseres
cheap, adj, barato
cheapen, v, abaratar, baratear
cheapening, n f, abaratamiento
cheapness, n f, baratura
cheat, n m, petardo, trampista
check, n m, pagaré
checkbook, n m, libro de pólizas, talonario
cheek, n f, mejilla
cheek, n m, carrillo
cheer, n m, aplauso
cheerful, adj, alegre
cheerfulness, n f, desenvoltura
cheese, n m, queso
cheesemaker, n m, quesero
chemical, adj, químico
chemise, n m, hipil
chemist, n m, químico
chemistry, n f, química
cherish, v, mantener
cherry tree, n m, cerezo
cherry, n f, cereza
chess, n m, ajedrez
chessboard, n m, jaquel
chest, n f, arca
chest of drawers, n f, cómoda
chestnut tree, n m, castaño
chestnut, n f, castaña
chew, v, mascar
chicken, n m, pollo
chief, adj, principal

chief, n m, jefe
child birth, n m, alumbramiento
child's cap, n m, capillo
child, n m, hijo
childish, adj, pueril
chill, n m, frío
chime, n m, carillón, repique
chime, v, repicar
chin, n f, barbilla
china, n f, china, porcelana
Chinaman, n m, chino
chinchilla, n f, chinchilla
Chinese, adj, chinesco
chip, n f, astilla
chirp, n m, chirrido
chisel, n m, cincel
chisel, v, cincelar
chivalry, n f, caballería
chlorate, n m, clorato
chloric, adj, clórico
chloride, n m, cloruro
chlorine, n m, cloro
chloroform, n f, cloroformo
chocolate, n m, chocolate
choice, n f, preferencia
choose, v, escoger, optar
chop, n f, chuleta
chough, n f, chova
Christ, n m, Cristo
Christian, adj, cristiano
Christmas Day, n f, Navidad
Christmas Eve, n f, Nochebuena
Christmas tree, n m, árbol de
  Navidad
chronic, adj, crónico
chrysanthemum, n m, crisantemo
chubby, adj, mofletudo
church, n f, iglesia
cider, n f, sidra
cigar case, n f, cigarrera
cigar seller, n m, cigarrero
cigar, n m, cigarro
cigarette butt, n f, colilla
cigarette, n f, cigarrillo, pitillo
cinnabar, n m, cinabrio
cinnamon, n f, canela

cipher, n f, cifra
cipher, v, cifrar
circle, n m, círculo
circle, v, circular
circuit, n m, circuito
circular, adj, circular
circulating, adj, circulante
circulation, n f, circulación
circumference, n f, circunferencia
circumference, n m, derredor, giro
circumnavigate, v, circunnavegar
circumscribe, circunscribir
circumspect, adj, circunspecto
circumstance, n f, circunstancia
circumstantial, adj, circunstanciado
circus, n m, circa
cistern, n f, cisterna
cistern, n m, aljibe
citadel, n f, ciudadela
citation, n f, citación
citizen, n m, ciudadano
citizenship, n f, ciudadanía
citrate, n m, citrato
citron, n f, cidra
city, n f, ciudad
civil, adj, civil, comedido
civility, n f, civilidad
civilization, n f, civilización
civilize, v, civilizar
civilized, adj, civilizado
civilly, adv, civilmente
claimant, n mf, demandante
clamor, n m, clamor
clamor, v, clamorear
clamorous, adj, clamoroso
clandestine, adj, clandestino
claret, n m, clarete
clarify, v, clarificar
clarinet, n m, clarinete
clarion, n m, clarín
clasp, n m, corchete, gafete
class, n f, clase
class, v, clasificar
classical, adj, clásico
classification, n f, clasificación
clause, n f, cláusula

claw, n f, garfa, garra, zarpa
claw, v, arranar
clay, n f, arcilla
clay, n m, barro
clean, adj, limpio, mondo
clean, v, limpiar, mondar
cleaner, n m, sacamanchas
cleanliness, n f, limpieza
cleanse, v, depurar, enjuagar
clear, adj, claro, raso
clear, v, aclarar, serenar
clearly, adv, claramente
clearness, n f, claridad
clearness, n m, claro
clemency, n f, clemencia
clench, v, remachar
clergy, n m, clero
clergyman, n m, clérigo
clerical, adj, clerical
clerk, n m, amanuense, dependiente
clever, adj, hábil
client, n m, cliente
clientele, n f, clientela
climate, n m, clima
climax, n m, clímax
climb, v, trepar
clinic, n f, clínica
clinical, adj, clínico
cloak, n m, capote
cloak, v, encapotar
cloaked, adj, encapado
clockmaker, n m, relojero
clog, n m, chanclo
cloister, n f, clausura
cloister, n m, claustra
close in, v, encerrar
close, adj, cerrado
close, n m, fenecimiento
close, v, cerrar, rematar
closet, n m, retrete
closing, adj, terminante
closing, n m, cierre
Cloth, n f, tela
cloth, n m, pañete, paño
clothe, v, vestir
clothes, n f, ropa, vestimenta

cloud, n f, nube
cloud, v, anublar
clown, n m, bufón
clue, n m, ovilla
coach, v, enseñar
coachman, n m, cochero
coal house, n f, carbonera
coal yard, n f, carbonería
coal, adj, carbonífero
coarse silk, n m, cadarzo
coast, n f, costa
coasting, n m, cabotaje
coat, n m, hábito
coax, v, mimar
cobalt, n m, cobalto
cobweb, n f, telaraña
cock, n m, gallo
cocoa, adj, coco
cocoa, n m, cacao
coconut fiber, n f, copra
coconut, n m, coco
cocoon, n m, capullo
code, n m, código
codfish, n m, abadejo, bacalao
codicil, n m, codicilo
coerce, v, refrenar
coercion, n f, coacción, coerción
coffee plantation, n m, cafetal
coffee pot, n f, cafetera
coffee, n m, café
coffin, n f, ataúd
cohesive, adj, cohesivo
coin, v, acuñar, amonedar
coinage, n m, monedaje
coincide, v, coincidir
colander, n m, coladero
cold meat, n m, fiambre
cold, adj, frío, fiambre
cold, n m, catarro, resfriado
coliseum, n m, coliseo
collaboration, n f, colaboración
collaborator, n m, colaborador
collapse, n m, colapso
collar, n f, collera
collate, v, comparar
collateral, adj, colateral

collation, n f, colación
colleague, n m, colega
collect, v, allegar, cobrar
collection, n f, cobranza
collection, n f, colección
collection, n m, cobro
collective, adj, colectivo
collector, n m, cobrador
college, n m, colegio
collide, v, chocar
collision, n f, colisión
colloquy, n m, coloquio
collusion, n f, colusión
colonel, n m, coronel
colonist, n m, colono
color, n m, color
color, v, colorar, matizar
colored red, adj, colorado
colored, adj, pintado, pinto
colorless, adj, incoloro
colossal, adj, colosal
column, n f, columna
comb one's hair, v, peinar
comb, n m, peine
combat, n m, combate
combat, v, combatir
combination, n f, combinación
combine, v, combinar
combustion, n f, quemazón
come back, v, volver
come down, v, bajar
come, v, venir
comedy, n f, comedia
comet, n m, cometa
comform, v, conformar
comfort, n f, confortación
comfortable, adj, acomodado
comfortable, adj, cómodo
comical, adj, cómico
comma, n f, coma
command, n f, comandancia
command, n m, mando
command, n mf, orden
command, v, comandar, imperar, mandar
commander, n f, comandante

commence, v, decentar
comment, n m, comento
comment, v, comentar
commentary, n m, comentario
commerce, n m, comercio
commercial, adj, comercial
commission, n f, comisión, encomienda
commission, n m, cometido
commission, v, comisionar
commit, v, cometer
committee, n m, comité
commodity, n f, comodidad
common, adj, común
commonly, adv, comúnmente
communicate, v, comunicar
communication, n f, comunicación
communication, n m, escrito
communion, n f, comunión
community, n f, comunidad
commute, v, conmutar
commuter train, n m, tranvia
compact, adj, compacta
companion, n m, compañero
company, n f, compañía
comparable, adj, comparable
compare, v, carear
compasionate, adj, compasivo
compassion, n f, compasión
compatibility, n f, compatibilidad
compel, v, compeler, precisar
compensate, v, compensar, recarsir
compete, v, competir, concurrir
competent, adj, competente
competition, n f, concurrencia
compile, v, compilar
complain, v, aquejar, quejarse
complaining, adj, quejumbroso
complaint, n f, queja, querella
complaint, n m, quejido
complete, adj, completo
complete, v, afinar, completar
completion, n f, acabamiento
complex, adj, complejo, complexo
complexion, n f, tez
compliance, n f, anuencia

complicate, v, complicar
complicated, adj, complicado
complicity, n f, complicidad
compliment, n m, parabién
comply, v, acceder
compose, v, componer
composer, n m, componedor
composition, n f, composición
compositor, n m, cajista
compound, n m, compuesto
comprehend, v, comprender
comprehension, n f, comprensión
comprise, v, englobar
compromise, comprometer
compromise, n m, compromiso
compulsory, adj, coactivo
computation, n m, tanteo
compute, v, computar
computer, n f, computista
comrade, n m, camarada
concave, adj, cóncavo
conceal, v, encubrir, ocultar, zampar
concealment, n m, encubrimiento
concede, v, conceder
conceivable, adj, concebible
conceive, v, concebir
concentrate, v, concentrar
concerned, adj, apesadumbrado
concert, n m, concierto
concise, adj, conciso
conclude, v, concluir
conclusion, n m, desenlace, remate
concrete, adj, concreto
condemn, v, condenar
condensation, n f, condensación
condition, adj, acondicionado
condition, n f, condición
conditional, adj, condicional
conduct, n f, conducta, gestión
conduct, v, conducir
conductor's baton, n f, batuta
cone, n m, cono
confer, v, confem
conference, n f, conferencia
confess, v, confesar
confession, n m, confesión

confidence, n f, confianza
confine, v, limitar
confirm, v, confirmar
confiscate, v, comisar, contiscar, decomisar
conflict, n f, lid
confraternity, n f, cofradía
confront, v, confrontar
confrontation, n m, careo
confusion, n f, behetría
congeal, v, helar
congestion, n f, congestión
congratulate, v, felicitar
congratulation, n f, enhorabuena, felicitación
conjecture, n m, barrunto
conjecture, v, barruntar
conjure, v, conjurar
connection, n m, conexión
conquer, v, conquistar, vencer
conqueror, n f, conquistador
conquest, n f, conquista
conscience, n f, conciencia
conscientious, adj, concienzudo
consent, n m, consentimiento
consent, v, consentir
conservation, n f, conservación
conserve, v, conservar
consider, v, considerar, mirar
considerate, adj, considerado, mirado
consideration, n m, miramiento
consign, v, consignar
consist, v, consistir
consistent, adj, consistente
conspicuous, adj, conspicuo
conspiracy, n f, conspiración
conspire, v, conspirar
constable, n m, alguacil
constancy, n f, constancia
constituent, n m, comitente
constrain, v, constreñir
constraint, n f, constreñimiento
construction, n f, construcción
consult, v, consultar
consume, v, desgastar

contact, n m, contacto
contain, v, contener
container, n m, recipiente
contemporary, adj, coetáneo
contempt, n f, vilipendio
contemptible, adj, despreciable
content, adj, contento
contents, n m, contenido
contest, n f, altercación
context, n m, contexto
contiguous, adj, colindante, lindero
continent, n f, continente
continual, adj, continuo
contour, n m, cantorno
contract, n m, contrato, pacto
contract, v, pactar
contrary, adj, contrario
contrast, n m, contraste
control, n m, gobierno
controversy, n m, certamen
convalescent, adj, convaleciente
convene, v, aplazar
convenient, adj, conveniente
conveniently, adv, apropiadamente, cómodamente
converge, v, convergir
conversation, n f, conversación, plática
converse, v, converso, platicar
convert, v, convertir
convocation, n m, aplazamiento
cook, n f, cocinera
cook, n m, cocinero
cook, v, cocinar, guisar
cool, adj, cachazudo
cool, v, enfriar, entibiar, resfriar
cooler, n f, garapiñera
coolness, n m, desapego
cooperate, v, cooperar
copier, n m, copiador
copious, adj, copioso
copper coin, n f, blanca
copper, n m, calderón, cobre
copy, n f, copra
copy, n m, traslado
copy, v, copiar, remedar

copyist, n m, copista
coral, n m, coral
cord, n m, cordel, torzal
cord, v, acordonar
corded, adj, acordonado
cordial, adj, cordial
core, n f, pepita
cork, n m, corcho, tapón
corkscrew, n f, sacacorchos
corn cob, n f, mazorca
corn field, n m, maizal
corn, n f, maíz
corn, n m, grano
corner, n f, ángulo
cornmeal, n f, maizena
coroner, n m, juez fiscal
corporal, n m, caporal
corps, n m, cuerpo
corpse, n m, cadáver
correct, adj, correcto
correct, v, corregir, enmendar
correction, n enmendación, enmienda
correspond, v, cartearse, corresponder
corridor, n m, corredor
corrode, v, corroer
corrupt, adj, corrupto, ímprobo
corrupt, v, empodrecer
corset, n m, corsé
cost, n m, precio
costly, adv, costoso
cotton plant, n m, algodonal
cotton, n m, algodón, cotón
couch, n f, cama
couch, n m, canapé
cough, n f, tos
cough, v, toser
count, n m, conde
count, v, contar
counterpoint, n m, contrapunto
country house, n f, casería, quinta
country, n m, país
county, n m, distrito
couple, n f, yunta
courage, n m, valor

courageous, adj, valiente
course, n f, corrida
course, n m, curso
court, n f, corte, curia
court, n m, corte, cortejo
courteous, adj, cortés
cousin (female only), n f, prima
cousin (male only), n m, primo
cover, n f, cobertura, cubierta
cover, v, cobijar, cubrir, tapar
cover one's face, v, embozar
cover with a hood, v, encapuchar
coverlet, n f, colcha
coverlet, n m, cobertor
covert, adj, cubierto
covet, v, codiciar
covetousness, n f, codicia
covey (birds), n f, bandada
cow, n f, ternera, vaca
coward, n mf, cobarde
cowardice, n f, cobardía
cowardly, adj, cobarde
cowhide, n f, vaqueta
cowl, n f, capucha
crab, n m, cangrejo
crack, v, cascar, chasquear, hender
craft, n m, arte
cram, v, embocar
cramp, n m, calambre
cranberry, n f, arándano
crane, n f, grúa
crane, n m, pescante
crank, adj, cigüeña
crash, n m, estallido
crash, v, fracaso
crate, n f, jaba
cravat, n f, chalina
crave, v, rogar
crayon, n m, clarión, lapíz
crazy, adj, loco
creak, v, rechinar
cream, n f, nata
create, crear
creature, n f, criatura
credible, adj, creíble
credit, n m, crédito

credit, v, acreditar, bonificar
creditor, n m, acreedor
creek, n f, cala
creek, n f, ensenada
crest, n f, cresta
crest, n m, copete
crestfallen, adj, cabizbajo
crevice, n f, grieta, rendija
crib, n m, pesebre
cricket, n m, grillo
criminal, n m, reo
crimson, adj, carmesí
cripple, v, baldar
crockery, n m, vidriado
crocodile, n m, cocodrilo
cross, n f, cruz
cross, v, atravesar, cruzar
crossroads, n f, encrucijada
crow, n f, cuerva
crow, n m, cuervo
crowd, n f, apretura, turba
crowd, n m, apretamiento, aprieto, gentío
crowd, v, agolparse
crown, n f, corona
crucifix, n m, crucifijo
crude, adj, crudo
cruel, adj, cruel
cruise, n m, corso
crumb, n f, miaja, miga
crumble, v, desmenuzar
crunch, v, machacar
crusade, n f, cruzada
crush, v, abrumar, chafar, triturar
crushed, adj, molido
cry out, v, clamar
cry, v, gritar
crypt, n f, cripta
crystal, n m, cristal
cube, n m, cubo
cuckoo, n m, cucú
cucumber, n m, cohombro, pepino
cuddle, v, abrazar
cudgel, n f, cachiporra
cudgel, n m, garrote
cult, n m, culto

cultivate, v, cultivar, laborear
cultivation of trees, n f, arboricultura
culture, n f, cultura
cumin plant, n m, comino
cunning, adj, ladino
cup, n f, copa, taza
cup, v, taza
cupid, n m, amor
curator, n m, celador
cure, n f, cura
cure, v, curar
curiosity, n f, curiosidad
curious, adj, curioso
curl, v, encrespar
curling iron, n m, encrespador
currant, n f, grosella
curry, v, zurrar
curse, n f, maldición
curse, v, maldecir
cursed, adj, maldito
curtain, n f, cortina
curve, n f, corva
curve, v, encorvar
cushion, n m, cojín, cojinete
custom, n f, costumbre
customs officer, n m, aduanero
customs' tariff, n m, arancel
cut oneself, v, cortarse
cut out, v, escotar
cut, n f, gema, taja
cut, n m, tajo
cut, v, cortar, tajar, tallar
cycle, n m, ciclio
cycling, n m, ciclismo
cyclist, n f, biciclista
cyclist, n m, ciclista
cylinder, n m, cilindro
cylinder, v, cilindrar
cylindrical, adj, cilíndrico
cymbal, n m, címbalo
cynic, n m, cínico
cynical, adj, cínico
cypress tree, n m, ciprés
czar, n m, czar

D

dagger, n f, daga
dagger, n m, puñal
daily, adv, diariamente
dairy, n f, vaquería
daisy, n f, margarita
dance, n f, danza
dance, v, bailar, danzar
dancer, n m, bailador
dancer, n mf, danzante
dare, v, atreverse, osar
daring, adj, osado
dark red, adj, granate
dark, adj, prieto
darken, v, anieblar, ofuscar
darkness, n f, cerrazón, tiniebla
dart, n m, dardo
data, n mpl, datos
date (fruit), n m, dátil
date, n f, data, fecha
date, v, datar, fechar
daub, v, embarrar
daughter, n f, hija
dauntless, adj, impávido
dawn, n f, alba, madrugada
dawn, v, amanecer
day, n m, día
dazzle, v, deslumbrar, encandilar
dead, adj, finado, muerto
deadbolt, pasador
deafen, v, ensordecer
deafness, n f, ensordecimiento
dear, adj, caro
dearly, adv, caro
death, n f, defunción, muerte
debate, n m, debate
debate, v, debatir
debilitate, v, debilitar
debilitation, n f, debilitación
debility, n f, debilidad
debit, n m, débito
debt free, adj, desempeñado
debt, n f, deuda
debtor, n m, debe, deudor
debtor, n mf, debiente
decade, n f, década
decagram, n f, m, decagramo

decameter, n f, m, decámetro
decamp, v, decampar
decant, v, decantar
decay, n f, decadencia, mengua
decay, v, decaer, desmedrar,
  menguar
decease, n f, m, fallecimiento
deceased, adj, fallecido
deceitful, adj, delusorio, tramposo
deceive, v, alucinar, embaucar,
  engañar
December, n m, diciembre
decency, n f, decencia
decent, adj, decente
decently, adv, decentemente
deception, n f, decepción
decide, v, decidir
decigram, n m, decigramo
deciliter, n m, decilitro
decimal, adj, decimal
decimeter, n m, decímetro
decipher, v, descifrar
decision, n f, decisión
decisive, adj, decisivo
declaim, v, declamar
declamation, n f, declamación
declaration, n f, declaración
declare, v, declarar
declared, adj, declarado
declarer, n m, declarante
declination, n f, declinación
decline, v, declinar
declining, adj, decadente
decompose, v, descomponer
decomposition, n f, descomposición
decorate, v, decorar, ornar
decoration, n f, decoración
decoration, n m, ornato
decorator, n m, decorador
decorous, adj, decoroso
decorum, n m, decoro
decrease, n f, decrecimiento
decrease, v, decrecer
decree, n m, decreto
decree, v, decretar
decrement, n f, decrecencia

decrement, n m, decremento
decrepit, adj, decrépito
dedicate, v, dedicar
dedication, n f, dedicación,
  dedicatoria
deduce, v, deducir
deduction, n f, deducción
deep, adj, profundo
deer, n m, ciervo, venado
defamatory, adj, difamatorio
defeat, v, desbaratar
defect, n f, falla, marra
defect, n f, m, defecto
defective, adj, defectuoso
defend, v, defender
defendant, n m, demandado
defender, n m, defensor
defense, n f, defensa
defenseless, adj, indefenso
defensible, adj, defendible
defensive, adj, defensivo
defensive, n f, defensiva
defer, v, deferir, retrasar
deference, n f, deferencia
deferent, adj, deferente
deficiency, n f, deficiencia
deficient, adj, deficiente
deficit, n m, déficit
defile, v, desfilar
define, v, definir
definite, adj, definido, definitivo
definition, n f, definición
definitively, adv, definitivamente
deform, v, afear, deformar
deformed, adj, deforme
defraud, v, defraudar
defrauder, n f, defraudador
defy, v, desafiar
degenerate, v, degenerar
degradation, n f, degradación
degrade, v, degradar
dejected, adj, abatido
delay, n f, demora, larga
delay, n m, retardo, retraso
delay, v, demorar
delegate, n f, delegado

delegation, n f, delegación
deliberate, v, deliberar
deliberation, n f, deliberación
delicacy, n f, delicadez
delicate, adj, delicado
delicateness, n f, delicadeza
delicious, adj, exquisito
delight, n f, delicia
delight, n m, deleite
delight, v, deleitar
delightful, adj, deleitable, deleitoso, delicioso
delineate, v, delinear
delinquent, n f, delincuente
delirium, n m, delirio
deliver, v, entregar
delivery, n f, entrega
deluded, adj, iluso
delusive, adj, delusivo
demagogue, n m, demagogo
demand, n f, demanda
demand, v, demandar
demarcate, v, demarcar
demarcation, n m, deslinde
dementia, n f, demencia
demerit, n m, demérito
democracy, n f, democracia
democrat, n m, demócrata
democratic, adj, democrático
demolish, v, demoler, derribar, derruir
demolition, n f, demolición
demon, n m, demonio
demonstrable, adj, demostrable
demonstrate, v, demostrar
demonstration, n f, demostración
demonstrative, adj, demostrativo
demoralize, v, desmoralizar
denial, n f, denegación
denominate, v, denominar
denomination, n f, denominación
denote, v, denotar
denounce, v, denunciar
dense, adj, denso
densely, adv, densamente
density, n f, densidad

dent, n f, abolladura
dented, adj, dentellado
dentifrice, n m, dentífrico
dentist, n m, dentista
denunciation, n f, denuncia, denunciación
deny, v, denegar, desmentir, renegar
department, n f, departamento
departure, n f, ida, partida
depend, v, depender, pender
dependence, n f, dependencia
dependent, adj, dependiente
deplorable, adj, deplorable
deplore, v, deplorar
deportation, n f, deportación
depose, v, deponer
deposit, n m, depósito, yacimiento
depositing, adj, depositante
deposition, n f, deposición
depositor, n depositador, depositante
depository, n f, depositaría
deprecate, v, deprecar
deprecatory, adj, deprecativo
depreciate, v, desapreciar, despreciar
depreciation, n f, depreciación
depress, v, deprimir
depression, n f, abatimiento
depression, n f, depresión
depressive, adj, depresivo
deprive, v, desapropiar, privar
deputize, v, delegar
deputy, n m, teniente
derail, v, descarrilar
deride, v, menospreciar
derision, n f, menosprecio
derisive, edj, irrisorio
derivation, n f, derivación
derive, v, derivar
derogate, v, derogar
derogatory, adj, derogatorio
descend, v, descender
descendant, n f, descendiente
descended, adj, bajado
descending, adj, descendente

descent, n f, descendencia, descensión
descent, n m, descenso
describe, v, describir
description, n f, descripción
descriptive, adj, descriptivo
desert, n m, desierto, yermo
desert, v, desertar
deserted, adj, desierto
desertion, n f, deserción
deserve, v, merecer
design, n m, designio
design, v, designar
designation, n f, designación
desirable, adj, apetecible, deseable
desire, n m, deseo, golondro
desire, v, desear
desirous, adj, deseoso, ganoso
desist, v, desistir
desolate, adj, desolado
desolate, v, desolar
desolation, n f, desolación
despair, n f, desesperación
despair, v, desahuciar, desesperar
desperate, adj, desesperado
despotic, adj, despótico
despotism, n m, despotismo
dessert, n f, tnpl, postres
destitute, adj, desacomodado
destitution, n m, desabrigo
destroy, v, desmoronar, destrozar, destruir
detail, n m, detalle, pormenor
detail, v, detallar
detention, n f, detención
deteriorate, v, deteriorar, menoscabar
deterioration, n f, deterioración
deterioration, n m, desperfecto, menoscabo
determinate, adj, determinado
determination, n f, determinación
detest, v, detestar
devastate, v, yermar
develop, v, desarrollar
development, n m, desarrollo, desenvolvimiento
devotion, n f, devoción
dexterous, adj, ducho
diamond, n m, diamante
dictate, v, dictar
dictionary, n dicciónario, tesauro
die, n m, dado
die, v, fallecer, finar, morir
diet, n f, dieta
differ, v, desdecir
difference, n desemejanza, diferencia
different, adj, diferente, distinto
difficult, adj, difícil, embarazoso
difficulty, n f, dificultad
difficulty, n m, berenjenal, inconveniente
dig, v, cavar
digest, v, digerir
dignity, n f, dignidad
diminish, v, achicar
dining room, n m, comedero
direct, v, dirigir, menear
dirty, adj, sucio
dirty, v, ensuciar
disadvantageous, adj, desaventajado
disaffected, adj, desafecto
disaffection, n f, desaficción
disagree, v, desconvenir
disagreeable, adj, desagradable
disagreeing, adj, desconforme
disagreement, n f, desconformidad
disagreement, n m, desacuerdo, desajuste
disappear, v, desaparecer, desparecer
disappearance, n f, desaparición
disappoint, v, malograr
disappointed, adj, fallido
disappointment, n m, malogro
disapprove, v, desaprobar
disarm, v, desarmar
disarmament, n m, desarmamiento
disarrange, v, desaliñar
disaster, n m, desastre

disbelieve, v, descreer
disburse, v, desembolsar
discard, v, descartar
discern, v, columbrar
discharge (firearm), v, descerrajar
discharge, n m, descargo
discharge, v, descargar
discolor, v, decolorar, descolorar
discompose, v, desconcertar,
  desmesurar
discomposure, n f, descompostura
disconcert, v, desavenir
disconsolate, adj, desconsolado
discontent, adj, descontento
discontent, v, descontentar
discontented, adj, malcontento
discontinue, v, descontinuar
discord, n f, cizaña
discord, n m, desagrado
discord, v, desconcordar
discordant, adj, desacorde
discount, n f, rebaja
discount, n m, descuento
discount, v, descontar
discourage, v, desalentar,
  desanimar
discouragement, n m, desaliento
discourtesy, n f, descortesía
discover, v, descubrir
discoverer, n f, descubridor
discovery, n f, descubrimiento
discredit, n m, descrédito
discredit, v, desacreditar
disdain, n m, desdén
disdain, v, desdeñar
disdainful, adj, desdeñoso
disembark, desembarcar
disembarkation, n f, desembarcación
disentangle, v, desenredar
disentanglement, n m, desenredo
disfavor, n m, desfavor
disfavor, v, desfavorecer
disfigure, v, desfigurar
disgust, n m, tedio
disgust, v, desazonar
dish, n m, plato

dishevelled, adj, descabellado
dishonor, n m, desdoro, deshonor
dishonor, v, deshonrar
dishonorable, adj, deshonroso
disinterested, adj, desinteresado
disjoint, v, desencajar
disk, n m, disco
dislocate, v, descoyuntar
dislocation, n m, descoyuntamiento
dislodge, v, desalojar
disloyal, adj, desleal
disloyalty, n f, deslealtad
dismantle, v, desmantelar
dismay, v, desmayar
dismount, v, descabalgar
disobey, v, desobedecer
disorder, n m, desarreglo,
  desconcierto, desorden
disorder, v, desordenar
disorderly, adj, desaforado,
  desconcertado
disown, v, desconocer
dispatch, v, despachar
displease, v, desagradar
dispose, v, acondicionar
dispossess, v, desposeer
dispute, v, porfiar
disquiet, v, desasosegar
disregard, v, desatender, desestimar
disregarded, adj, desairado
disrespect, n f, desestimación
disrespect, n m, desacato
dissent, v, desconformar
dissimilar, adj, desemejante
dissolve, v, descuajar
distance, n f, distancia, lejanía
distant, adj, lejano
distaste, n m, fastidio
distill, v, alambicar
distilled, adj, alambicado
distribute, v, erogar, ratear, repartir
distribution, n m, rateo, reparto
district, n f, comarca
district, n m, barrio
distrust, n f, desconfianza,
  inconfidencia

distrust, v, desconfiar
distrustful, adj, desconfiado
disturb, v, alborotar, desgobernar, molestar
ditch, n f, zanja
diversion, n m, deporte
divide, v, compartir, departir, dividir
divine, v, vaticinar
dock, n f, dársena
doctor, n m, doctor, médico
dog, n m, can, perro
dollar, n m, dólar, duro
domestic, adj, casero, doméstico
domestic, n m, familiar
domicile, n m, domicilio
dominant, adj, dominante
dominion, n m, dominio
donkey, n m, burro
door, n f, puerta
doormat, n m, felpudo
dose, n f, dosis
double, n m, duplo
double, v, redoblar
doublet, n m, coleto
doubt, n f, duda
doubt, v, dudar
dough, n m, amasijo
dove, n f, paloma
dovetail, v, empalmar
dowel, n f, cabilla
down, n m, vello
downy, adj, felpudo, velloso
dowry, n mf, dote
dozen, n f, docena
drab, adj, pardo
drain, n m, desagüe
drain, v, desaguar
draught, n m, trago
draw, v, dibujar
drawer, n f, gaveta
drawer, n m, cajón, girador
dreadful, adj, temible
dream, v, soñar
dredge, v, dragar
dress, n m, terno, traje, vestido
dress, v, aderezar, adobar

dried, adj, enjuto
drink, n f, bebida
drink, v, beber
drinker, n m, bebedor
drive away, v, ahuyentar
drive in, v, encajar
drive out, v, expulsar
driver, n m, botador
drone, n m, zángano
drop, n f, gota
drop, v, gotear
drug, n f, droga
druggist, n m, droguero
drum, n m, tambor
drummer, n m, tambor
drunk, adj, beodo, borracho
drunkenness, n f, borrachera
dry, adj, seco
dry, v, desecar, enjugar, secar
dryly, adv, secamente
duck, n mf, ánade
due, adj, debido
duel, n m, duelo
duke, n m, duque
dull, adj, desanimado, embotado
duly, adv, debidamente
dungeon, n m, calabozo
duplicate, v, duplicar
duplicity, n f, duplicidad
during, adv, durante
dust, n m, palvo
dusty, adj, polvoroso
duty, n m, deber, impuesto
dwarf, n m, enano
dye, v, teñir

E

eager, adj, afanoso
eagle, n f, águila
ear, n f, oreja
ear, n m, oído
early, adj, temprano
earnestness, n m, ahínco
earring, n m, zarcillo
earthen jar, n m, cangilón

earthen jug, n f, aljofaina

earthen pot, n m, cacharro

earthquake, n m, terremoto

ease pain, v, desahogar

ease, n f, holgura

ease, n m, desahogo, desenfado

easily deceived, adj, engañadizo

easily, adv, descansadamente, fácilmente

east, n m, este

Easter, n f, Pascua

easy, adj, dable, fácil

eat, v, comer

eating house, n m, bodegón

ebb, n m, reflujo

ebb, v, refluir

ebony, n m, ébano

echo, n m, eco

eclipse, n m, eclipse

eclipse, v, eclipsar

economical, adj, económico

economics, n f, economía

economist, n m, economista

economize, v, ahorrar

economize, v, economizar

edible, adj, comedero, comestible

edict, n m, edicto

edification, n f, edificación

edifice, n m, edificio

edify, v, edificar

edition, n f, edición

editor, n m, redactor

editorial, adj, editorial

editorial, n m, editorial

educate, v, educar

education, n f, educación

eel, n f, anguila

effect, n m, efecto

effect, v, efectuar

effective, adj, efectivo

effectively, adv, efectivamente

effects, n mpl, efecto

effervescence, n f, efervescencia

efficacious, adj, eficaz

efficaciously, adv, eficazmente

efficacy, n f, eficacia

efficiency, n f, eficiencia

efficient, adj, eficiente

effigy, n f, efigie

effusion, n derramamiento, efusión

egg shell, n m, cascarón

egg, n m, huevo

eight, n f, ocho

either, adj, sendos

elaborate, adj, elaborado

elaborate, v, elaborar

elaboration, n f, elaboración

elapse, v, transcurrir

elastic, adj, elástico

elasticity, n f, elasticidad

elation, n m, engreimiento

elbow, n m, coda

elbow, v, codear

elect, adj, electo

elect, v, elegir

election, n f, elección

elector, n m, elector

electorate, n m, electorado

electric, adj, electrico

electrician, n m, electricista

electricity, n f, electricidad

electrify, v, electrizar

electro-magnet, n m, electroimán

elegance, n f, elegancia

elegant, adj, apuesto, elegante

element, n m, elemento

elementary, adj, elemental

elephant, n mf, elefante

elevate, v, elevar

elevation, n f, alteza, elevación

elevator, n m, elevador

eleven, n, once

eligible, adj, elegible

eliminate, v, eliminar

elm tree, n m, olmo

elocution, n f, elocución

eloquence, n f, elocuencia

eloquent, adj, elocuente

elude, v, eludir

emanate, v, emanar

emancipate, v, emancipar

embargo, n m, embargo

embarkation, n f, embarcación
embarrass, v, avergonzar
embarrassment, n m, embarazo, vergüenza
embassy, n f, embajada, legación
embellish, v, embellecer
embellishment, n m, embellecimiento
emblem, n m, emblema
emboss, v, abollar
embrace, n m, abrazo
embrace, v, abarcar, abrazar
embroider, v, bordar
embroiderer, n m, bordador
embroiderv, n m, bordado
embroidery, n f, bordadura
embroil, v, embrollar
embryo, n m, embrión
emergency, n f, emergencia
emetic, adj, emético
emigrant, n m, emigrado, emigrante
emigrate, v, emigrar
emigration, n f, emigración
eminence, n f, eminencia
eminent, adj, eminente
emissary, n m, emisario
emission, n f, emisión
emit, v, emitir
emolument, n m, emolumento
emotion, n f, emoción
empale, v, empalar
emperor, n m, emperador
emphasis, n m, énfasis
emphatic, adj, enfático
empire, n m, imperio
empirical, edj, empírico
employ, v, emplear
employed, adj, empleado
employee, n m, empleado
employer, n m, patrón
employment, n m, empleo
emporium, n m, emporio
empower, v, apoderar
empowered, adj, apoderado
empress, n f, emperatriz
empty, v, vaciar
emulate, v, emular

emulation, n f, emulación
emulsion, n f, emulsión
encamp, v, campar
encampment, n m, campamento
encase, v, engastar
encasing, n m, encaje
enchanted, adj, encantado
enchanter, n m, encantador
enclose, v, cercar
enclosed, adj, adjunto, incluso
enclosure, n f, adjunta, cerca
enclosure, n m, encierro
encouraging, adj, halagüeño
encyclopedia, n f, enciclopedia
enemy, v, enemistar
end, n m, dejo, éxito, fin
end, v, terminar, ultimar
endeavor, n m, canato
endive, n f, endibia
endorse, v, endosar, respaldar
endure, v, perdurar
enemy, n m, enemigo
energetic, adj, enérgico
energy, n f, energía
enforced, adj, vigente
engender, v, engendrar
England, n f, Inglaterra
English (language), n f, inglés
English, adj, inglés
engrave, v, entallar, grabar
engraver, n m, entallador, tallador, tallista
enhancement, n m, encarecimiento
enigma, n m, enigma
enigmatical, adj, enigmático
enjoy, v, gozar, saborear
enjoyment, n m, goce
enlarge, v, agrandar
enlargement, n f, ampliación
enlistment, n m, enganche
enmity, n f, enemistad
ennoble, v, ennoblecer
enormity, n f, enormidad
enormous, adj, enorme
enormously, adv, enormemente
enough, adj, bastante

enrage, v, embravecer, enloquecer
enrich, v, enriquecer
ensign, n m, alférez
entangle, v, enredar
entangled, adj, enredado
enter, v, entrar
entering, adj, entrante
enterprise, n f, empresa
enterpriser, n m, emprendedor
enterprising, adj, emprendedor
entertain, v, entretener
entertainment, n m, entretenimiento
enthusiasm, n m, entusiasmo
enthusiastic, adj, entusiasta
entire, adj, entero
entirely, adv, enteramente
entirety, n f, entereza
entity, n f, entidad
entity, n m, ente
entrail, n f, entraña
entrance, n f, entrada
entry, n f, bocacalle
enumerate, v, enumerar
enunciate, v, enunciar
envelope, n m, sobre
envelopment, n m, envolvimiento
enviable, adj, envidiable
envious, adj, envidioso
environs, n fpl, afueras
environs, n mpl, alrededores
envoy, n m, enviado
envy, n f, envidia
envy, v, envidiar
epaulette, n f, charretera
epidemic, adj, epidémico
epidemic, n f, epidemia
epidermis, n f, epidermis
epigram, n m, epigrama
epilogue, n m, epílogo
episode, n m, episodio
epistle, n f, epístola
epitaph, n m, epitafio
epithet, n m, epíteto
epitome, n m, epítome
epitomize, v, epitomar
epoch, n f, epoca

equal, adj, igual, par, parejo
equal, n m, igual
equal, v, empatar
equality, n f, igualdad
equality, n m, empate
equalization, n f, igualación
equalize, v, igualar
equally, adv, igualmente
equator, n m, ecuador
equilateral, adj, equilátero
equilibrate, v, equilibrar
equilibrium, n m, equilibrio
equip, v, equipar
equitable, adj, equitativo
equity, n f, equidad
era, n f, era
eradicate, v, desarraigar
eradication, n f, erradicación
eradication, n m, desarraigo, descuajo
erase, v, borrar
eraser, n m, raspador
erect, adj, enhiesto
erect, v, erguir
err, v, errar
errant, adj, errante
erratic, adj, errático
erroneous, adj, erróneo
erroneously, adv, erradamente, erróneamente
error, n f, errata
error, n m, descamino, error, yerro
eruption, n f, erupción
escape, v, fugarse, zafar
essence, n f, esencia
estate, n f, finca
estimate, v, presupuestar
eternal, adj, eternal, eterno
eternity, n f, eternidad
ethical, adj, ético
ethics, n f, ética
etiquette, n f, etiqueta
Europe, n f, Europa
European, adj, europeo
evacuate, v, evacuar
evade, v, evadir

evaporate, v, evaporar
evaporation, n f, evaporación
evasion, n f, evasión
evasive, adj, evasivo
event, n m, acontecimiento, caso, evento
eventual, adj, eventual
evergreen oak, n f, encima
everlasting, adj, sempiterno
every, pro, cada
everything, pro, todo
eviction, n f, evicción
eviction, n m, desahucio
evil, n m, mal
exact, adj, ajustado
exactly, adv, cabalmente
exalt, v, ensalzar
examination, n m, examen
examine closely, v, aquilatar
examine, v, recorrer, revisar
example, n m, ejemplar, ejemplo
exasperate, v, exasperar
exasperated, adj, exasperado
excavate, v, ahuecar, excavar
exceed, v, rebasar
exceeding, adj, excedente
exceedingly, adv, encarecidamente
excel, v, campear, descollar
excellent, adj, primoroso
except, adv, excepto
except, v, exceptuar
excess, n f, demaseia
excess, n m, desafuero
excessive height, n m, descuello
excessive, adj, demasiado, descompasado
excessively, adv, demasiadamente
exchange, n f, permuta
exchange, n m, cambio, canje
exchange, v, permutar
excise, n f, alcabala
excite, v, excitar
exclaim, v, exclamar
exclude, v, excluir
excuse, n f, excusa
excuse, v, dispensar

executable, adj, ejecutable
execute, v, ejecutar
execution, n f, ejecución
executioner, n m, verdugo
executive, adj, ejecutivo
exemplary, adj, ejemplar
exempt from punishment, adj, impune
exercise, n m, ejercicio
exercise, v, ejercer, ejercitar
exhaust, v, agotar
exhaustible, adj, agotable
exist, v, existir
expect, v, aguardar
expedition, n f, expedición
expenditure, n m, desembolso
expense, n m, gasto
experience, experimentar
experienced, adj, veterano
expert, adj, experto
expert, n m, perito
expiration, n f, vencimiento
expire, v, expirar
explain, v, aclarar, explicar
explanation, aclaración, explicación
exploit, n f, hazaña
explore, v, explorar
explorer, n m, explorador
export, v, exportar
exportation, n f, exportación
expose, v, exponer
express, n m, expreso, rápido
expressible, adj, decible
extent, n f, amplitud
external, adj, externo
extinguisher, n m, apagador
extravagance, n f, extravagancia
extravagance, n m, desatino
extravagant, adj, destinado, extravagante
extreme, adj, extremo
extreme, n m, extremo
extremity, n f, extremidad
eye, n m, ojo
eye, v, ojear
eyebrow, n f, ceja

eyeglass, n m, ocular
eyeglasses, n mpl, quevedos
eyelash, n f, pestaña
eyelid, n m, párpado

F

fable, n f, fábula
fabricate, v, fabricar
fabrication, n f, fábrica, fabricación
fabulous, adj, fabuloso
face, n f, cara, fachada, faz
face, n m, cariz, gesto
face, v, afrontar, encara
faced, adj, encarado
facility, n f, facilidad
facsimile, n m, facsímile
fact, n m, hecho
factor, n m, factor
factory, n f, factoría
faculty, n f, facultad
failing, n m, achaque
failure, n m, fiasco
fainting, n f, desfallecimiento
fair, n f, feria
fairy, n f, hada
fairy, n m, duende
faith, n f, fe
faithful, adj, fiel
faithfully, adv, fielmente
falcon, n m, halcón
fall away, v, desfallecer
fall ill, v, enfermar
fall, n f, baja, caída
fall, v, caer
fallow, n m, barbecho
false, adj, falso, mentiroso
falsehood, n f, falsedad, patraña
falsely, adv, falsamente
falsification, n f, falsificación
falsify, v, falsear, falsificar
fame, n f, fama
familiar, edj, familiar
familiarity, n f, familiaridad
familiarize, familiarizar
familiarly, adv, familiarmente

family, n f, alcurnia, familia
famous, adj, famoso
fan, n m, abanico
fan, v, abanicar
fanatical, adj, fanático
fanaticism, n m, fanatismo
fancy, n f, fantasía
fancy, v, fantasear
fantastic, adj, fantástico
far, adv, lejos
farce, n f, farsa
farce, n m, sainete
farewell, n m, vale
farm house, n f, alquería
farm, n f, quintería
farmer, n m, granjero, labrador,
  quintero
farming, n f, granjería
fascinate, v, fascinar
fascinating, adj, fascinador
fascination, n f, fascinación
fastener, n m, afianzador
fastidious, adj, melindroso
fat, adj, gordo, grueso
fat, n f, grosura
fat, n m, graso
fatal, adj, fatal
fatality, n f, fatalidad
fate, n m, hado
father, n m, padre
fatigue, n f, fatiga
fatigue, v, fatigar
fatten, v, engordar
fatuous, adj, fatuo
fault, n f, culpa, tacha
fault, n m, delito
favor, n m, favor, amparo
favor, v, favorecer, apoyar
favorable, adj, favorable
favorer, n m, favorecedor
favorite, adj, favorito
favorite, n m, favorito
fawn, n m, cervato
fear, n m, miedo, pavor, temor
fear, v, temer
fearful, adj, medroso, miedoso

feasible, adj, practicable, factible, hacedero
feast, n f, fiesta
feast, n m, festín
feast, v, festejar
feather, n f, pluma
feature, n m, lineamiento
February, n m, febrero
fecundity, n f, fecundidad
federal, adj, federal
federation, n f, federación
feeble, adj, endeble
feed, v, alimentar, cebar
feeding, n f, alimentación
feel pain, v, doler
feel, v, manosear, palpar
feign, v, aparentar, fingir
feigned, adj, fingido
felt, n m, fieltro
female, n f, hembra
feminine, adj, femenino
fence, v, vallar
ferment, n m, fermento
ferment, v, fermentar
ferocious, adj, feroz
ferocity, n f, ferocidad
ferrous, adj, férreo
fertile, adj, feraz
fervent, adj, férvido
fervor, n m, fervor
festive, adj, festivo
festivity, n f, festividad
fetid, adj, fétido
fever, n f, calentura, fiebre
fiber, n f, fibra, hebra
fibrous, adj, fibroso
fiction, n f, ficción
fictitious, adj, ficticio
fidelity, n f, fidelidad
fierce, adj, fiero
fierceness, n f, fiereza
fiery, adj, fogoso
fifteen, n f, quince
fifty, n f, cincuenta
fig, n m, higo
fight, v, lidiar, luchar, pelear

figurative, adj, figurativo
figure, n f, figura
figure, v, figurar
filament, n m, filamento
file, n m, legajo
file, v, limar
filigree, n f, filigrana
filings, n f, cizalla
fill up, v, henchir
fill, v, llenar
fillet, n m, filete
film, n f, pelicula
filter, n m, envasador, filtro
filter, v, filtrar
final, adj, final, terminal
finalize, v, finalizar
finally, adv, finalmente
find, v, hallar
fine, adj, fino
fineness, n f, fineza
finery, n m, aderezo
finger, n m, anillo, dedo
finish, n m, acabado
finish, v, acabar, retocar
finished, adj, acabado
finisher, n f, aprestador
fire extinguisher, n m, matafuego
fire, n m, fuego, incendio
fireman, n m, bombero
first, adj, primero
first, adv, antes
fiscal, adj, fiscal
fish hook, n m, anzuelo
fish, n m, besugo, pescado
fish, v, pescar
fishing tackle, n f, jarcia
fishing, n f, pesca
fist, n m, puño
fit, adj, acertado, idóneo
five, n f, cinco
fix, v, fijar
fixation, n f, fijación
fixed, adj, fijo, reglamentado
fixedly, adv, fijamente
flag staff, n m, zanco
flagrant, adj, flagrante

flake, n f, vedija

flake, n m, copo

flaming, adj, flamante

flank, n f, ijada

flank, n m, flanco, ijar

flat, adj, chato

flatten, v, aplastar

flatter, v, lisonjear

flatterer, n m, lisonjero

flattering, adj, lisonjero

flattery, n f, lisonja

flattery, n m, halago

flaxen, adj, blondo

fleece, n m, vellón

fleet, n f, flota

fleshy, adj, carnoso

flexible, adj, flexible

flight, n f, zafada

float, v, flotar

floating, adj, flotante

flock, n f, grey, manada

flock, n m, rebaño

floodgate, n m, arbollón

floor, n m, piso

florescence, n f, florescencia

Florida, n f, Florida

florist, n m, florista

flounce, n f, farfalá

flounce, n m, falbalá

flour, n f, harina

flourish, v, florecer

flourishing, adj, floreciente

flow in, v, afluir

flow into, v, desembocar

flow, v, fluir

flower pot, n m, florero, tiesto

flower, n f, flor

flowered, adj, floreado

flowery, adj, florido

flowing, adj, caudaloso

fluctuation, n m, vaivén

fluent, adj, fluente, lenguaraz

fluid, n m, fluido

fly, n f, mosca

fly, v, volar

focus, v, enfocar

fog, n f, niebla

fold, n f, plegadura

fold, v, plegar

foliage, n m, follaje

folio, n m, folio

follow, v, alcanzar, seguir

following, adj, siguiente

folly, n f, sandez

fond, adj, aficiónado

food, n f, comida, vianda

food, n m, alimento, cebo, manjar

fool, n m, bobo, mentecato, tonto

foolish speech, n f, bobería

foolish, adj, majadero, mentecato

foolish, n f, calaverada

foolishly, adv, bobamente

foolishness, n f, tontería

foot, n f, pata

foot, n m, pie

football, n m, balompié, balón

footlights (theater), n fpl, candilejas

footman, n m, lacayo

footstep, n f, pisada

footstool, n m, escabel

footwear, n f, calzado

for, prep, para, por

force, n f, fuerza, vigencia

force, v, mechar

forcing, adj, impelente

ford, n m, vado

forearm, n m, antebrazo

forehead, n f, testera

foreign, adj, advenedizo, extranjero

foreigner, n m, gringo

foremost, adj, delantero

forest, n f, floresta, selva

foretell, v, adivinar

forge, n f, herrería

forger, n m, falsificador

forget, v, olvidar

forgetfulness, n m, olvido

form, n f, banca

form, v, formar

formula, n f, fórmula

fort, n m, fuerte

fortitude, n f, fortaleza

fortunate, adj, afortunado, hadado
fortune, n f, andanza, fortuna
fortune, n m, caudal
forty, n f, cuarenta
forward, adv, adelante
found, v, cimentar, fundar
foundation, n m, cimiento, fundamento
fountain, n f, fuente
four, n f, cuatro
fourteen, n f, catorce
fox, n f, zorra
fox, n m, raposo, zorro
fracture, n f, quebrantamiento
fracture, n f, quiebra
frail, n f, espuerta
frame, n m, bastidor
France, n f, Francia
fraud, n f, baratería, defraudación
fraud, n m, chivo, embrollo, embuste
free will, n m, arbitrio
free, adj, desahogado, desenfadado, zafo
free, adv, gratis
free, v, desembarazar, librar
freedom, n f, desembarazo
freely, adv, libremente
freight, n m, flete
freighter, n m, fletador
French (language), n f, francés
French, adj, francés
frequent, v, cursar
fresh, adj, fresco
fretful, adj, mohino
friar, n m, fraile
friction, n f, friega
Friday, n m, viernes
fried, adj, frito
friend, n f, amigo
friendly, adj, amistoso
frighten, v, amedrentar, amilanar
frizzle, v, frisar
frog, n f, rana
from, prep, desde
front, n f, delantera
frontier, n f, frontera

frost, n f, helada
frost, n m, hielo
frown, n m, ceño
frowning, adj, ceñudo
frozen, adj, helado
fruit, n f, fruta
fruitfulness, n f, feracidad
full, adj, lleno, plenario, pleno
fully, adv, plenamente
funds, n mpl, fondos
funnel, n m, embudo
furnace, n m, calorífero
furnish, v, amueblar
furnished, adj, fornido
furniture, n m, ajuar, menaje
furniture, n mpl, trastos
furtive, adj, furtivo
fury, n f, furia
futile, adj, fútil
future, adj, venidero
future, n m, porvenir

G

gain, n f, ganancia
gain, n m, granjeo
gain, v, ganar, granjear
gala, n f, gala
gale, n m, ventarrón
gall, n f, hiel
gallant, adj, galán
gallant, n m, bizarro, galán
gallantry, n f, bizarría, galantería
galleon, n m, galeón
gallery, n f, galería
gallop, n m, galope
gallop, v, galopar
galosh, n f, galocha
galvanize, v, galvanizar
game, n m, juego
gamut, n f, gama
gander, n m, ganso
gap, n m, boquete
garden, n m, jardín
gardener, n m, jardinero
gardening, n f, jardinería

garlic, n m, ajo
garnet, n m, granate
garret, n m, zaquizamí
garrulous, adj, gárrulo
gas, n m, gas
gaseous, adj, gaseoso
gather, v, acopiar, colegir
gathering, n m, acopio
gaudy, adj, charro
gauge, v, aforar
gauntlet, n m, guantelete
gauze, n f, gasa
gauze, n m, rengue
gay, adj, donoso, gallardo
gazette, n f, gaceta
gear, n m, engranaje
gear, v, engranar
gelatine, n f, jaletina
gelatinous, adj, gelatinoso
genealogy, n f, genealogia
general, adj, general
generality, n f, generalidad
generalize, v, generalizar
generally, adv, generalmente
generosity, n f, generosidad
generous, adj, dadivoso, generoso
genius, n m, genio
gentility, n f, gentileza
gentle, adj, paulatino
gently, adv, paulatinamente
genuine, adj, genuino
geography, n f, geografía
geology, n f, geología
geometry, n l, geometría
geranium, n m, geranio
germ, n m, germen
German, adj, alemán
Germany, n f, Alemania
germinate, v, germinar
gesticulation, n f, qesticulación
gesture, n m, ademán
giant, n m, gigante
gibberish, n f, jerigonza
gift, n f, dádiva, merced
gifts, n mpl, dote
gigantic, adj, gigante

ginger, n m, jengibre
gird, v, ceñir, cinchar
girl, n f, muchacha, niña
girth, n f, cincha
give nicknames, v, apodar
give possession, v, aposesionar
give satisfaction, v, desagraviar
give, v, dar, regalar
glance, n f, mirada, ojeada
glance, n m, vistazo
gland, n f, glándula
glare, n m, deslumbramiento
glass bead, n m, abalorio
glass, n m, vidrio
glaze, v, vidriar
glazier, n m, vidriero
glee, n m, júbilo
glen, n f, cañada
globe, n m, globo, redondo
glorify, v, glorificar
glorious, adj, glorioso
glory, n l, gloria
glossary, n m, glosario
glove, n m, guante
glucose, n f, glucosa
glue, v, encolar
glut, n m, abarrotamiento
gnaw, v, carcomer
go out, v, salir
go, v, andar, ir, marchar
goat, n f, cabra
gobble, v, engullir
God, n m, Dios
godfather, n m, compadre
going, adj, andante
gold, n m, oro
golden, adj, dorado
goldfinch, n m, jilguero
good bye, adv, agur
good gracious, int, caramba
good natured, adj, bonachón
good, adj, buena
good-bye, int, adiós
goodness, n m, bien
goose, n f, oca
goose, n m, pato

gossip, n f, habladuría
gothic, adj, gótico
govern, v, gobernar
government, n f, gobernación
governor, n m, gobernador, regido
gown, n f, bata
grace, n f, gracia
graceful, adj, gracioso, grato
gracefulness, n m, garbo
graciously, adv, gratamente
gradation, n f, gradación
gradual, adj, gradual
gradually, adv, gradualmente
graduated, adj, graduado
graduation, n f, graduación
grain, n f, grana
grainy, adj, granoso
grammar, n f, gramática
grammatical, adj, gramatical
granary, n m, granero
grand, adj, grandioso
grandfather, n m, abuelo
grandmother, n f, abuela
grandson, n m, nieto
grange, n f, granja
grant, v, impartir
granulate, v, granular
granulation, n f, granulación
grape skin, n f, casca
grape, n f, uva
graphic, adj, gráfico
grapple, v, aferrar
grasp, v, agarrar, apañar, empuñar
grate, n f, verja
grateful, adj, agradecido
gratefulness, n m, adecimiento
gratification, n f, gratificación
gratify, v, gratificar
gratitude, n f, gratitud
gratuitously, adv, gratuitamente
grave, adj, grave, tétrico
gravedigger, n m, enterrador
gravel, n m, cascajo
gravitation, n f, gravitación
gravity, n f, gravedad
gray, adj, gris

graze, v, apacentar, pacer
grease, n f, gordura, grasa
grease, n m, unto
grease, v, engrasar, ensebar
greasy, adj, grasiento, lardoso, seboso
great (size), adj, tamaño
great grandfather, n m, bisabuelo
great grandson, n m, biznieto
great, adj, gran, magno
greatly, adv, grandemente
greatness, n f, grandeza, grandura
greedy, adj, codicioso
green (color), adj, verde
greenish, adj, verdusco
greens, n f, verdura
grey hair, n f, cana
greyhound, n m, galgo, lebrel
grieve, v, penar
grievous, adj, gravoso
grind, v, moler
grinder, n m, moledor
groan, n m, gemido
groan, v, gemir
grocer, n m, abacero
grocery, n f, abacería
groin, n m, empeine
groove, n f, ranura
gross, adj, grosero
grossness, n f, grosería
ground floor, n m, suelo
group, n m, grupo
group, v, agrupar
grouse, n f, ganga
grove, n f, alameda
grow dark, v, anochecer
grow feeble, v, flaquear
grow grey, v, encanecer
grow light, v, clarear
grow sour, v, ahilarse
growing, adj, naciente
growl, v, regañar
grudge, n f, rencilla
grumbling, adj, regañón
guarantee, n f, fianza
guarantee, n m, garante

guarantee, v, afianzar, garantir
guarantor, n m, fiador
guard, n f, guarda
guard, n m, resguardo
guide, n m, guía
guide, v, encaminar, enderezar, guiar
guitar, n f, guitarra
gulf, n m, golfo
gum, n f, encía, goma
gummed, adj, engomado
gun, n m, fusil
gush, v, chorrear
gust, n f, ráfaga
gutter, n f, gotera
gutter, n m, canalón
gymnasium, n f, palestra
gymnasium, n m, gimnasio
gymnast, n mf, gimnasta
gypsy, n m, gitano

H

habilitation, n f, habilitación
habitation, n f, habitación
habitual, adj, habitual
habituate, v, habituar
habitude, n f, habitud
hail, n m, granizo
hail, v, granizar, salve
hair, n m, pelo
hairpin, n f, horquilla
hairy, adj, peloso
half, adj, medio
half, n f, mitad
hall, n f, sala
hall, n m, salón
halt, int, alto
halter, n m, cabestro
ham, n m, jamón, jarrete
hammer, n m, martillo
hammer, v, amartillar, macear, martillar
hammock, n f, hamaca
hand, n f, mano
handbook, n f, vademécum

handcuff, v, maniatar
handful, n m, puñado
handkerchief, n m, pañuelo
handle, n f, manivela
handle, n m, mango, manubrio
handsaw, n m, serrucho
hang up, v, colgar
hang, v, ahorcar
hanging, adj, colgante
happen, v, acaecer, acontecer
happily, adv, felizmente
happiness, n f, dicha, felicidad
happy, adj, beato, fausto, feliz
hard rain, n m, chaparrón
hard, adj, duro, endurecido
harden, v, empedernir, endurecer
hardened, adj, encallecido
hardness, n f, dureza
hardness, n m, endurecimiento
hardware store, n f, ferretería
hardware, n f, quincalla, quincallería
harm, n m, daña
harmful, adj, dañoso
harmony, n f, armonía
harness, n m, jaez
harvest, n f, mies, siega
hasten, v, activar, apresurar
hastily, adv, apresuradaente
hasty, adj, apresurado
hat, n m, sombrero
hatch, v, empollar
hatchet, n m, machado
hate, v, malquerer, odiar
hated, adj, malquisto
hateful, adj, odioso
hatred, n f, malquerencia
hatred, n m, odio
haughtiness, n f, altanería
haughty, adj, altivo, entonado
Havana cigar, n m, habano
Havana tobacco, adj, habano
have supper, v, cenar
have, v, haber, tener
hawker, n m, chalán
hay, n m, heno
he, pro, él

head stock, n m, cabezal
head, n f, cabecera, cabeza
headache, n f, jaqueca
headshake, n f, cabezada
heal, v, cicatrizar, sanar
health, n f, salud
healthful, adj, saludable
healthy, adj, salubre
heap up, v, aglomerar, amontonar, colmar
heap, n m, colmo, montón
hear, v, oír
hearing, n m, oyente
heart, n m, corazón
hearth, n f, chimenea
hearth, n m, fogón, hogar
heat, n m, calor
heating, n f, calefacción
heavily, adv, pesadamente
heavy rain shower, n m, aguacero
heavy, adj, pesado
hectare, n f, hectárea
heel, n m, tacón, talón, zancajo
height, n f, altura, alzada
height, n m, alto
heir, n m, heredero
helm, n f, celada
helmet, n m, yelmo
help, n f, ayuda
help, v, ayudar, coadyuvar
hem, n f, bastilla
hemisphere, n m, hemisferio
hemp, n m, cáñamo
hen, n f, gallina
her, pro, la
herald, n m, heraldo
heraldry, n m, blasón
herb, n f, hierba
herbaceous, adj, herbáceo
herd (of cattle), n m, hato
herd (of cows), n m, vaquero
here, adv, acá, aquí
hereditary, adj, hereditario
hermit, n m, ermitaño
hermitage, n f, ermita
hero, n m, héroe

heroic, adj, heroico
hesitate, v, hesitar, titubear
hesitation, n f, hesitación
hidden, adj, oculto
hide, n m, cuero
hide, v, esconder
hierarchy, n f, jerarquía
hieroglyphic, adj, geroglífico, jeroglífico
hieroglyphic, n m, geroglífico
hieroglyphs, n m, jeroglífico
high, adj, alto, elevado, encumbrado
highly, adv, altamente
highway, n f, carretera
hill, n f, colina
hill, n m, cerro
him, pro, le, lo
himself, pro, sí
hinge, n f, bisagra, charnela
hinge, n m, gozne, quicio
hip, n f, cadera
his, adj, su
hiss, v, chirriar
historian, n f, historiador
historic, adj, histórico
history, n f, historia
hit the mark, v, acertar
hoard, v, hacinar
hoarse, adj, ronco
hoarseness, n f, carraspera
hoary, adj, canoso
hobble, v, manear
hobby, n f, chifladura
hogshead, n m, bocoy
hoist, v, arbolar, izar
holder, n m, tenedor
hole, n m, agujero
home, n f, morada
honey, n f, miel
honeycomb, n m, panal
honeysuckle, n f, madreselva
honor, n m, honor
honor, v, honrar
honorable, adj, honrado
hood, n f, caperuza, toca
hood, n m, capirote, capucho

ook, n f, gafa
ook, n m, gancha, garfio
ook, v, enganchar, garabatear
oop, n m, cerco, fleje
ope, v, esperar
orn, n f, bocina
orse, n f, cabalgadura
orse, n m, caballo, corcel
orsemanship, n f, equitación
ose, n f, manguera
ospital, n m, hospital
ost, n m, hueste
ot weather, n m, bochorno
ot, adj, cálido
otel, n m, hotel
ound, n m, podenco
our, n f, hora
ouse, n f, casa
ouse, n m, apeadero
ouse, v, posar
ow much, adv, cuánto
ow, adv, cómo
uman, adj, humano
umming, n m, zurrido
umor, n m, humor
ump, n f, corcova
undred, n f, centena
unger, n f, hambre
ungry, adj, hambriento
unt, v, cazar
unter, n f, saboneta
unter, n m, cazador
urricane, n m, huracán
urry, n f, prisa
urt, adj, leso
urt, v, dañar, lastimar, lesionar
urtful, adj, dañino
usband, n m, marido
ut, n f, casucha, choza
yacinth, n m, jacinto
ydraulics, n f, hidráulica
ydrochloric, n m, clorhídrico
ydrogen, n m, hidrógeno
yena, n f, hiena
ygiene, n f, higiene
ymn, n m, himno

hypocrisy, n f, gazmoñería, hipocresía
hypocrite, n m, mojigato
hypocritical, adj, gazmoño

I

I, pro, yo
Iberian, n m, ibero
ice cream, n m, helado
ice, v, garapiñar
Iceland, n f, Islandia
idea, n f, idea
ideal, adj, ideal
ideal, n m, ideal
identically, adv, idénticamente
identify, v, identificar
identity, n f, identidad
idiom, n m, idioma, idiotismo, modismo
idiosyncrasy, n f, idiosincrasia
idiot, adj, idiota
idle, adj, holgazán, ocioso, poltrón
idle, v, haraganear
idler, n m, haragán
if, conj, si
ignition, n f, ignición
ignominious, adj, ignominioso
ignominy, n f, ignominia
ignorance, n f, ignorancia
ignorant, adj, desentendido, ignorante
ill, adj, enfermo
illegal, adj, ilegal, ilegítimo
illegality, n f, ilegalidad
illegible, adj, ilegible
illicit, adj, ilícito
illiterate, adj, iliterato
illogical, adj, ilógico
illuminate, v, iluminar
illuminated, adj, iluminado
illumination, n f, iluminación
illuminative, adj, iluminativo
illusive, adj, ilusivo
illusory, adj, ilusorio
illustrate, v, ilustrar

illustration 44 *imprudence*

illustration, n f, ilustración
illustrator, n m, ilustrador
illustrious, adj, ilustre
image, n f, imagen
imaginable, adj, imaginable
imaginary, adj, imaginario
imagination, n f, imaqinación
imagination, n m, magín
imaginative, adj, imaginativo
imagine, v, imaginar
imbecility, n f, imbecilidad
imbibe, v, embeber, empapar
imitable, adj, imitable
imitate, v, imitar
imitated, adj, imitado
imitation, n f, imitación
immediately, adj, inmediatamente
immense, adj, inmenso
immoderate, adj, desarreglado
immodesty, n f, deshonestidad
impacted, adj, impacto
impair, v, empeorar
impartial, adj, imparcial
impartiality, n f, imparcialidad
impartially, adv, imparcialmente
impassibility, n f, imposibilidad
impassible, adj, impasible
impatience, n f, impaciencia
impatient, adj, impaciente
impeccable, adj, impecable
impede, v, empachar, impedir
impediment, n m, impedimento
impel, v, impeler, impulsar
impeller, n m, impulsor
impenetrable, adj, impenetrable
imperative, adj, imperativo
imperceptible, adj, imperceptible
imperfect, adj, imperfecto
imperfectbn, n f, imperfección
imperial, adj, imperial
impermeable, adj, impermeable
impersonal, adj, impersonal
impertinence, n f, impertinencia
impertinent, adj, impertinente
impervious, adj, impermeable
impetuous, adj, impetuoso

impetus, n m, ímpetu
implicate, v, implicar
implicated, adj, implicado
implication, n f, implicación
implicit, adj, implícito
implore, v, implorar
impolite, adj, descortés
impolitic, adj, impolítico
import, v, importar
importance, n f, importancia
important, adj, importante
importation, n f, importación
importer, n m, importador
importune, v, importunar
impose, n f, leva
imposed, adj, impuesto
imposing, adj, imponente
imposition, imposición
impossibility, n f, imposibilidad
impossible, adj, imposible
impostor, n m, embustero,
  engañador, impostor
imposture, n f, impostura
impotence, n f, impotencia
impotent, adj, impotente
impoverish, v, empobrecer
impoverishment, n m,
  empobrecimiento
impracticable, adj, impracticable
imprecate, v, imprecar
impregnate, v, impregnar
impress, v, impresionar
impression, n f, impresión
imprevision, n f, imprevisión
imprison, v, aprisionar, encarcelar
imprisonment, n f, carcelería,
  encarcelación
improbability, n f, improbabilidad
improbable, adj, improbable
improper, adj, impropio
impropriety, n f, impropiedad
improve, v, mejorar
improved, adj, aprovechado
improvement, n f, mejora
improvident, adj, impróvido
imprudence, n f, imprudencia

imprudent, adj, imprudente
impudence, n f, desfachatez, impudencia
impudence, n m, descaro
impudent, adj, impudente
impugn, v, impugnar
impulse, n m, impulso
impulsion, n f, impulsión
impulsive, adj, impulsivo
impunity, n f, impunidad
impure, adj, impuro
impurity, n f, impureza
imputable, adj, imputable
imputation, n f, imputación
in advance, adv, anticipadamente
in front of, prep, delante
in haste, adv, aprisa
in love, adj, enamorado
in, prep, a, en
inaccessible, adj, inaccesible
inaction, n f, inacción
inactive, adj, inactivo
inactivity, n f, inactividad
inadequate, adj, inadecuado
inadmissible, adj, inadmisible
inadvertence, n f, inadvertencia
inadvertent, adj, inadvertido
inapplicable, adj, inaplicable
inattentive, adj, desatento
inaugurate, v, inaugurar
inauguration, n f, inauguración
Inca, n m, inca
incalculable, adj, incalculable
incandescence, n f, incandescencia
incandescent, adj, candente, incandescente
incapable, adj, incapaz
incapacity, n f, incapacidad
incarnate, adj, encarnado
incarnate, v, encarnar
incautious, adj, incauto
incautiously, adj, incautamente
incendiary, n m, incendiario, quemador
incentive, n m, incentivo
incertitude, n f, incertidumbre

incessant, adj, incesante
incidence, n f, incidencia
incident, n m, incidente
incidental, adj, incidental, incidente
incision, n f, incisión
incite, v, incitar
incivility, n f, incivilidad
inclemency, n f, inclemencia
inclement, adj, inclemente
inclination, n f, inclinación
incline, v, inclinar
inclined, adj, inclinado
include, v, incluir
including, adv, incluso
inclusion, n f, inclusión
inclusive, adj, inclusivo
inclusively, adv, inclusive
incoherency, n f, inconexión
incombustible, adj, incombustible
incomparable, adj, incomparable
incompatibility, n f, incompatibilidad
incompatible, adj, incompatible
incompetency, n f, incompetencia
incompetent, adj, incompetente
incomplete, adj, incompleto
incomprehensibility, n f, incomprensibilidad
incomprehensible, adj, incomprensible
inconceivable, adj, inconcebible
incongruity, n f, incongruencia
incongruous, adj, incongruo
inconsequence, n f, inconsecuencia
inconsequent, adj, inconsecuente, inconsiguiente
inconsiderable, adj, inconsiderable
inconsiderate, adj, desacertado, desconsiderado, inconsiderado
inconsiderately, adv, desatinadamente
inconsideration, n f, inconsideración
inconsistency, n f, inconsistencia
inconsistent, adj, inconsistente
inconsolable, adj, inconsolable
inconstancy, n f, inconstancia
inconstant, adj, inconstante

incontestable, adj, inconcuso,
　incontestable
incontrovertible, adj, incontrovertible
inconvenience, n f, descomodidad,
　incomodidad, inconveniencia
inconvenient time, n f, deshora
inconvenient, adj, descómodo,
　incómodo, inconveniente
incorporate, v, incorporar
incorporation, n f, incorporación
incorrect, adj, incorrecto
incorrigible, adj, incorregible
increase, n f, engrandecimiento
increase, v, abultar, acrecentar,
　acrecer
incredibility, n f, incredibilidad
incredible, adj, increíble
incredulity, n f, incredulidad
incredulous, adj, incrédulo
increment, n m, incremento
incriminate, v, incriminar
incubator, n f, incubadora
inculcate, v, inculcar
inculpable, adj, inculpable
incumbency, n f, incumbencia
incur, v, incurrir
indecency, n f, indecencia
indecent, adj, indecente
indecision, n f, indecisión
indefensible, adj, indefensible
indefinite, adj, indefinido
indelible, adj, indeleble
indemnity, n f, indemnidad
independence, n f, independencia
independent, adj, independiente
Indian, n m, indio
indicate, v, indicar
indispensable, adj, imprescindible
indivisible, adj, impartible
industrious, adj, diligente, trabajador
inebriated, adj, ebrio
inequality, n f, desigualdad
inexhaustible, adj, inagotable
inexpressible, adj, indecible
inferior, adj, mascabado
infirmary, n f, enfermerfía

inflame, v, enconar, entervorizar,
　incendiar
inflamed, adj, encendido
inflammation, n m, encendimiento
inflate, v, hinchar
influenza, n m, trancazo
inform, v, enterar
ingot, n m, tejo
inhabit, v, habitar, morar
inhabitant, n m, habitante
inherit, v, heredar
inheritance, n f, herencia
inhuman, adj, desalmado
inject, v, inyectar
injure, v, malear
injured, adj, descalabrado
ink, v, entintar
inkwell, n m, tintero
inlay, n m, embutido
inlay, v, embutir
inn, n f, fonda
inn, n m, mesón
innkeeper, n m, mesonero, vemero
innocent, adj, inocente
inquiry, n f, indagación, pesquisa
inscription, n m, letrero
insect, n m, bicho
inseparable, adj, inseparable
insertion, n m, metido
insignificance, n f, insignificación
insipidity, n m, desabor,
　desabrimiento, desazón
insist, v, insistir
insolent, adj, insolente
inspection, n f, inspección
inspire, v, inspirar
instance, n f, instancia
instigation, n f, instigación
instinct, n m, instinto
instruct, v, amaestrar, instruir
instructor, n m, educador
instrument, n f, instrumento
insufficient, adj, insuficiente
insulator, n m, aislador
insult, n m, denuesto
insult, v, denostar, insultar

insupportable, adj, inaguantable
insurmountable, adj, incontrastable
integrity, n f, integridad
intellect, n m, intelecto
intellectual, adj, intelectual
intelligent, adj, inteligente
intensity, n f, intensidad
intent, n m, intento
intentional, adj, intencional
intercede, v, interceder
intercept, v, interceptar
interdiction, n m, entredicho
interest, n f, usura
interest, n m, interés
interest, v, interesar
interesting, adj, interesante
interference, n m, entremetimiento
interminable, adj, inacabable
intermittent, adj, intermitente
internal, adj, interno
international, adj, internacional
interpose, v, entreponer, interponer
interpret, v, interpretar
interpretation, n f, interpretación
interrogation, n f, interrogación
interrupt, v, interrumpir
intersection, n f, intersección
intervene, v, intervenir
interview, n f, entrevista
intimacy, n f, intimidad
intimate, adj, entrañable, íntimo
intimidate, v, intimidar
intolerable, adj, intolerable
intolerant, adj, intolerante
intoxicate, v, emborrachar,
  embriagar
intoxicated, adj, embriagado
intoxication, n f, embriaguez
intrepidity, n f, impavidez
intrigue, v, intrigar
intrinsic, adj, intrínseco
introduce, v, introducir
introduction, n f, introducción
inundate, v, anegar
invade, v, invadir
invalid, adj, inválido

invariable, adj, invariable
inventor, n m, fabricador, inventor
inventory, n m, inventario, recuento
inverse, adj, inverso
invert, v, invertir
invest, v, envestir, investir
investigate, v, indagar, investigar
investigation, n f, investigación
invigorate, v, vigorar
invincible, adj, invencible
invisible, adj, invisible
invitation, n f, invitación
invite, v, invitar
invoice, n f, factura
invoice, v, facturar
invoke, v, invocar
involuntary, adj, involuntario
involved, adj, envuelto
iodine, n f, yodina
iodine, n m, iodo, yodo
ire, n f, ira
iris, n m, iris
Irish (language), n f, irlandés
Irish, adj, irlandés
iron (clothes), v, planchar
iron bar, n m, barrote
iron clad, adj, blindado
iron cladding, n m, blindado
iron, n m, fierro, hierro
iron, v, aplanchar
ironclad (battleship), n m, acorazado
ironic, adj, irónico
ironing, n m, planchado
irony, n f, ironía
irrecoverable, adj, incobrable
irregular, adj, irregular
irreparable, adj, irreparable
irresistible, adj, irresistible
irresolute, adj, irresoluto
irresponsibility, n f, irresponsabilidad
irrevocable, edj, irrevocable
irrigation, n f, regadura
irritable, adj, enfadadizo, irritable
irritate, v, enfurecer, irritar
irritation, n f, irritación
island, n f, isla

islet, n f, isleta
isolate, v, aislar
isolated, adj, aislado
isthmus, n m, istmo
it, pro, ello
Italian (language), n f, italiano
Italian, adj, italiano
italic, adj, grifado
itinerary, n m, itinerario
ivory, n m, marfil
ivy, n f, yedra

J

jack, n m, bolillo, bolín
jacket, n f, chaqueta, jaqueta
jacket, n m, jubón
jailer, n m, carcelero
jam, n f, compota
jamb, n m, batiente
January, n m, enero
Japan, n f, Japón
Japanese (language), v, japonés
Japanese, adj, japonés
jar, n m, tarro
jargon, n f, jerigonza
jaw, n f, mandíbula, quijada
jealous, adj, celoso
jeer, n f, befa, chufleta
jelly, n f, jalea, melcocha
jest, n f, chanza, chunga, guasa
jest, v, chancear
jesting, adj, chancero
jettison, n alijamiento
jettison, n f, echazon
jewel, n f, alhaja, joya
jeweler, n m, joyero
jewelry, n f, joyería, bisutería
join, v, acoplar, compaginar, unir
joining, n m, empalme
joint heir, n m, coheredero
jointly, adv, unidamente
joke, n f, matraca
joke, n m, chasco, chiste
journal, n m, diario
journalism, n f, periodismo

journalist, n m, periodista
journey, n f, jornada
journey, n m, recorrido, viaje
joy, n m, gozo
joyful, adj, gozoso
jubilee, n m, jubileo
judge, n m, juez
judge, v, fallar, juzgar
judgement, n m, juicio, falio
judicial, adj, judicial
judicious, adj, juicioso, sentado
jug, n f, jarra
julcy, adj, jugoso, zumoso
July, n m, julio
jump, n f, cabriola
jump, v, saltar
June, n m, junio
juniper, n m, enebro
just, adj, cabal, justo
justice, n f, justicia

K

keel, n f, quilla
keep, v, cumplir, guardar
keg, n f, barrica
kernel, n f, almendra
kettle, n f, marmita
key, n f, clave, llave
keyboard, n m, teclado
keyring, n m, llavero
khaki, adj, caqui, kaki
kick, n f, patada
kick, v, cocear, patear
kidney bean, n f, habichuela, judía
kidskin, n f, cabritilla
kill, v, matar
kilogram (abbr,), n m, kilo
kilogram, n f, kilogramo
kiloliter, n m, kilolitro
kilometer, n m, kilómetro
kilowatt, n m, kilovatio
kind reception, n m, agasajo
kind, adj, bondadoso
kind, n m, genero
kindle, v, enardecer, encender

kindness, n f, benignidad, bondad
king, n m, rey
kingdom, n m, reino
kiosk, n m, kiosco
kitchen, n f, cocina
kite, n f, cometa
kitten, n m, gatillo
knavery, n f, bellaquería
knead, v, amasar, heñir
kneel, v, arrodillarse
knife, n f, faca
knife, n m, cuchillo
knot, v, anudar
know, v, saber
knowingly, adv, adrede, adredemente, sabiendas

L

labor, n f, labor
labor, n m, laboreo
laborious, adj, laborioso, trabajoso
labyrinth, n m, laberinto
lace, v, encordonar, lacear
lacerate, v, lacerar
lack, n f, carencia
lack, v, carecer
ladder, n f, escala
lady typist, n f, dactilógrafa
lady, n f, dama, señora
lake, n m, lago
lamb skins, n mpl, añinos
lamb, n m, borrego
lame, adj, cojo, zopo
lament, v, lamentar, plañir, querellarse
lamentable, adj, lamentable
lamentation, n m, lamento
lamp lighter, n m, farolero
lamp, n f, lámpara
lamp, n m, candil, quinque
lance, n f, lanza
land owner, n m, hacendado
land surveyor, n m, apeador
land, n f, campiña, hacienda
land, n m, terreno

landed, adj, hacendado
landing, n m, desembarco, desembarque
landlord, n m, casero
landmark, n m, hito, linde
landscape, n m, paisaje
lane, n f, callejón
language, n m, lenguaje
languid, adj, lánguido
lantern, n f, linterna
lantern, n m, fanal, farol
lap, n m, gremio
lapse, n m, lapso
laquer, n f, laca
larceny, n f, ratería
lard, n m lardo
large basket, n m, banasto
large chest, n m, arcón
large coach, n f, carroza
large cushion, n m, almohadón
large drum, n m, bombo
large house, n m, caserón
large, adj, granado, grande, lato
largely, adv, ampliamente, largamente
last night, adv, anoche
last year, adv, antaño
last, adj, postre, postrero, último
last, v, durar
lastly, adv, ultimamente
latch, n f, taravilla
late, adj, tardío
late, adv, tarde
latent, adj, latente
lateral, adj, lateral
latitude, n f, latitud
latrine, n f, letrina
laudable, adj, laudable
laugh, v, reir
launch, n f, lancha
launch, v, varar
launching, n f, botadura
launderer, n f, quitamanchas
laundress, n f, aplanchadora, lavandera
laundry, n m, lavadero

lavatory, n m, lavatorio
law, n f, ley
lawful, adj, lícito
lawn, n m, linón, prado
lawsuit, n m, litigio
lawyer, n m, abogado, letrado
lax, adj, flojo, laxo
laxity, n f, laxitud
lay down, v, acostar
lay, v, imponer
layer, n f, tongada
laziness, n f, pereza
lazy, adj, perezoso
lead, n m, plomo
leaden, adj, aplomado
leader, n m, mayoral
leaf, n f, hoja
league, n f, legua
leak, v, derramar
leakage, n m, derrame
lean, adj, macilento
leap, n mf, salto
learn, v, aprender
learned, adj, entendido
learning, n f, sabiduría
learning, n m, saber
leather wine bag, n m, borracha
leave, v, dejar
left hand, n f, siniestra
left, adj, izquierdo, zurdo
leg, n f, pierna
legacy, n m, legado
legal, adj, legal
legality, n f, legalidad
legalization, n f, legalización
legalize, v, legalizar
legally, adv, legalmente
legend, n f, leyenda
legible, adj, legible, leíble
legislate, v, legislar
legislation, n f, legislación
legislative, adj, legislativo
legislator, n m, legislador
legislature, n f, legislatura
legitimacy, n f, legitimidad
legitimate, adj, legítimo

leisure, n f, desocupación
leisure, n m, ocio
lemon, adj, limonado
lemon, n m, limón
lemonade, n f, limonada
lend, v, prestar
lender, n m, usurero
lending, n m, empréstito
length, n f, largueza, largura
length, n m, largor
lengthen, v, alargar
leniency, n f, lenidad
lens, n mf, lente
lentil, n f, lenteja
less, adj, menos
lessen, v, aminorar, apocar
lesson, n f, lección
let, v, alquilar
letter, n f, letra
lettuce, n f, lechuga
level, n m, nivel, ras
level, v, allanar, emparejar, nivelar
lever, n f, alzaprima, báscula, palanea
levity, n f, levedad, liviandad, vaguedad
liar, n m, mentiroso
libel, n m, libelo
liberal, adj, liberal
liberality, n f, liberalidad
liberate, v, libertar
liberation, n f, liberación
liberty, n f, libertad
librarian, n f, bibliotecario
library, n f, biblioteea, librería
license, n f, licencia
lick, v, lamer
lid, n f, tapa
lie, n f, mentira
lie, v, mentir, yacer
lie in ambush, v, acechar
life, n f, vida
lift, v, engreir
lifting, n m, levantamiento
ligament, n m, ligamenta
light, adj, leve, ligero, liviano

light, n f, luz
light, v, alumbrar
lighten, v, aligerar, aliviar
lighter, n f, gabarra
lighter, n m, lanchón
lighthouse, n m, faro
lighting, n m, alumbrado
lightly, adv, levemente
lightness, n f, ligereza
likelihood, n f, verosimilitud
likely, adj, verosímil
liking, n m, agrado
lilac, n f, lila
lily, n m, lirio
limb, n m, miembro
lime, n f, lima
limit, n m, límite
limitation, n f, limitación
limited, adj, limitado
line, n f, línea
line, n m, renglón
line, v, aforrar, linear
lineage, n m, linaje
lineal, adj, lineal
linen, n m, lienzo, lino
lingual, adj, lingual
linguist, n m, lingüista
linguistic, adj, lingüistico
lining, n m, aforro, forro
link, n m, engarce, vínculo
link, v, engarzar, enhebrar
linoleum, n m, linóleo
lion, n m, león
lip, n m, labia
liquid, adj, líquido
liquidate, v, liquidar
liquor, n m, licor
list, n m, empadronamiento,
   escalafón
listen, v, escuchar
liter, n m, litro
literal, adj, literal
literary, adj, literario
literate, adj, literato
literature, n f, literatura
lithium, n m, litio

litigate, v, litigar
litigation, n m, pleito
litter, n f, litera
little bird, n m, pajarillo
little brother, n m, hermanito
little child, n m, niñito
little finger, n m, dedillo
little girl, n f, chica
little kiss, n m, besito
little mouth, n f, boquilla
little sister, n f, hermanita
little, adj, chico, pequeño, poco
little, adv, poco
little, n m, poco
live, v, vivir
liver, n m, hígado
livid, adj, amoratado, lívido
lizard, n m, lagarto
llama, n m, llama
Impertous, adj, imperioso
load, v, cargar
loaded, adj, cargado
loader, n m, cargador
loan, n m, préstarmo
loathing, n m, hastío
lock, n f, cerradura
locksmith, n m, cerrajero
locust, n f, langosta
lodge, v, albergar, alojar
lodging, n m, albergue, alojamiento
log, n f, toza
log, n m, leña
loitering, adj, callejero
long hair, n f, cabellera
long, adj, largo
long, v, antojarse
look, n m, semblante
lookout, n m, vigía
loop, n f, presilla
loose, adj, desatado, holgado
loosen, v, desasir, desligar, largar
lord, v, enseñorear
lose, v, perder
loser, n m, perdedor
loss, n f, pérdida
lottery, n f, lotería

loud laughter, n f, carcajada
loud, adv, alto
love, n m, amor
love, v, amar
lover, n mf, amante
lovingly, adv, amante
low tide, n f, bajamar
low, adj, bajo
lowness, n f, bajeza
loyal, adj, leal
loyalty, n f, lealtad
lucky, adj, venturoso
lucrative, adj, ganancioso
lull, n m, recalmón
lumber yard, n m, leñero
lumberjack, n m, leñador
lump, n m, terrón
lunch, n f, merienda
lunch, v, merendar
luster, n m, prensado
lustre, n m, relumbrón
lying, adj, mentiroso, yacente

M

macaroni, n m, macarrón
mace, n f, maza
machete, n m, machete
machine gun, n f, ametralladora
machine, n f, máquina
mad, adj, demente
made, adj, hecho
maggot, n m, gusano
magic, adj, mágico
magic, n f, magia
magician, n m, mágico, mage
magistrate, n f, magistrado
magnate, n m, magnate
magnet, n m, imán
magnetic, adj, magnético
magnetism, n m, magnetismo
magnetize, v, imanar
magnificence, n f, magnificencia
magnificent, adj, magnífico
magnitude, n f, magnitud
mahogany, n f, caoba

mail, n f, mala, valija
mailman, n m, cartero
maim, v, mancar
maimed, adj, manco
maintenance, n f, manutención
majestic, adj, majestuoso
majesty, n f, majestad
majority, n f, mayoria
make bitter, v, amargar
make blind, v, cegar
make easy, v, facilitar
make fat, v, engrosar
make good, v, abonar
make impossible, v, imposibilitar
make merry, v, alegrar
make old, v, añejar, envejecer
make progress, v, aprovechar
make vain, v, envanecer
make, v, hacer
maker, n m, fabricante
malefactor, n m, malhechor
malevolence, n f, malevolencia
malevolence, n m, encono
malevolent, adj, malévolo
malice, n f, malicia
malicious, adj, malicioso, malvado
malignant, adj, maligno
malleable, adj, maleable
mallet, n f, maceta
mallet, n m, mazo
mamma, n f, mamá
man, n m, hombre, varón
manage, v, gestionar, manejar
manageable, adj, manejable
management, n m, manejo
manager, n m, gerente
mandate, n m, mandado, mandamiento, mandato
mane, n f, melena
maneuver, n f, maniobra
maneuver, v, maniobrar
mania, n f, manía
manifest (shipping), n f, manifiesto
manifest, adj, manifiesto
manifest, v, manifestar
manifestation, n f, manitestación

manipulate, v, manipular
manipulation, n f, manipulación
manly, adj, varonil
mannequin, n m, maniquí
manner, n f, manera
mansion, n f, mansión
manual, adj, manual
manual, n m, manual
manufacture, v, manufacturar
manuscript, n m, manuscrito
map, n m, mapa
maraud, v, merodear
marble, n m, mármol
marbled, adj, marmóreo
March, n m, marzo
mare, n f, yegua
margin, n mi, margen
marine, adj, marino
mark (German currency), n m, marco
mark, n f, marca
mark, v, marcar
markedly, adv, marcadamente
market, n m, mercado
market, v, mercadear
marketer, n m, mercader
marksman, n m, tirador
marmalade, n f, mermelada
marriage, n f, boda
marriage, n m, casamiento,
  matrimonio
marrow, n f, médula
marrow, n m, meollo
marry, v, casar, casarse, maridar
marsh, n f, ciénaga
marshal, n m, mariscal
martingale, n f, gamarra
marvel, v, pasmar
marvelous, adj, maravilloso
masculine, adj, macho, masculino
mask, n f, carátula, careta, máscara
mason, n m, albañil
masonry, n f, albañilería
mass, n f, masa, misa
massive, adj, macizo
master, n m, amo
masterly, adj, magistral

mastery, n f, maestría
mastery, n m, magisterio
match, n f, mecha
match, n m, fósforo
match, v, aparear, hermanar, parear
mate, n f, pareja
material, adj, material
material, n m, material
maternal, adj, materno
mathematical, adj, matemático
mathematician, n m, matemático
mathematics, n f, matemática
matrix, n f, matriz
matrix, n m, clisé
mattress, n m, colchón, jergón
maturation, n f, maduración
mature, adj, maduro
mature, v, madurar
maturity, n f, madurez
mausoleum, n m, mausoleo
maxim, n f, máxima
maximum, adj, máximo
maximum, n m, máximo
May, n m, mayo
mayor, n m, alcalde
me, pro, me, mí
meadow, n f, pradera, vega
meagre, adj, magro
mean, adj, mezquino, tacaño, vil
meaning, n m, significado
meanness, n f, mezquindad, vileza
meanwhile, adv, entretanto
measure, n f, medida, mesura
measure, v, graduar, medir, tantear
measured, adj, mesurado
measurement, n f, medición
meat pie, n f, empanada
meat, n f, carne
mechanic, n m, mecánico
mechanical, adj, mecánico
mechanism, n m, mecanismo
medal, n f, medalla
medallion, n m, medallón
mediate, v, mediar
mediation, n f, mediación, tercería
mediator, n m, mediador

medicinal, adj, medicinal
medicine, n f, medicina
mediocre, adj, mediocre
mediocrity, n f, mediocridad
meditate, v, meditar
meditation, n f, meditación
Mediterranean, adj, mediterráneo
meek, adj, manso
meet, v, abocar, encontrar
meeting, n m, encuentro, mitin
melancholy, adj, melancólico
melancholy, n f, melancolía
melody, n f, melodía
melon, n m, melón
membrane, n f, membrana
memorable, adj, memorable
memorial, n m, memorial
memory, n f, memoria
mend, v, remendar
mental hospital, n m, manicomio
mental, adj, mental
mention, n f, mención
mention, v, mentar, mencionar
mentor, n m, mentor
mercantile, adj, mercante
mercenary, n m, mercenario
merchandise, n f, mercadería,
  mercancía
merchant, n m, marchante,
  mercante, traficante
merciless, adj, desapiadado
mere, adj, mero
merely, adv, meramente
meridian, n m, meridiano
meringue, n m, merengue
merit, n m, merecido,
  merecimiento, mérito
meritorious, adj, benemérito
merrily, adv, alegremente
merriment, n m, alborozo
merry, adj, alegre
mesh, n f, malla
message, n m, mansaje, recado
messenger, n m, mandadero,
  mensajoro
metal, n m, metal

metallic, adj, metálico
meter, n m, metro
method, n m, método
methodical, adj, metódico
metric, adj, métrico
metropolis, n f, metrópoli
metropolitan, adj, metropolitano
Mexico, Méjico, México
microscope, n f, microscopio
middle, n m, medio
middling, adj, entrefino
migration, n f, migración
migratory, adj, migratorio
mile, n f, milla
militant, adj, militante
military or naval station, n m,
  apostadero
military, adj, militar
military, n m, militar
militia, n f, milicia
milk, n f,leche
milky, adj, lácteo
mill, n m, molino
millenium, n m, milenario
million, n m, millón
millionaire, n m, millonario
minced meat, n m, gigote
mind, n f, mente
mindful, adj, memorioso
mine (minerals), v, zapar
mine, adj, mía, mío
mine, n f, mina
mine, v, minar
miner, n m, minador
mineral, n m, mineral
miniature, n f, miniatura
minimum, adj, mínimo
minimum, n m, mínimum
minister, n m, ministro
minister, v, ministrar
ministry, n m, ministerio
minor, adj, menor
minor, n m, menor
minority, n f, menoría
mint, n f, hierbabuena, menta
minute (time), n m, minuto

minute, adj, menudo
minute, n f, minuta
minutely, adv, menudamente
miracle, n m, milagro
miraculous, adj, milagroso
mirage, n m, miraje
mire, n m, fango
mirth, n f, alegría
miserable, adj, miserable
misery, n f, miseria
misery, n m, malestar
misfortune, n f, desdicha, desgracia, malaventura
misfortune, n m, descalabro, desmán
misgiving, n m, recelo
misgovernment, n m, desgobierno
misguided, adj, descaminado
mislead, v, descaminar, descarriar, extraviar
misshapen, adj, malhecho
mission, n f, misión
missionary, n m, misionero
Mississippi, n f, Misisipí
mist, n f, neblina
mistake, n f, equivocación, falta, trabacuenta
mistake, n m, desacierto, engaño
mistake, v, desacertar
mistake, v, equivocar
mistaken, adj, engañado, errado
misty, adj, nebuloso
mitigate, v, mitigar
mitten, n m, mitón
mix, v, mezclar, mixturar
mixed, adj, mixto
mixture, n f, mezcla, mixtura
mob, n f, canalla
mobile, adj, móvil
mobility, n f, movilidad
moccasin, n m, mocasín
mocha, n f, moca
mock, v, befar, fisgar
mockery, n f, mofa
mode, n m, modo
model, n f, plantilla
model, n m, figurín

model, v, modelar
moderate, adj, bonancible, mediano, moderado
moderate, v, moderar
moderately, adv, medidamente
moderation, n f, medianía, moderación
modern, adj, moderno
modest, adj, modesto
modesty, n f, modestia
modification, n f, modificación
modify, v, modificar
modulate, v, modular
modulation, n f, modulación
modulation, n m, módulo
moisten, v, emblandecer, mojar
molasses, n f, melaza
mold, n m, molde
mold, v, enmohecer, moldear
moldy, adj, mohoso
mole, n m, topo
moleskin, n f, angola
molest, v, desacomodar
moment, n m, momenta, santiamén
momentous, adj, momentáneo
monarch, n m, monarca
monastery, n m, monasterio
Monday, n m, lunes
money, n f, moneda
money, n m, dinero
mongrel, adj, mestizo
monk, n m, monje
monopolize, v, acaparar
monopoly, n acaparamiento, acopiamento, monopolio
monster, n m, monstruo
monstrous, adj, monstruoso
month, n m, mes
monthly, adj, mensual
monthly, adv, mensualmente
monument, n m, monumento
moon, n f, luna
Moor, n m, mora
moorings, n f, amarradura
moral, adj, moral
morality, n f, moralidad

morals, n f, moral
more, adv, más
moreover, adv, además
morning, n f, mañana
morsel, n m, bocado
mortal, adj, mortal
mortality, n f, mortalidad
mortally, adv, mortalmente
mortar, n m, mortero
mortgage, n f, hipoteca
mortification, n f, mortificación
mosaic, adj, mosaico
mosque, n f, mezquita
mosquito, n m, mosquito
moss, n m, moho
moth eaten, adj, apolillado
mother, n f, madre
motion, n f, moción
motivate, v, motivar
motive, n m, motivo
motor, n m, motor
motorcycle, n m, motociclo
motto, n m, lema, mote
mount, v, montar
mountain, n f, montaña
mountain, n m, monte
mountainous, adj, cerril, enriscado, montañés
mouse, n m, ratón
mousetrap, n f, ratonera
moustache, n m, bigote
mouth of river, n m, desembocadero
mouth, n f, boca
mouthpiece, n f, embocadura
movable, adj, movible
move, v, mover
movie, n m, cine
mow, v, guadañar
much, adj, mucho
much, n m, mucho
mud hole, n m, barrizal
mud, n f, lama
mud, n m, cieno
muddle, v, enturbiar
muddy, adj, fangoso, limoso
muffling, n m, embozo

mug, n m, pichel
mule, n f, acémila
mummy, n f, momia
murder, n m, homicidio
murderer, n m, matador
murmuring, n f, querellante
museum, n m, museo
music, n f, música
muslin, n f, muselina
mustard, n f, mostaza
musty, adj, enmohecido
mutiny, n m, motín
mutter, v, chistar
my, adj, mi
mystery, n m, misterio
mystical, adj, místico

N

nail, n f, uña
nail, v, clavar, enclavar
naked, adj, desnudo
name, n m, nombre
name, v, apellidar, nombrar
named, adj, apellidado
namesake, n m, tocayo
napkin, n f, servilleta, toalleta
narcotic, adj, naróotico
narrate, v, narrar
narration, n f, narración
narrow, adj, angosto
narrowness, n f, angostura
nastiness, n f, porquería
nation, n f, nación
national, adj, nacional
nationality, n f, nacionalidad
native country, n f, patria
native, adj, natal, native
native, n m, natural
natural, adj, natural
naturally, adv, naturalmente
nature, n f, naturaleza
near, adj, cerca
near, adv, cerca, cerquita
nearly, adv, aproximadamente
neat, adj, mono, neto

neatly, adv, lindamente
neatness, n f, lindeza
necessary, adj, necesario
necessity, n f, necesidad
necessity, n m, menester
neck, n m, cuello, pescuezo
necklace, n f, gargantilla
necklace, n m, collar
necktie, n f, corbata
need, v, necesitar
needle, n f, aguja
needy, adj, menesteroso
nefarious, adj, nefario
negation, n f, neqación
negative, adj, negativo
negative, n f, negativa
neglect, v, descuidar
neglectful, adj, omiso
negligence, n f, incuria, negligencia
negligent, adj, negligente
negociator, n m, negociador
negotiable, adj, negociable
negotiate, v, negociar
negotiation, n f, negociación
neighbor, n m, vecino
neighborhood, n f, cercanía, redonda
neighborhood, n m, vecindario
neighboring, adj, circunvecino,
  rayano, vecino
neither, adv, tampoco
neither, conj, ni
nephew, n m, sobrino
nerve, n m, nervio
nervous, adj, nervioso
nest, n m, nido
net, n f, red
neuter, adj, neutro
neutral, adj, neutral
never, adv, jamás, nunca
new, adj, nuevo
newspaper, n m, periodico
next, adj, proximo
nice, adj, amable, simpático
nicer, adj, mejor
nicety, n f, quisquilla
niche, n m, nicho

nickel, n m, níquel
nickname, n m, apodo
nicotine, n f, nicotina
niece, n f, sobrina
night before last, adv, anteanoche
night, n f, noche
nightlight, n f, lamparilla
nightmare, n f, pesadilla
nine, n f, nueve
nitrogen, n m, nitrógeno
no one, pro, nadie
no, adv, no
nobility, n f, hidalguía
noble, adj, caballeroso, noble
nobleman, n m, hidalgo
nobleness, n f, caballerosidad
nocturnal, adj, nocturno
nod (to sleep), v, cabecear
noise, n f, baraúnda
noise, n m, ruido
nominal, adj, nominal
nominated, adj, nombrado
nomination, n f, nombramiento
nominee, n m, nómino
none, adj, ninguno
nonsense, n f, majadería
noon, n m, mediodía
north, n m, norte
nose, n f, nariz
notary, n m, escribano
notch, n f, mella
note, n m, billete, membrete
note, v, anotar
notebook, n m, cuaderno
nothing, n f, nada
notice, v, advertir
noticed, adj, advertido
notion, n f, noción
notwithstanding, adv, obstante
nourishment, n m, pábulo
November, n m, noviembre
now, adv, ahora
noxious, adj, nocivo
nudity, n f, desnudez
number, n m, número
numerous, adj, numeroso

nun, n f, monja
nurse, n f, enfermera, nodriza
nut cracker, n m, cascanueces
nut, n f, nuez
nutritious, adj, alimenticio

O

oar, n m, remo
obedience, n f, obediencia
obedient, adj, obediente
obese, adj, obeso
obey, v, obedecer
obituary, n m, obituario
object, n m, objeto
object, v, objetar
objection, n f, objeción
objectionable, adj, reparable
objective, adj, objetivo
obligation, n f, obligación
obligation, n m, empeño
obligatory, adj, obligatorio
oblige, v, obligar
oblique, adj, oblicuo
oblong, adj, oblongo
obscure, adj, obscuro
obscure, v, obscurecer
obscurely, adv, obscuramente
obscurity, n f, obscuridad
obsequious, adj, obsequioso
observant, adj, observante
observation, n f, observación
observation, n m, apuntamiento
observatory, n m, observatorio
observe, v, observar
observer, n m, apuntador
obstacle, n f, traba
obstacle, n m, óbice, quite
obstinate, adj, obstinado, porfiado,
　testarudo
obstinately, adv, tercamente
obstruct, v, obstar, obstruir
obtain, v, obtener, reportar
obtainable, adj, obtenible
obtuse, adj, obtuso
obvious, adj, obvio

occasion, n f, ocasión
occasional, adj, ocasional
occupation, n f, ocupación
occupation, n m, quehacer
occupied, adj, ocupado
occupy, v, ocupar
occur, v, ocurrir
occurrence, n f, ocurrencia
ocean, n m, océano
octave, n f, octava
October, n m, octubre
ocular, adj, ocular
odd, adj, non
odometer, n m, odómetro
of, prep, de
offence, n m, agravio
offend, v, delinquir, ofender
offender, n m, ofensor
offense, n f, ofensa
offensive, adj, enojoso, ofensivo
offer, n f, oferta
offer, n m, ofrecimiento
offer, v, deparar, ofrecer
office, n f, oficina
official, adj, oficioso
official, n m, oficial
officially, adv, oficialmente
officiate, v, oficiar
oh!, int, ...ay!
oil cloth, n m, encerado
oil, n m, aceite, óleo
oily, adj, oleoso, aceitero
old age, n f, vejez
old man, n m, anciano
old, adj, anciano, añejo, viejo
older, adj, mayor
olive, n f, aceituna, oliva
omelet, n f, tortilla
ominous, adj, ominoso
omission, n f, omisión
on, prep, sobre
one hundred, adj, cien
one, adj, uno
one, n m, uno
one, pro, se
onerous, adj, oneroso

onion, n f, cebolla
only, adj, solamente, sólo
only, adv, únicamente
opaque, adj, opaco
open, adj, abierto, libre
open, v, abrir, zanjar
opened, edj, escotado
opening, n f, abertura
opening, n m, portillo
openly, adv, abiertamente
opera, n f, opera
operable, adj, operable
operate, v, operar
operation, n f, operación
operator, n m, operario
opinion, n f, opinión
opinion, n m, parecer
opponent, n m, opositor
opportune, adj, oportuno
opportunely, adv, acertadamente
opportunity, n f, oportunidad
oppose, v, oponer
opposite, adj, enfrente, opuesto
opposition, n f, oposición
oppress, v, agobiar, oprimir
oppression, n f, opresion
oppressive, eoi, opresivo
oppressor, n m, opresor
optical, adj, óptico
optics, n f, óptica
optimism, n f, optimismo
optimist, n m, optimista
option, n f, opción
optionally, adv, facultativamente
opulence, n f, opulencia
opulent, adj, opulento
or, conj, o
oral, adj, oral
orange tree, n m, naranjo
orange, adj, naranjado
orange, n f, naranja
orchestra, n f, orquesta
order, n m, pedido
order, v, ordenar
ordinarily, adv, ordinariamente
ordinary, adj, ordinario

ordinary, n m, ordinario
ore, n m, quijo
organ, n m, órgano
organic, adj, orgánico
organization, n f, orqanización
organize, v, organizar
Orient, n m, oriente
oriental, adj, oriental
orifice, n m, orificio
ornament, n m, ornamento, tocado
orphanage, n f, orfandad
oscillate, v, oscilar
ostentation, n m, boato
ounce, n f, onza
our, adj, nuestro
outline, n m, recorte
outpour, n m, chorrillo
outrage, n m, ultraje
outrage, v, ultrajar
oval, adj, oval
oval, n m, óvalo
overcast, adj, anublado
overdone, adj, rendido
overflow, v, desbordar, redundar
overflowed, adj, anegado
overseer, n m, capataz, veedor
overthrow, n m, trastorno
overturn, v, trastornar
overwhelmed, adj, abrumado
overwhelming, adj, abrumador
owe, v, deber
owl, n f, lechuza
owl, n m, chucho
owner, n f, dueña
owner, n m, dueño
ox, n m, buey
oxidation, n f, oxidación
oxidize, v, oxidar
oxygen, n m, oxígeno
oyster, n f, ostra

P

Pacific, n f, Pacífico
pacify, v, pacificar
pack, n f, paca

pack, v, embalar, empacar, empaquetar
package, n m, paquete
packer, n m, embalador
packing, n m, embalaje, empaque, empaquetado
pad, n f, hombrera
paddle, n m, canalete
padlock, n m, candado
page, n f, página
pain, n m, pena
painful, adj, penoso
paint, n m, tinte
paint, v, pintar
painter, n m, pintor
painting, n f, pintura
pair, n m, par
palace, n m, palacio
pale, adj, desmayado, pálido
palisade, n f, empalizada
palm tree, n f, palma
palpable, adj, palpable
palpitate, v, palpitar
pamphlet, n m, impreso
Panama, n f, Panamá
panel, n m, entrepaño
panic, n m, pánico
pants, n m, pantalón
pants, n mpl, calzoncillos
papa, n m, papá
paper, n m, papel
paperweight, n m, pisapapeles
parachute, n f, paracaídas
parade, n f, parada
paradise, n m, paraíso
paradox, n f, paradoja
paraffin, n f, parafina
paragon, n m, parangón
paragraph, n m, párrafo
parallel, adj, paralelo
parallel, n m, paralelo
paralyze, v, paralizar
paralyzed, adj, paralizado
parasite, n m, mogollón
parasol, n f, sombrilla
parasol, n m, parasol, quitasol

parcel, n m, lío
parchmenf, n m, parche
pardon, n f, venia
pardon, n m, perdón
pardon, v, perdonar
parent, n m, deudo
parenthesis, n m, paréntesis
parishioner, n mi, feligrés
parity, n f, paridad
park, n m, parque
parliament, n m, parlamento
parrot, n m, papagayo
parsley, n m, perejil
part, n f, parte
part, v, apartar, desemparejar
partial, adj, parcial
partiality, n f, parcialidad
participate, v, participar
participation, n f, participación
particular, adj, descontentadizo, particular
particularly, adv, particularmente
partition, n f, partición
partition, n m, tabique
party (political), n m, partido
pass judgment, v, enjuiciar
pass, n m, pase
pass, v, pasar
passable, adj, pasadero
passage, n f, pasada
passage, n m, palenque, pasaje, tránsito
passenger, n m, pasajero
passion, n f, pasión
passive, adj, pasivo
passport, n m, pasaporte
past, adj, pasado
paste, n f, pasta
paste, n m, empaste, engrudo
paste, v, empastar
pastime, n m, pasatiempo
pasture, n f, dehesa
pasture, n m, pasto
patch, n m, remiendo
patent, adj, patente
patent, v, patentar

patented, adj, patentado

paternal, adj, paterno

path, n f, senda, vereda

path, n m, trámite

pathetic, adj, patético

patience, n f, paciencia

patient, adj, paciente

patiently, adv, pacientemente

patriot, n m, patriota

patriotic, adj, patriótico

patriotism, n m, patriotismo

patrol, n f, patrulla

patrol, v, patrullar

patron, n m, patrón

patronage, n f, partrocinio

patronize, v, patrocinar

pause, n f, pausa

pause, v, pausar

pave, v, empedrar

pavement, n m, empedrado, pavimento

pavillion, n m, pabellón

pawn, v, empeñar

pay, v, adeudor, pagar

payment, n f, paga

payment, n m, pagamento

pea, n m, garbanzo, quisante

peace, n f, paz

peach, n m, albérchigo, melocotón

pear, n f, pera

pearl, n f, perla

pebble, n m, guijarro

peculiar, adj, peculiar

pedal, n m, pedal

peddler, n m, baratillero

pedestal, n f, repisa

pedestal, n m, pedestal

peel, n f, piel

pelts, n f, corambre

penalty, n f, penalidad

pencil, n m, pincel

pendant, adj, colgadizo, pendiente

pendulum, n f, péndola

penetrable, adj, penetrable

penetrate, v, calar, desentrañar, penetrar

penetrating, adj, penetrante

penetration, n f, penetración

peninsula, n f, península

penitence, n f, penitencia

penknife, n m, cortaplumas

penman, n m, calígrafo

penny, n m, penique

pension, n f, cesantía, pensión

pensive, adj, pensativo

people, n f, gente

pepper, n f, pimienta

percentage, n m, porcentaje

perceptible, adj, perceptible

perception, n f, percepción

perch, n f, percha

perennial, adj, perenne

perfect, adj, perfecto

perfect, v, perfecciónar

perfection, n f, perfección

perfectly, adv, perfectamente

perforation, n f, perforación

performance, n m, desempeño

perfumed, adj, oloroso

perhaps, adv, quizás

peril, n m, peligro, trance

perilous, adj, peligroso

period of time, n m, período

periodical, adj, periódico

periodically, adv, periódicamente

periphery, n f, periferia

perish, v, perecer

perishable, adj, perecedero

perjure, v, perjurar

permanence, n f, permanencia

permanent, adj, permanente

permissible, adj, permisible

permission, n f, permisión

permission, n m, permiso

permit, v, licenciar, permitir

perpendicular, adj, perpendicular

perpetrate, v, perpetrar

perpetual, adj, perdurable, perpetuo

perpetuate, v, perpetuar

perplex, v, intrincar

perplexed, adj, perplejo

persecution, n f, persecución

persecutor, n f, perseguidor
perseverance, n f, perseverancia
persevere, v, perseverar
persist, v, persistir
persistence, n f, persistencia
persistent, adj, perseverante, persistente
person, n f, persona
personal, adj, personal
personality, n f, personalidad
personally, adv, personalmente
perspective, n f, perspectiva
persuade, v, persuadir
persuasive, adj, persuasivo
persuation, n f, persuasión
pertinance, n f, pertenencia
pertinant, adj, perteneciente
pertinent, adj, pertinente
perturb, v, perturbar
Peru, n f, Perú
perverse, adj, perverso
perversion, n f, perversión
perversity, n f, perversidad
pervert, v, pervertir
peseta (Spanish currency), n f, peseta
pest, n f, peste
pester, v, apestar
pestered, adj, apestado
petition, n f, petición
petition, n m, pedimento
petition, v, libelar
petroleum, n m, petróleo
petticoat, n fpl, enaguas
phantom, n m, fantasma
pharmacy, n f, farmacia
pheasant, n f, faisán
Philippines, n fpl, Filipinas
philosophy, n f, filosofía
phonograph, n m, fonógrafo
photograph, n f, fotografía
physical, adj, físico
physician, n m, físico
physics, n f, física
piano, n m, piano
pick, v, picar, recoger

pickle, n m, escabeche
pickle, v, encurtir, escabechar
pickled, adj, adobado, encurtido
pickles, n mpl, encurtidos, pepinillos
picture, n m, cuadro
picturesque, adj, pintoresco
pie, n m, pastel
piece, n f, pieza
piece, n m, pedazo, tramo, trozo
pierce, v, acribillar, agujerear
pig, n m, lechón, marrano
pigeon holes, n m, casillero
pigeon, n m, pichón
pigment, n m, pigmento
pike, n m, chuzo
pile up, v, apilar
pile, n m, pilón
pillar, n m, pilar
pillow, n f, almohada, almohadilla
pilot, n m, pilato
pin case, n m, alfiletero
pin, n f, clavija
pin, n m, alfiler, bolo, perno
pincers, n fpl, pinzas, tenacillas
pine, n m, pino
pineapple, n f, anana, piña
pinnacle, n m, pináculo
pious, adj, piadoso, pío
pipe, n f, cachimba, cañería, pipa
pipe, n m, cañuto, pita
piper, n m, gaitero
pippin, n f, camuesa
piracy, n f, piratería
pirate, n m, pirata
pistol, n f, pistola
piston, n m, émbolo, pistón
pit, n m, tragadero
pitcher, n f, cántara, piqueta
pitcher, n m, bocal, cántaro
pity, n f, lástima, piedad
pity, v, apiadarse, compadecerse
pivot, n m, pivote
placable, adj, aplacable
placard, n m, cartel
placate, v, aplacar
place, n m, paraje

place, v, colocar
placement, n f, colocación
placid, adj, plácido
plague, n f, plaga
plague, v, plagar
plain, adj, llano, plano
plain, n f, planada
plan, n m, plan, plano
plan, v, plantear
planet, n f, planeta
plank, n m, tablón
plank, v, entablar
planks, n m, tablazón
plant, n f, planta
plant, v, plantar
plantation, n f, plantación
planter, n m, plantador
plaster, n m, emplasto
plaster, v, emplastar
plate, n f, placa, plancha
plate, v, chapear, planchear
plates, n f, vajilla
platform, n f, plataforma
platinum, n m, platino
plausible, adj, plausible
play, n f, jugada
play, v, jugar
player, n m, jugador
plead, v, pleitear
pleasant, adj, ameno, chusco, placentero
please, v, complacer, gustar, placer
pleasure, n m, gusto, placer
pledge, v, pignorar
plentiful, adj, pingüe
pliable, adj, plegable
plot, n m, complot
plough, n m, arado
plough, v, arar
ploughing, n f, aradura
ploughman, n m, arador
pluck, v, pelar
plum, n f, ciruela
plumage, n m, plumaje
plumber, n m, plomero
plunge, v, zabullir

plural, adj, plural
plurality, n f, pluralidad
plush, adj, afelpado
poach eggs, v, escalfar
pocket, n f, faltriquera
poem, n m, poema
poet, n m, poeta
poetry, n f, poesía
point, n m, punto
pointed, adj, apuntado
poison, n m, veneno
poison, v, emponzoñar, envenenar
polar, adj, polar
pole, n f, pértiga
pole, n m, polo
police station, n f, comisaría
police, n f, policía
policy, n f, póliza
polish, v, acicalar
polisher, n m, alisador
politeness, n f, urbanidad
political, adj, político
politics, n f, política
poll tax, n f, capitación
poll, n m, padrón
pomegranate, n f, granada
pompous, adj, pomposo
pond, n f, laguna
ponder, v, ponderar
pony, n f, haca
pool, n f, balsa
pool, n m, charco
poor, adj, apurado, pobre
Pope, n m, papa
populace, n m, poblacho
popularity, n f, popularidad
popularize, v, popularizar
populate, v, poblar
population, n f, población
populous, adj, populoso
porch, n m, portal, zaguán
pork sausage, n m, chorizo
porous, adj, poroso
portable, adj, portátil
portfolio, n f, carpeta, cartera
portion, n f, porción, toma

portrait, n m, retrato
Portuguese (language), n f,
 portugués
Portuguese, adj, portugués
posession, n f, tenencia
position, n f, posición
positive, adj, positivo
possess, v, poseer
possession, n f, posesión
possessor, n m, poseedor
possibility, n f, posibilidad
possible, adj, posible
post office, n f, posta
post office, n m, correo
post, n m, poste
postage, n m, porte
postal, adj, postal
posterity, n f, posteridad
posthumous, adj, póstumo
postpone, v, posponer
postscript, n f, posdata
postulate, v, postular
posture, n f, postura
pot, n m, pote
potable, adj, bebedero
potassium, n m, potasio
potato, n f, patata
potent, adj, potente
potential, adj, potencial
potion, n f, poción
potter, n m, alfarero
pottery, n f, ollería, alfarería
pound, n f, libra
pound, v, machar
poverty, n f, pobreza
power, n f, potencia
power, n m, poder
powerful, adj, poderoso
practical, adj, práctico
practically, adv, prácticamente
practice, n f, práctica
practice, v, practicar
praise, n f, alabanza
praise, n m, elogio, encomio
praise, v, alabar, elogiar
pray, v, orar, rezar

prayer, n m, rezo
preamble, n m, preámbulo
precarious, adj, precario
precede, v, anteceder, preceder
precedence in order of time, n f,
 antelación
preceding, adj, precedente
precious, adj, precioso
precipitate, v, derrumbar, precipitar
precipitation, n f, precipitación
precipitation, n m, derrumbamiento
precise, adj, preciso
precisely, adv, precisamente
precision, n f, precisión
precursor, n m, precursor
predecessor, n m, antecesor,
 predecesor
predict, v, antedecir, predecir
prediction, n f, predicción
prediction, n m, vaticinio
predominant, adj, predominante
predominate, v, predominar
preface, n m, prefacio
prefer, v, anteponer, preferir
preferable, adj, preferible
preference, n f, prelación
prefix, n m, prefijo
prejudge, v, prejuzgar
prejudice, n m, desabono, prejuicio
preliminary, adj, preliminar
prelude, n m, preludio
premature, adj, prematuro
premise, n f, premisa
premium, n f, prima
premium, n m, agio, agiotaje
preoccupation, n f, preocupación
preoccupy, v, preocupar
preparation, n f, preparación
preparation, n m, aparejo, apresto
prepare, v, aparejar preparar,
 prevenir
prepared, adj, aparejado
prescribe, v, prescribir, recetar
prescribed, adj, prescripto
prescription, n f, prescripción, receta
presence, n f, presencia

resent, adj, presente

resent, adv, ora

resent, n m, presente, regalo

resent, v, presentar

resentation, n f, presentación

resently, adv, presentemente

reservation, n f, preservación

reserve, v, preservar, resguardar

reside, v, presidir

resident, n m, presidente

ress, n f, prensa

ress, v, apremiar, aprensar, prensar

resser, n m, aprensador

ressure, n f, premura, prensadura, presión

ressure, n m, apremio, apretón

restige, n m, prestigio

restigious, adj, prestigioso

resume, v, presumir

resumed, adj, presunto

resumption, n f, presunción

retend, v, pretender

retense, n f, pretensión

retext, n m, pretexto

retty good, adj, bonico, bonito

retty, adj, linda

revent, v, precaver

reventive, adj, preventivo

revious, adv, anterior

reviously, adv, anteriormente, previamente

prevoius, adj, previo

prick, v, aguijar

pride, n f, ufanía

pride, n m, fasto, orgullo

primacy, n f, primacía

primarily, adv, máxime

primitive, adj, primitivo

prince, n m, príncipe

princess, n f, princesa

principal inhabitant, n f, cacique

principal, adj, cardinal, primario

principal, n m, director

principally, adv, mayormente, principalmente

print, n f, zaraza

print, v, imprimir

printed, adj, impreso

printer, n m, impresor, tipógrafo

printing, n f, imprenta, tipografía

prior, adj, prior

priority, n f, prioridad

prison, n f, cárcel, prisión

prisoner, n f, m, preso, prisionero

private, adj, privado

privation, n f, privación

privilege, n m, privilegio

prize, n m, premio

probability, n f, probabilidad

probable, adj, probable

probably, adv, probablemente

probation, n f, probación

proclamation, n m, bando

product, n m, producto

profit, n m, cómodo, pro, usufructo

program, n m, programa

progress, n f, adelantamiento

progress, n f, medra

progress, v, medrar

prohibit, v, vedar

prohibition, n m, interdicto

promise, n f, promesa

promise, v, prometer

promissory note, n m, abonaré

pronounce, v, pronunciar

prophetic, adj, fatídico

proposal, n f, manda

prosecute, v, proseguir

prosperity, n bienandanza, bonanza

protect, v, abrigar, proteger

proud, adj, orgulloso, ufano

prove, v, probar

proverb, n m, refrán

provide, v, abastecer

providing, n f, apercibimiento

provision, n m, abastecimiento

provoke, v, encarnizar

prudence, n f, sensatez

prudent, adj, recatado

prune, v, podar

public school, n m, liceo

publish, v, publicar
publisher, n m, editor
publishing, n f, redacción
Puerto Rico, n f, Puerto Rico
pull out, v, arrancar
pulley, n f, garrucha, polea
pulverize, v, polvorizar
pump, n f, bomba
pumpkin, n f, calabaza
punch (drink), n m, ponche
punch, v, punzar
punctual, adj, puntual
punctuality, n f, puntualidad
punctually, adv, apuradamente,
  puntualmante
punctuate, v, puntuar
punctuation, n f, puntuación
puncture, n f, picada, puntura
punishment, n m, castigo
punster, n m, chulo
pupil (eye), n f, pupila
pupil (school), n m, pupilo,
  discípulo, alumno
puppy, n m, cachorro
purchase, n f, compra, merca
pure blooded, adj, castizo
pure, adj, caste, lirondo, puro
purely, adv, puramente
purge, v, purgar
purification, n f, depuración
purify, v, acendrar, apurar, purificar
purity, n f, pureza, puridad
purple, n f, púrpura
purse, n f, bolsa
purse, n m, bolsillo, portamonedas
push, n m, empellón
push, v, empujar
put, adj, metido
put, v, meter, poner
putrid, adj, pútrido
pyramidal, adj, apiñado

Q

quack, n m, empírico
quagmire, n m, cenagal

quail, n f, codorniz
qualification, n f, calificación
qualified, adj, habilitado
qualify, v, calificar, habilitar
quality, n f, calidad
quantity, n f, cantidad
quarrel, n f, camorra, pendencia
quarrel, v, reñir
quarry, n f, cantera
quarter, v, descuartizar
queen, n f, reina
quench, v, apagar
querulous, adj, quejoso
question, n f, cuestión, pregunta
question, v, cuestionar
quick, adj, presto
quickness, n f, presteza
quiet, adj, encalmado, quedo, quieto
quiet, v, aquietar
quietly, adv, quietamente,
  tranquilamente
quietness, n f, quietud
quilt, v, colchar
quilting, n m, acolchado
quinine, n f, quinina
quintuple, adj, quíntuplo
quit, v, desocupar, quitar
quota, n f, cuota
quote, v, citar

R

rabble, n f, gentío
rabid, adj, rabioso
race, n f, ralea, raza
racket, n f, raqueta
radiant, adj, radiante
radiation, n f, radiación
radical, edj, radical
radish, n m, rábano
radius, n m, radio
rafter, n m, cabrio
rag, n m, andrajo, harapo, trapo
rage, n f, rabia
rage, v, rabiar
railroad switch, n f, cambiamano

railroad, n f, ferrocarril
rain, n f, lluvia
rain, v, llover
raincoat, n f, impermeable
raise price, v, encarecer
raise, v, empinar, levantar, realzar
raisin, n f, pasa
raising, n m, alzamiento
raisins, n fpl, uva pasa
ramification, n f, ramificación
ramrod, n f, baqueta
ranch, n m, rancho
rancher, n m, ranchero
rancid, adj, rancio
rancor, n m, rencor
rancorous, adj, rencoroso
rank, n m, rango
ransom, n m, rescate
ransom, v, rescatar
rapair, v, reparar
rapidity, n f, rapidez
rapidly, adv, rápidamente
rare, adj, raro
rareness, n f, rareza
rarify, v, rarificar
rarity, n f, raridad
rascal, n m, perillán
rash, adj, temerario
rasp, n f, raspa
rasp, v, raspar
rat, n f, rata
rate, n f, tasa
ratification, n f, ratificación
ratify, v, ratificar
ration, n f, ración
rational, edj, racional
rationality, n f, racionalidad
rave, v, delirar
raw sugar, n m, cogucho
raw, adj, bisoño
ray, n m, rayo
razor handle, n f, cacha
re-elect, v, reelegir
re-election, n f, reelección
re-examine, v, reexaminar
reaction, n f, reacción

read, v, leer
reader, n m, lector
reading, n f, lectura
ready, adj, apercibido, dispuesto, listo
real, adj, real
reality, n f, realidad
reality, n fpl, veras
realize, v, realizar
really, adv, realmente
reap, v, segar
reappear, v, reaparecer
reappearance, n f, reaparición
reason, n f, razón
reason, v, raciocinar, razonar
reasonable, adj, razonable
reasoning, n m, raciocinio
reassurance, n m, reaseguro
reassure, v, reasegurar
rebel, n m, rebelde
rebel, v, rebelar
rebellion, n f, rebelión
rebellious, edj, rebelde
rebound, v, resaltar
receipt, n f, quitanza
receipt, n m, recibí
receive, v, percibir, recibir
receiver, n m, recibidor
recent, adj, reciente
recently, adv, recién, recientemente
receptacle, n receptáculo
reception, n f, acogida, recepción
recess, n m, recreo
recipient, n m, receptor
reciprocal, adj, recíproco
reciprocate, v, reciprocar
recite, v, recitar
reclaim, v, reclamar
recline, v, reclinar, recostar
recognition, n f, descubierta
recognition, n m, reconocimiento
recognize, v, reconocer
recognized, adj, reconocido
recollect, v, recapacitar
recollection, n f, recolección
recommend, v, encargar,

encomendar, recomendar
recommendable, adj, recomendable
recommendation, n f,
recomendación
reconcile, v, reconciliar
reconciliation, n f, reconciliación
recorder, n m, archivero
recount, v, recontar
recourse, n m, recurso
recover, v, recobrar, recuperar,
reivindicar
recoverable, adj, cobradero
recovered, adj, cobrado
recovery, n f, recuperación
recovery, n m, desquite, recobro
recreation, n f, recreación
recruit, n m, recluta
recruit, v, reclutar
rectification, n f, rectificación
rectify, v, rectificar
rectitude, n f, derechura, rectitud
recur, v, recurrir
red color, adj, cardenal
red, adj, punzó, rojo
reddish, adj, bermejizo
redeem, v, desempeñar, redimir
redemption, n f, redención
redouble, v, replegar
reduce, v, rebajar, reducir
reduced, adj, reducido
reduction, n f, reducción
redundant, adj, redundante
reel, v, bambolear
reeling, n m, bamboleo
reestablish, v, restablecer
refer, v, referir
reference, n f, referencia
refine, v, acrisolar, refinar
refined, adj, refinado
reflect, v, reflectar, reflejar,
reflexionar
reflection, n f, reflexión
reflective, adj, reflexivo
reflex, n m, reflejo
reform, n f, reforma
reform, v, reformar

refresh, v, refrescar
refreshment, n f, refacción
refreshment, n m, refresco, refrigerio
refrigeration, n m, enfriamiento
refrigerator, n m, enfriador,
refrigerador
refuge, n m, refugio
refuse, n f, zupia
refuse, v, desechar, rehusar
refused, adj, desechado
refute, v, refutar
regal, adj, regio
regimen, n m, régimen
regiment, n m, regimiento
region, n f, región
register, n m, registro
register, v, encabezar, registrar
registered, adj, registrado
registrar, n f, registrador
regret, v, sentir
regular, adregular
regularity, n f, regularidad
regularly, adv, regularmente
regulate, v, regular
regulated, adj, regulado
regulation, n f, regulación
regulation, n m, reglamento
regulator, n m, regulador
rehabilitate, v, rehabilitar
reign, n m, reinado
reign, v, reinar
reigning, adj, reinante
reimburse, v, embolsar, reembolsar
reindeer, n m, reno
reinforcement, n m, refuerzo
reintegrate, v, reintegrar
reiterate, v, reiterar
reject, v, repulsar
rejection, n m, rechazo
rejoice, v, regocijarse
rejoicing, n m, regocijo
relapse, n f, recaída
relapse, v, recaer
relate, v, relacionar, relatar
relation, n m, relato
relative, adj, relativo

relatively, adv, relativamente
relax, v, amainar, cejar, relajar
relegate, v, relegar
relevant, adj, relevante
relief, n f, relevación
relief, n m, desagravio, relieve
relieve, v, relevar
religion, n f, religión
religious, adj, religioso
religiously, adv, religiosamente
reload, v, recargar
remain, v, permanecer
remainder, n m, restante
remedy, n m, remedio
remedy, v, remediar
remember, v, recordar
remind, v, recordar
remiss, adj, remiso
remission, n f, remisión
remit, v, remitir
remnant, n m, remanente
remorse, n m, remordimiento
remote, adj, remoto
remotely, adv, remotamente
remount, v, remontar
remove, v, escotar, desmontar, remover
rendition, n f, rendición
renew, v, reanudar
renounce, v, renunciar
renovate, v, renovar
renovation, n f, renovación
renown, n m, renombre
renowned, adj, renombrado
rent, n f, renta
rent, n m, desgarro
rent, v, rentar
renter, n m, rentero
renunciation, n f, renuncia
reopen, v, reabrir
reorganize, v, reorganizar
repaint, v, repintar
repair, n m, reparo
repair, v, rehacer
repairing a ship, n f, carena
repairs, n f, recorrida

repay, v, repagar
repeat, v, menudear, repetir
repeated, adj, repetido
repeatedly, adv, repetidamente
repel, v, rechazar, repeler
repetition, n f, repetición
replace, v, reemplazar, reponer
replaced, adj, repuesto
replete, adj, replete
reply, n f, réplica
reply, v, replicar
report, n f, relación
report, n m, informe
reporter, n m, relator
repose, n m, repose
represent, v, representar
representation, n f, representación
representative, n m, representativo
repression, n f, represión
reprimand, n f, reprimenda
reproach, n m, reproche
reproach, v, increpar, reprochar
reproduce, v, reproducir
reproduction, n f, reproducción
reprove, v, reprobar
republic, n f, república
republican, adj, republicano
repudiate, v, repudiar
repugnant, adj, repugnante
reputation, n f, nombradía, reputación
repute, v, reputar
request, n m, requerimiento
request, v, requerir
requisition, n f, requisición
rescind, v, rescindir
research, n f, rebusca
resemblance, n f, semejanza
resemble, v, semejar
resent, v, resentirse
resentful, adj, resentido
resentment, n f, resentimiento
reserve, n f, reserva
reserve, v, reservar
reserved, adj, reservado
reside, v, residir

residence, n f, residencia
resident, adj, residente
residue, n m, desecho, residuo
resign, v, resignar
resignation, n f, dejación,
  resignación
resin, n f, resina
resist, v, resistir
resistance, n f, resistencia
resistant, adj, resistente
resolute, adj, resolute, resuelto
resolution, n f, resolución
resolve, v, acordar
resort, n f, manida
resound, v, zumbar
respect, n m, respecto, respeto
respect, v, acatar, respetar
respectable, adj, abonado,
  apreciable, respetable
respectful, adj, respetuoso
respective, adj, respective
respectively, adv, respectivamente
resplendent, adj, esplendente
respond, v, responder
response, n f, respuesta
responsibility, n f, responsabilidad
responsible, adj, responsable
rest, n m, descanso, resto
rest, v, descansar, holgar, reposar
restaurant, n m, restaurant
restitution, n f, restitución, torna
restlessness, n m, desasosiego
restoration, n f, restauración
restore, v, restaurar, restituir
restrain, v, restringir
restrict, v, coartar
restriction, n f, restricción
result, n f, resulta
result, n m, resultado
result, v, resultar
resume, v, reasumir, resumir
retail store, n m, menudeo
retail, v, revender
retailer, n m, detallista
retain, v, retener
retaliate, v, talionar

retard, v, retardar
retire, v, rehuir, retirar
retired official, n m, cesante
retired, adj, retirado
retort, n f, retorta
retort, v, retorcer
retract, v, retractar
retraction, n f, retracción
retreat, n f, retirada
retreat, n m, recogimiento, retiro
retribution, n f, retribución
retrieve, v, desquitar, retraer
return, n f, vuelta
return, n m, regreso, retorno
return, v, regresar, retornar, tornar
reunion, n f, reunión
reunite, v, reunir
reveal, v, revelar
revenge, n f, venganza
revenue, n m, rédito
reverse, n m, reverso
reversible, adj, reversible
review, n f, reseña, revista
review, n m, alarde
review, v, repasar, reseñar
revile, v, vilipendiar
revise, v, releer
revision, n f, revisión
revision, n m, repaso
revive, v, revivir
revoke, v, revocar
revolution, n f, revolución
revolve, v, girar
revolver, n m, revolver
reward, n m, recambio
reward, v, premiar, remunerar
rewards, n fpl, albricias
rhyme, n f, rima
ribbon, n m, listón
rice, n m, arroz
rich, adj, acaudalado, rico
riches, n f, riqueza
riddle, n f, quisicosa
ride, v, cabalgar
ridge, n m, caballete
right hand, n f, derecha, diestra

right, adj, derecho
right, n m, derecho
rightly, adv, derechamente, rectamente
ringleader, n f, cabecilla
risk, v, peligrar
river's mouth, n m, embocadero
river, n m, río
riverbed, n m, cauce
road, n f, rada
road, n m, camino
robber, n m, bandolero, hurtador
robbery, n f, rapacidad
robbery, n m, latrocinio
robust, adj, membrudo
rock salt, n f, sal gema
rock, n f, peña, roca
rocket, n m, cohete
rocky, adj, peñascoso
rod, n f, vara
rogue, n m, bellaco
roll, v, aplanar, laminar
roller, n f, aplanadera
rolling (ship), n m, bandazo
rolling pin, n m, zurrullo
Roman, adj, romano
roof, n m, techado
roof, v, techar
room, n m, aposento, cuarto
root, n f, cepa, raíz
rope, n f, maroma
rope, n m, dogal
rose, n f, rosa
rosebush, n m, rosal
rotary, adj, giratorio
rouge, n m, afeite
rough draft, n m, borrador
rough, adj, acerbo, escabroso, tosco
roughness, n f, tosquedad
round, adj, redondo
rout, v, derrotar
route, n f, ruta
row, n f, andana, fila, hila
row, v, remar
rowing, n f, boga
royalty, n f, realeza

rubbish, n cachivache, cascote
rudder, n m, gobernalle
rude, adj, descomedido, malcriado
ruffled shirt, n f, camisola
rug, n m, tapete
ruin, n f, ruina
rule, n f, regla
rule, v, dominar, regir, reglar
rumor, n f, hablilla
run aground, v, encallar, zabordar
rural, adj, campesino
rust, n m, orín
rustic, adj, villano
rut, n m, carril
rye, n m, centeno

S

sabbath, n m, sábado
sable, n f, cebellina
sabre, n m, sable
saccharine, adj, sacarino
saccharine, n f, sacarina
sack, n m, saco
sack, v, saquear
sacrament, n m, sacramento
sacred, adj, sagrado
sacrifice, n m, sacrificio
sacrifice, v, sacrificar
sacrilege, n m, sacrilegio
sad, adj, lastimero, triste
sad, n f, turba
sad, n m, césped
sadden, v, entristecer
saddle, v, ensillar
sadness, n f, tristeza
safe, adj, salvo
safe, n m, segura
safeguard, n f, salvaguardia
safety pin, n m, imperdible
saffron, n m, azafrán
sagacity, n f, sagacidad
sage, n m, filósofo
sail, n f, salvia
sail, v, navegar, navigar, zarpar
sailboat, n m, velero

sailing, adj, velero
sailor, n m, marinero
sails, n m, velaje
saint, n mf, santo
saintly, adj, santo
salad bowl, n f, ensaladera
salad, n f, ensalada
salary, n m, gaje, salario
sale, adj, único
sale, n f, venta
salient, adj, saliente
saline, adj, salina
salmon, n m, salmón
salt, n f, sal
salt, v, salar
salty, adj, salado
salutary, adj, salubre
salutation, n f, salutación
salute, n m, saludo
salute, v, saludar
salvage, n m, salvamento
same, adj, idéntico, mismo
sample, n f, muestra
sample, n m, dechado
sanctify, v, santificar
sanction, n f, sanción
sanction, v, sancionar
sanctuary, n m, santuario
sand, n f, arena
sand, v, enarenar
sandal, n f, sandalia
sandbag, n m, saco de arena
sandwich, n m, emparedado
sandy, adj, arenoso
sane, adj, sana
sanguine, adj, sanguíneo
sanitary, adj, sanitario
sanity, n f, sanidad
sap, n f, savia
sap, n m, jugo, zumo
sapling, n m, renuevo
sapphire, n m, zafir
sarcasm, n m, sarcasmo
sarcastic, adj, sarcástico
sardine, n f, sardina
sarsaparilla, n f, zarzaparilla

sash, n f, cinta
satan, n m, satán
satanic, adj, satánico
satellite, n m, satélite
satiate, v, saciar
satiated, adj, harto
satin, n m, raso, satín
satire, n f, sátira
satirical, adj, satírico
satirist, n mf, satírico
satisfaction, n f, satistacción
satisfactory, adj, satisfactorio
satisfied, adj, satisfecho
satisfy, v, satisfacer
saturate, v, saturar
Saturday, n m, sábado
sauce, n f, salsa
saucepan, n f, cacerola, cazuela
saucer, n f, salsera
saucer, n m, platillo
sausage, n m, embuchado
savage, adj, salvaje
savage, n m, cafre, salvaje
save, v, salvar
saving, adj, ahorrativo
Savior, n m, salvador
savory, adj, sabroso
saw, n f, sierra
saw, v, serrar
sawdust, n m, serrín
say, v, decir
saying, n m, decir, dicho
scabbard, n f, vaina
scaffold, n m, andamio, cadalso
scald, v, escaldar, tiña
scale, n f, balanza, escama
scale, v, escalar, escamar
scalpel, n m, escalpelo
scamp, n m, ganapán
scamper, v, correr
scan, v, escudriñar
scandal, n m, escándalo
scant, adj, escaso
scapegoat, n m, chivo emisario
scar, n f, cicatriz
scarce, adj, escaso

scarcely, adv, apenas
scarcity, n f, carestía
scare, n m, espanto
scare, v, espantar
scarecrow, n m, espantajo
scatter, v, disipar
scavenger, n m, basurero
scene, n f, escena
scenic, adj, escénico
scent, n m, olfato, perfume
scent, v, perfumar
scentless, adj, inodoro
sceptre, n m, cetro
schedule, n f, cédula
scheme, n m, proyecto
scholar, n m, escolar
scholarly, adj, erudito
scholastic, adj, escolástico
school, n f, escuela
school, v, amaestrar
schoolroom, n f, aula
science, n f, ciencia
scientific, adj, científico
scissors, n fpl, tijeras
scoff (mock), v, mofar
scold, v, reñir
scoop, n m, cucharón
scoop, v, achicar
scope, n m, alcance
score, n f, muesca
score, v, escoplear
scoundrel, n m, pícaro
scour, v, fregar
scout, n m, batidor
scrap, n f, migaja
scrap, n m, retazo, tasajo
scrape, n f, raedura
scrape, v, raer
scraped, adj, raído
scraper, n m, rascador
scratch, n f, rascadura
scratch, n m, araño, rasguño
scratch, v, arañar, rascar, rasguñar
scream, n m, chillido
scream, v, chillar
screen, n f, pantalla, zaranda

screen, n m, biombo
screen, v, cibar
screw, n m, tornillo
screw, v, atornillar
scribble, v, emborronar
scroll, n m, rollo
scrub, v, frotar
scrupulous, adj, escrupuloso
scrutiny, n f, escrutinio
sculpt, v, esculpir
sculptor, n m, escultor
sculpture, n f, escultura
scum, n f, espuma
scupltor, n m, labrante
scythe, n f, guadaña
sea salt, n m, sal marina
sea weed, n f, alga
sea, n mf, mar
seagull, n f, gaviota
seal (animal), n m, foca
seal, n m, sello, sigilo, timbre
seal, v, sellar, sigilar
seam, n f, costura
seaport, n m, puerto, puerto de mar
search, n f, busca
search, v, buscar, rebuscar
seasickness, n m, mareo
season, n f, sazón
season, n m, temporal
season, v, sazonar
seasonable, adj, estaciónal
seasoned, adj, sazonado
seasoning, n f, salazón
seasoning, n m, condimento
seat, n m, asiento
seaweed, n f, alga
secluded, adj, recogido
seclusion, n f, apartamiento
second (time), n m, segundo
second, adj, segundo
secondary, adj, secundario
secrecy, n m, secreto
secret, adj, secreto
secretary, n m, secretario
secrete, v, secretar
secretive, adj, misterioso

secretly, adv, encubiertamente, ocultamente
sect, n f, secta
section, n f, sección
section, v, seccionar
secular, adj, secular
secure, v, asegurar
security, n f, seguridad
sedate, adj, serio
sedative, n f, mt, sedativo
sediment, n f, sedimento
seduce, v, seducir
seduction, n f, seducción
seductive, adj, seductivo
see, v, ver
seed, n f, semilla
seed, v, granar
seedling, n m, retoño
seeing, n f, vista
seeing, n m, ver
seem, v, parecer
seen, adj, visto
seer, n m, profeta
segment, n m, segmento
segregate, v, segregar
seize, v, apresar, asir, prender
seizure, n m, secuestro
seldom, adv, raramente
select, adj, selecto
selection, n f, selección
self, n mf, mismo
self-deception, n f, ilusión
self-defense, n f, defensa propia
selfish, adj, egoísta, ensimismado, interesado
selfishness, n m, egoísmo
sell, v, vender
sellable, adj, vendible
seller, n m, vendedor
semi-annual, adj, semianual
semicircle, n f, semicírculo
semicolon, n, punto y coma
seminary, n m, seminario
senate, n m, senado
senator, n m, senador
send a telegraph, v, telegrafiar

send, v, enviar
sending, n m, envío
senile, adj, caduco, senil
sensation, n f, sensación
sense, n m, sentido
senseless, adj, insensible
sensibility, n f, sensibilidad
sensible, adj, sensato, sensible
sentence, n f, frase, oración, sentencia
sentiment, n f, sentimiento
sentry, n mi, centinela
separate room, n m, apartado
separate, v, desagregar, separar
separated, adj, apartado
separation, n f, apartamiento
September, n m, septiembre
septic, adj, séptico
sepulchre, n m, sepulcro
sequel, n f, secuela
sequence, n f, seguida
serenade, n f, serenata
serenely, adv, serenamente
serenity, n f, serenidad
serial, adj, consecutive
series, n f, serie
seriously, adv, de veras, seriamente
seriousness, n f, seriedad
sermon, n m, sermón
serpent, n f, serpiente, sierpe
serpentine, adj, serpentino
serrated, adj, dentado
servant, n f, criada
servant, n m, criado, gañán
serve, v, servir
service, n f, m, servicio
serviceable, adj, servible
session, n mt, sesión
set, n m, surtido
settlement, n f, colonia
seven, n f, siete
seventy, n f, setenta
several, adj, diverse
severe, adj, severo
sew, v, coser, zurcir
sewer, n f, cloaca

sewer, n m, albañal, alcantarillado, vertedero
shade, n f, sombra
shade, n m, matiz
shady, adj, sombrío
shaft, n f, flecha
shaggy, adj, afelpado, felpado
shake, v, sacudir
shaky, adj, titubeante
shallow, adj, somero
shallow, n m, bajío
sham, n m, fingimiento
shame, n f, vergüenza
shame, v, avergonzar
shameful, adj, bochornoso, vergonzoso
shampoo, n m, champú
shamrock, n m, trébol
shank, n f, zanca
shank, n m, empalmo
shape, n f, forma
shape, n m, talle
shapely, adj, simétrico
share, v, distribuir
shark, n m, tiburón
sharp, adj, afilado, agudo, picante
sharpen, v, afilar, aguzar
sharply, adv, agudamente
sharpshooter, n m, certero
shave, v, afeitar, rapar
shaving, n f, acepilladura, rasura, viruta
shaving, n m, rape
shawl, n m, chal
she, pro, ella
shear, v, trasquilar
sheathe, v, envainar
shed, n m, sotechado
sheep, n f, oveja
sheep, n m, carnero
sheepish, adj, ovejuno
sheepskin, n m, zamarro
sheet, n f, sábana
sheet, n m, pliego
shelf, n m, anaquel, andén
shell, n f, concha

shellfish, n f, coquina
shellfish, n m, marisco
shelter, n m, abrigo, cobertizo
shelter, v, amparar, refugiar
shelving, n f, inclinado
shepherd, n m, ovejero, pastor
shield, n m, escudo
shield, v, escudar
shift, v, mudar
shin, n f, tibia
shine, n m, brillo
shine, v, lucir, relucir
shiny, adj, luminoso
ship's course, n f, deriva, derrota
ship's course, n m, derrotero
ship, n f, nave
ship, n m, buque, navío
ship, v, embarcar
shipment, n m, embarque
shipwreck, n m, naufragio
shipyard, n f, verga
shipyard, n m, varadero
shirk, v, esquivar
shirt, n f, carnisa, camiseta
shirting, n f, bogotana
shiver, v, tiritar
shivering fit, n m, calofrío
shock, n f, sacudida
shock, n m, choque
shock, v, escandalizar
shoe shop, n f, zapatería
shoe, n f, herradura
shoe, n m, zapato
shoehorn, n m, calzador
shoelaces, n f, majuela
shoemaker, n m, zapatero
shoot, n m, tallo
shorn, adj, chamorro
short cut, n m, atajo
short space of time, n m, rato
short, adj, corto
short, adv, breve
shorten, v, acortar, recortar
shorthand, n f, taquigrafía
shortly, adv, luego
shot, n m, balazo

shoulder, n f, espalda
shoulder, n m, hombro
shout, n f, aclamación
shout, n m, alarido, hocico
shout, v, aclamar
shovel, n f, pala
shovel, n m, legón
show window, n m, escaparate
show, n m, espectáculo
show, v, mostrar
shred, n f, lira
shrew, n f, regañona
shrewd, adj, astuto
shrill, adj, agudo
shrimp, n m, camarón
shrine, n m, relicario
shrink, v, encoger, estrechar
shrivel, v, arrugar
shrub, n m, arbusto
shrug, n m, encogimiento
shudder, v, estremecerse
shuffle, v, mezclar, tergiversar
shy, adj, huraño, timido
shyness, n f, timidez
sickening, adj, asqueroso
sickly, adj, enfermizo
sickness, n f, enfermedad
side, n m, lado
sidepost, n m, quicial
sidewalk, n f, acera
sideways, adj, de lado
siding, n m, apartadero
siege, n m, sitio
sieve, n f, criba
sieve, n m, cedazo
sieve, n m, tamiz
siezure, n f, presa
sift, v, cerner, tarnizar, zarandear
sigh, n m, suspiro
sigh, v, suspirar
sight, n f, vista
sign, n f, seña
sign, n m, signo
sign, v, firmar, señalar
signal, n m, señalado
signature, n f, firma

significance, n f, significación
significant, adj, significante
signify, v, significar
signpost, n m, poste de señales
silence!, int, ...chito!
silence, n f, callada
silence, n m, silencio
silence, v, acallar
silent, adj, callado, silencioso
silently, adv, calladamente
silhouette, n f, silueta
silk, n f, seda
silky, adj, sedoso, sérico
silly, adj, chiflado, tonto
silver plated, adj, plateado
silver plating, n f, plateadura
silver, n f, argentino, plata
silver, v, platear
similar, adj, parecido, semejante, similar
simple, adj, simple
simplicity, n f, sencillez
simplify, v, simplificar
simply, adv, simplemente
simulate, v, simular
simultaneous, adj, simultáneo
sin, n m, pecado
sin, v, pecar
since, adv, desde que, puesto que
sincere, adj, sincero
sincerely, adv, sinceramente
sincerity, n f, sinceridad
sine, n m, seno
singe, v, chamuscar
singer, n f, cantarina
singer, n m, cantor
single, adj, sencillo
singly, adv, solamente
singular, adj, singular
singularity, n f, singularidad
sinister, adj, siniestro
sink, n f, sentina
sink, v, hundir
sinner, n m, pecador
sinus, n m, seno
sip, n m, sorbo

sip, v, sorber
sir, n m, señor
siren, n f, sirena
sirloin, n m, solomo de buey
sister, n f, hermana
sit, v, sentar
site, n m, sitio
situate, v, situado
situation, n f, ubicación
six, n f, seis
sixty, v, sesenta
size, n m, grandor, tamaño
size, v, ajustar
skate, n m, patín
skate, v, patinar
skating rink, n m, salon de patinar
skating, n f, patinación
skeleton, n m, esqueleto
skeptic, n mf, escéptico
skeptical, adj, escéptico
skepticism, n f, escepticismo
sketch, n m, boceto, bosquejo, esbozo
sketch, v, bosquejar, esquiciar
skiff, n m, esquife
skill, n f, arte, maña, pericia
skill, n m, tino
skillful, adj, perito
skin, n m, cutis
skirmish, n f, escaramuza
skirt, n f, falda, saya
skit, n f, burla
skull, n f, calavera
skull, n m, casco, cráneo
skunk, n f, mofeta
sky light, n f, claraboya, tragaluz
sky, n m, cielo
slab, n f, baldosa
slacken, v, aflojar, flojear
slag, n f, escoria
slander, n f, calumnia, maledicencia
slander, v, calumniar
slang, n f, jerga
slant, adj, sesgo
slap, n f, manotada
slaughter, n f, matanza

slave, n m, esclavo
sleek, adj, pulido
sleep, n m, sueño
sleep, v, dormir
sleeping, adj, durmiente
sleet, n f, aguanieve
sleeve, n f, manga
slender, adj, delgado
slice, n f, rebanada, tajada
slice, n m, cacho
slice, v, rebanar
slide, n m, resbaladero
slide, v, resbalar
slight, n m, desaire
slight, v, desairar
slip, n m, desliz
slip, v, deslizar
slipper, n f, babucha, chinela, zapatilla
slippery, adj, resbaladizo
sloe, n m, arañón
sloop, n f, balandra
slope, n m, declive
slot, n f muesca
slouch, v, encorvarse
slow, adj, lento, pausado, tardo
slowly, adv, lentamente, lerdamente, pausadamente
slowness, n f, lentitud, tardanza
slum, n f, callejuela
slumber, n m, sueño ligero
sly, adj, socarrón, taimado
small basket, n f, canastilla
small bed, n f, camilla
small bell, n f, campanilla
small bridge, n f, alcantarilla
small carriage, n m, carrito
small cart, n m, carretón
smallness, n f, cortedad
smallpox, n fpl, viruelas
smart, adj, agudo
smattering, n f, tintura
smear, n f, mancha
smear, v, manchar
smell (bad), n m, husmo
smell, n m, olor

smell, v, oler
smile, n f, sonrisa
smile, v, sonreir
smiling, adj, risueño
smith, n m, herrero
smoke, n f, fumarada
smoke, n m, humo
smoke, v, ahumar
smoked, adj, ahumado
smoker, n f, fumador
smoky, adj, fumosos, humoso
smolder, v, arder sin llama
smooth, adj, liso, terso
smooth, v, allanar, enrasar
smoothing, n f, alisadura
smoothly, adv, lisamente
smoothness, n f, tersura
smuggle, v, matutear
smuggler, n m, matutero
smuggling, n m, contrabando,
  matute
snag, v, dentadura
snail, n m, caracol
snake, n f, culebra
snap, v, estallar
snare, n m, garlito, lazo
snare, v, enmarañar
snarl, n m, enredo
snarl, v, gruñir
sneak, v, arrastrar
sneer, n f, fisga
sneeze, n m, estornudo
sneeze, v, estornudar
sniff, v, husmear
snob, n f, afectado
snooze, v, dormitar
snore, n m, ronquido
snore, v, roncar
snort, v, resoplar
snow, n f, nieve
snow, v, nevar
snowfall, n f, nevada
snowstorm, n f, nevasca
snug, adj, abrigado
so much, adv, tanto
so, adv, así, tan

so-and-so, n m, zutano
soak, v, recalar, remojar
soap, n m, jabón
soap, v, enjabonar, jabonar
soaring, adj, altanero
sober, adj, sobrio
sociable, adj, sociable
social, adj, social
society, n f, sociedad
sock, n m, calcetín
socket, n f, mechero
soda, n f, soda
sofa, n f, sofá
soft, adj, blando, mole, suave
soften, v, blandear, enmollecer,
  suavizar
softly, adv, blandamente,
  suavemente
softness, n f, blandura, terneza
soil, n f, tierra
soil, v, emporcar
soldier, n m, soldado
solemn, adj, solemne
solicit, v, agenciar, solicitar
solid, adj, sólido
solidify, v, solidificar
solitary, adj, solitario
solitude, n f, soledad
solution, n f, mf, solución
solve, v, resolver
some, adj, algún, alguno
somebody, n f, alguien
somehow, adv, de algún modo
someone, pro, alguien
something, pro, alguna cosa
sometimes, adv, algunas veces
somewhat, adv, algo, alguna
somewhere, adv, en alguna tanto
son-in-law, n m, yerno
song, n f, canción
song, n m, cantar
sonnet, n m, soneto
soon, adv, presto, pronto
soot, n m, hollín
soothe, v, calmar
sorcerer, n m, hechicero

sordid, adj, sórdido
sore, adj, doloroso
sorrow, n m, pesar
sorrowful, adj, pesaroso
sorry, adj, apenado
soul, n f, alma
sound, n mf, sana
sound, v, sonar
soup, n f, sopa
sour, adj, acre, agrio
sour, v, agriar
source, n m, manantial
south, n m, sur
southwest, n m, suroeste
souvenir, n m, recuerdo
sow, n f, cochina
sow, v, sembrar
space, n f, cabida
space, n m, espacio
spacious, adj, espacioso
spade, n f, zapa
Spain, n f, España
Spanish (language), n f, español
Spanish fly, n f, cantárida
Spanish, adj, español, hispano
spare, v, preservar
spark, n f, centella, chispa
spark, n m, centelleo
sparkle, v, centellar, chispear, relumbrar
sparrow, n m, gorrión
spasm, n m, espasmo
speak, v, hablar
speaker, n f, mi, orador
special, adj, especial
specify, v, especificar
speck, n f, peca
spectator, n f, espectador
spectrum, n f, espectro solar
speculate, v, especular
speech, n f, habla
speech, n m, discurso
speechless, adj, mudo
speed, n m, andar
speed, v, expedir
speedy, adj, pronto

spell, v, deletrear
spelling, n m, deletreo
spend, v, despender, gastar
spendthrift, n m, derrochador, gastador
sperm whale, n m, cachalote
sphere, n f, esfera
sphinx, n f, esfinge
spice, n f, especie
spice, v, especiar
spices, n fpl, especias
spider, n f, araña
spill, v, verter
spin, v, hilar
spinach, n fpt, espinacas
spindle, n f, troncho, varilla
spine, n f, espina
spiral, n f, espiral
spirit, n m, ánimo, espíritu
spirited, adj, alentado, animado
spiritless, adj, exánime
spit, v, escupir
spite, n f, ojeriza
spite, n m, despecho
splash, n f, salpicadura
splash, v, chapotear, salpicar
splendid, adj, espléndido
splendor, n m, esplendor, resplandor, fausto
splinter, n f, raja
split, v, hendir, partir, rajar
spoil, v, ajar, malbaratar, viciar
spoiled, adj, mimado
sponge, n f, esponja
sponge, v, esponjar
spongy, adj, esponjoso
spontaneous, adj, espontáneo
spool, n m, carrete
spoon, n f, cuchara
sportsman, n m, sportsman
spot, n f, pinta
spot, n m, deslustre
spot, v, lugar
spotless, adj, inmaculado
spouse, n mi, esposo
sprain, n f, dislocación

spread, v, extender
spring, n f, primavera
spring, n m, brinco
spring, v, brotar
spur on, v, aguijonear
sputter, v, chisporrotear
spy glass, n m, anteojo
spy, n mf, espía
spy, v, espiar
squadron, n f, escuadra
squall, n m, grito
squander, v, desperdiciar
square, n f, plaza
square, n m, cuadrado
square, v, escuadrar
squash, v, aplastar
squat, v, agacharse
squeamish, adj, fastidioso
squeeze, v, apretar, recalcar
squint, v, bizco
squire, n m, caballero
squirrel, n f, ardilla
stable, adj, estable
stable, n f, caballeriza, cuadra
stack, n f, pila
stack, v, apilar
staff, n m, bastón
stag, n m, ciervo
stage, n m, tablado
stagnant, adj, estancado
stain, v, amancillar, tiznar
stair step, n f, grada
staircase, n f, escalera
stairstep, n m, peldaño
stake, n f, estaca
stake, v, envidar
stall, n f, butaca
stamp, n m, bocarte
stamp, v, timbrar
stand (of trees), n f, arboleda
stand, n f, mesita
standard, n f, enseña
standard, n m, modele
standardize, regularizar
staple, n m, cerradero
star, n f, estrella

starch, n f, fécula
starch, n m, almidón
starch, v, almidonar
starling, n m, estornino
starry, adj, estrellado
start, n f, salida
start, v, lanzar
startle, v, asustarse
starvation, n f, inanición
state, n m, estado
state, v, establecer
statement, n f, exposición
station, n f, estación
stationery, n f, papeleria
statue, n f, estatua
stature, n f, estatura, talla
statute, n m, estatuto
stay, v, quedar
steady, adj, firme
steal, v, hurtar
steam, n m, vaho
steel, n m, acero
steep, adj, escarpado
steeple, n m, campanario
steering, n m, timón
stem, n m, tronco, vástago
stench, n m, hedor
step, n m, grado, paso
step, v, andar
step-daughter, n f, entenada
step-son, n m, entenado
stepfather, n m, padrastro
stepmother, n f, madrastra
stereotype, v, estereotipar
sterile, adj, estéril
sterility, n f, esterilidad
stew, n mf, estofado
stew, v, cocer
stick, n f, porra
stick, n m, bastón, palo
sticky, adj, pegajoso
stiff, adj, tieso, yerto
stiffness, n f, tiesura
stifle, v, ahogar
stifled, adj, ahogado
still, n m, alambique

stimulate, v, estimular
sting, n m, aguijón
sting, v, pinchar
stink, v, heder
stir, v, agitar, mecer
stitching, n m, zurcido
stock, n m, retén
stocking, n f, media
stomach, n m, estómago
stone, n f, piedra
stool, n f, banqueta, taburete
stop, v, detenerse, parar
stoppage, n m, para
storage, n m, almacenaje
store, n f, tienda, almacén
store, v, almacenar
storekeeper, n m, tendero
storm, n f, borrasca
stormy NW wind, n f, galerna
stormy, adj, borrascoso,
  tempestuoso
story, n m, cuento
stove, n f, estufa
straight, adj, recto
strain, n m, esfuerzo
strain, v, colar
strand, n m, grao
strange, adj, extraño
stranger, n desconocido,
  extranjero, forastero
strangle, v, estrangular
strap, n f, correa, tiradera
straw, n f, paja
straw, n m, bledo
strawberry, n f, fresa
streak, n f, raya
streak, v, rayar
stream, n f, corriente
street, n f, calle
strengthen, v, fortificar, reforzar
stress, n f, violencia
stretch, v, extenderse, tender
strict, adj, estricto
strike, v, golpear, rasar
string, n f, cuerda
strip, n f, lista

strip, n m, jirón
strip, v, desguarnecer
striped, adj, listado, rayado, veteado
stroke, n m, rasgo
stroke, v, acariciar
stroll, n m, paseo
strong wind, n m, vandaval
strong, adj, fuerte, recio
strongly, adv, reciamente, recio
structure, n f, animadversión
struggle, n f, lucha
stubbornness, n f, terquedad
stucco, n m, estuco
stud, n m, clavo
student, n m, estudiante
studious, adj, aplicado
study, n m, estudio
study, v, estudiar
stuff, v, emborrar, hartar
stumble, v, tropezar
stun, v, aturdir
stupefy, v, embobecer, embrutecer,
  entorpecer
stupendous, adj, prodigioso
stupid, adj, estúpido, necio
stupidity, n f, estupidez
sturdy, adj, brusco
style, n f, moda
style, n m, estilo
subdivide, v, subdividir
subdue, v, subyugar
subdued, adj, vencido
subject, n f, materia
subject, n m, asunto, sujeto
subject, v, someter
sublime, adj, sublime
submarine, n m, submarino
submerge, v, sumergir
subscribe, v, subscribir
subscriber, n m, abonado
subscription, n f, subscripción
subside, v, sumergirse
subsist, v, subsistir
substance, n f, substancia
substantial, adj, sustancial
substitute, v, sustituir

substitution, n m, remplazo
subterfuge, n m, efugio
subterranean, adj, subterráneo
subtle, adj, sutil
subtract, v, restar, sustraer
subtraction, n m, sustracción
suburb, n f, barriada
suburb, n m, suburbio
subversion, n f, subversión
subversive, n f, subversivo
subway, n f, galería subterránea
succeed, v, tener éxito
successful, adj, próspero
successor, n mf, sucesor
such, adj, tal
suck, v, chupar, mamar
sudden, adj, de pronto, repentino
suddenly, adv, repentinamente
sue, v, perseguir
suffer, v, adolecer, padecer, sufrir
suffering, n f, padecimiento
sufficient, adj, suficiente
sufficiently, adv, bastantemente
suffocate, v, sotocar
sugar candy, adj, cande
sugar, n m, azúcar
suggest, v, sugerir
suggestion, n f, sugestión
suicide, n m, suicidio
suitcase, n f, maleta
suite, n f, comitiva
sulfur, n m, azufre
sulfuric, adj, sulfúrico
sullen, adj, malhumorado
sully, v, desdorar
sultry, adj, caluroso
sum, n f, suma
sum, v, sumar
sumac (tree), n m, zumaque
summary, n m, sumario
summer house, n f, glorieta
summer, adj, veraniego
summer, n m, verano
summit, n f, cima, cumbre
summon, v, emplazar, notificar
summons, n m, emplazamiento

sun, n m, sol
Sunday, n m, domingo
sunflower, n m, girasol, mirasol, tornasol
sunny, adj, soleado
sunrise, n f, salida del sol
sunset, n f, puesta del sol
superintendent, n m, gestor
superior, adj, superior
supernatural, n f, sobrenatural
superstition, n f, superstición
supervise, v, revisar
supper, n f, cena
supplant, v, suplantar
supplier, n f, abastecedor
suppliment, n f, suplemento
supply, n f, provisión
supply, n m, abasto, aprovisionamiento
supply, v, suplir
support, n m, apoyo, sostén
support, v, apadrinar, soportar
suppose, v, suponer
suppression, n f, supresión
supress, v, suprimir
sure, adj, segura
surely, adv, seguramente
surf, n f, ola
surge, n f, sarga
surgeon, n m, cirujano
surgery, n f, cirugía
surgical instrument, n m, bisturí
surname, n m, apellido
surpass, v, sobrepujar
surplus, n m, exceso
surprise, n f, sorpresa
surprise, n m, rebato
surprised, adj, sorprendido
surprising, adj, sorprendente
surrender, v, rendir
surround, v, circundar, rodear
survey, n m, apeo, peritaje
survey, v, deslindar, examinar
surveying, n f, agrimensura
surveyor, n f, agrimensor
survival, n f, supervivencia

survive, v, sobrevivir
suspect, v, recelar, sospechar
suspend, v, suspender
suspended, adj, colgado
suspenders, n mpl, tirantes
suspense, n f, suspensión
suspicion, n f, sospecha
suspicious, adj, sospechoso
sustain, v, aguantar, sostener
swaddle, v, empañar
swallow (bird), n f, golondrina
swallow, v, tragar
swamp, n m, pantano
swan, n m, cisne
swarm, n m, enjambre
swarm, v, enjambrar
sway, v, agitar
swear, v, jurar
sweat, n m, sudor
sweat, v, sudar
Swede, n m, sueco
Sweden, n f, Suecia
Swedish, adj, sueco
sweep, v, barrer
sweeper, n m, barrendero
sweepings, n f, basura
sweet, adj, dulce
sweeten, v, dulcificar, endulzar
sweetheart, n f, mf, enamorado
sweetness, n f, dulzura
swell, v, entumecer, inflar
swelling, n f, hinchazón
swift, adj, rapido
swiftly, adv, aprisa, ligeramente
swim, v, nadar
swimmer, n mf, nadador
swimming, n f, nado
swindle, timar
swing, n m, columpio
swing, v, columpiar
switch, n f, aguja
swollen, adj, hinchado
swoon, n m, desmayo
sword, n f, espada
syllable, n f, sílaba
symbol, n m, símbolo

sympathize, v, simpatizar
sympathy, n f, simpatía
symptom, n m, síntoma
synagogue, n f, sinagoga
syndicate, n m, sindicato
synonym, n m, sinónimo
synonymous, adj, sinónimo
syphilis, n f, sífilis
syringe, n f, jeringa
syrup, n m, almíbar, jarabe
system, n f, sistema

T

table salt, n f, sal blanca
table, n f, mesa
table, n m, elenco
tablecloth, n f, mantel
tablet, n f, tableta
tacit, adj, tácito
tack, n f, bordada
tack, n m, clavete, clavito
tact, n m, aplomo
tactics, n f, táctica
taffeta, n m, tafetán
tail, n f, cola
tail, n m, rabo
tailor, n m, sastre
take, v, tomar
talc, n m, talco
talent, n m, talento
talented, adj, talentoso
talk, v, parlamentar
talkative, adj, hablador
tall, adj, esbelto
tallow, n m, sebo
tally, n f, tarja
tally, v, tarjar
tame, v, amansar, domar
tangible, adj, tangible
tank, n m, tanque
tanner, n m, zurrador
tannery, n f, tenería
tap, n m, grito
tape, n f, lienza
taper, n m, blandón

tapestry, n f, colgadura, tapicería
tapestry, n m, tapiz
tapioca, n f, tapioca
tar, n f, pez
tar, n m, alquitrán
tar, v, alquitranar, embrear
tardiness, n f, cachaza
target, n m, blanco
tariff, n f, tarifa
tarnish, v, deslucir
tarpaulin, n m, alquitranado, embreado
task, n f, faena, tarea
tassel, n f, borla
taste, n m, sabor
taste, v, catar, libar
tasteless, adj, desabrido
taster, n m, catador
tasty, adj, gustoso
tattle, v, chismear
taught, adj, amaestrado
tavern, n f, taberna
tax assessment, n f, amillaramiento
taxi, n m, taxi
tea, n m, té
teacher, n f, maestra, profesora
teacher, n m, maestro, profesor
teaching, n f, enseñanza
teak (wood), n f, teca
teapot, n f, tetera
tear, n f, lágrima
tear, v, rasgar
teaspoon, n f, cucharita
technical, adj, técnico
technique, n f, técnica
tedious, adj, tedioso
telegram, n m, telegrama
telegraph, n m, telégrafo
telephone call, n m, telefonema
telephone, n m, teléfono
telephone, v, telefonar
telescope, n m, telescopio
temerity, n f, temeridad
temper, v, temperar, templar
temperament, n m, temperamento
temperance, n f, templanza
temperate, adj, templado

temperature, n m, temple
temple, n f, sien
temporal, adj, temporal
temporary, adj, temporario
ten, n f, diez
tenacious, adj, tenaz
tenacity, n f, tenacidad
tenacity, n m, tesón
tendency, n f, tendencia
tenderize, v, reblandecer
tenderness, n f, molicie, ternura
tenor, n m, tenor
tense, adj, tenso
tension, n f, tensión
tentative, adj, tentativo
tenth, adj, denario
tepid, adj, tibio
term, n m, plazo, término
terminate, v, fenecer
termination, n f, terminación
terrace, n f, terraza
terrace, n m, terrado
terrestrial, adj, terrenal, terrestre
terrible, adj, terrible
territorial, adj, territorial
territory, n m, territorio
terror, n m, terror
testament, n f, testamento
testify, v, testificar, testimoniar
testimonial, n m, testimonial
testimony, n m, testimonio
text, n m, tema, texto
textile, adj, textil
texture, n f, tejedura, textura
texture, n m, tejido
thank, v, agradecer
thankless, adj, ingrato
thanks, n fpl, gracias
that is enough, int, basta
that one, adj, aquel
that, adj, eso
that, pro, esa
thaw, n f, derretimiento
thaw, v, deshelar
the Netherlands, n f, Países Bajos
the, art, el, la, lo
theater manager, n m, empresario

theater, n m, teatro
theft, n m, hurto
them, art, los
them, pro, las, los
then, adv, entonces, pues
theoretical, adj, teórico
theory, n f, teoría
there is, adv, hay
there, adv, ahí, allá, allí
thermometer, n m, termómetro
these, adj, estos
these, art, las
thesis, n f, tesis
thick, adj, espeso
thickness, n m, grosor
thief, n m, ladrón
thimble, n m, dedal
thin, adj, tenue
thing, n f, cosa
think, v, pensar
thinness, n f, delgadez
third person, n m, tercero
third, adj, tercero, tercio
thirst, n f, sed
thirsty, adj, sediento
thirteen, n f, trece
thirty, n f, treinta
this year, adv, hogaño
this, adj, esto
this, pro, este
thistle, n m, cardo
thong, n f, zurriaga
thorn, adj, espina
those, pro, aquellas
thou, pro, tú
thought, n f, pensamiento
thoughts, n fpl, mientes
thousand, adj, mil
thousand, n m, millar
thread, n m, hila
threat, n f, amenaza
threaten, v, amenazar
three, n f, tres
threshold, n m, umbral
thrift, n m, ahorro
throat, n f, garganta

throttle, n m, gaznate
throw down, v, abatir, soltar
throw, v, botar, echar, tirar
Thursday, n m, jueves
thy, adj, tu
thyme, n m, tomillo
ticket office, n f, casilla, taquilla
ticket, n f, viñeta
ticket, n m, boletín, boleto
ticking, n m, terliz
tide, n f, marea
tie, n f, igualada
tie, v, amarrar, liar, ligar
tie down, v, abarrotar
tight, adj, tirante
tighten, v, apretar
tightly, adv, apretadamente
tightness, n f, tirantez
tilde, n m, tilde
tile, n f, teja
time, n f, vez
time, n m, tiempo
timid, adj, empachado, temeroso
timidity, n m, empacho
tin, n f, hojalata
tinder, n f, yesca
tint, n f, tinta
tipper, n f, beca
tissue, n m, tisú
tithe, v, diezmar
title, n m, título
title, v, titular
to be, v, ser
toast, n fpl, tostadas
toast, v, tostar
toasted, adj, tostado
tobacco, n m, tabaco
today, adv, hoy
together, adj, junto
toil, v, alanar, afanarse
toilet, n m, tocador
tolerable, adj, tolerable
tolerance, n f, tolerancia
tolerant, adj, tolerante
tolerate, v, tolerar
toll, n m, peaje

tomato, n m, tomate
tomboy, n f, marimacho
ton, n f, tonelada
tone, n m, tono
tongs, n fpl, tenazas
tongue, n f, lengua
tonic, n m, tónico
tonnage, n m, tonelaje
too, adv, demasía
tool, n f, herramienta
tool, n m, apero
tooth pain, n f, dentera
tooth, n m, diente
toothed, adj, serrado
toothpick, n f, mondadientes
top (toy), n f, peonza
top, n m, tope
topaz, n m, topacio
topic, n m, tópico
torch, n f, antorcha, tea
torment, n m, tormento
torpedo, n m, torpedo
torpid, adj, torpe
torpor, n m, entorpecimiento
torrent, n m, raudal, torrente
tortoise shell, n m, carey
tortoise, n f, tortuga
tortuous, adj, tortuoso
total, adj, total
total, n m, total
totality, n f, totalidad
totally, adv, totalmente
touch, n m, tacto, tiento, toque
touch, v, toear
tow, v, remolcar
toward, adv, hacia
towel, n f, toalla
tower, n f, torre
town, n f, villa
town, n m, poblado
toy, n m, juguete
trace, n m, rastro
trace, v, calcar, rastrear, trazar
tracing, n f, traza
tracing, n m, calco
track, n f, andada, pista
traction, n f, tracción

trade, v, comerciar, marchantear, traficar
traffic, n m, tráfago, tráfico
tragedy, n f, tragedia
tragic, adj, trágico
train, n m, tren
train, v, entrenar
traitor, n m, traidor
trample, v, pisotear
tranquility, n f, tranquilidad
transaction, n f, transacción
transatlantic, adj, transatlántico
transcribe, v, transcribir
transcription, n f, transcripción
transfer, n f, transferencia
transfer, v, transferir
transferable, adj, transferible
transform, v, transformar
transformation, n f, transformación
transitory, adj, transeúnte
translate, v, traducir, verter
translation, n f, traducción, traslación
transmission, n f, transmisión
transmit, v, transmitir
transparent, adj, límpido, transparente, traslúcido
transpire, v, transpirar
transplant, v, transplantar
transport, n m, transporte
transport, v, deportar, entusiasmar, transportar
transpose, v, transponer
trap, n f, trampa
trash, n f, maula
travel, v, transitar, viajar
traveler, n m, viajero, caminante
travelling, adj, viajante
tray, n f, bandeja, batea, salvilla
treacherous, adj, traidor
treachery, n f, felonía
tread, v, pisar
treason, n f, traición
treasurer, n m, tesorero
treasury, n f, tesorería
treatment, n m, trato
tree, n m, árbol
trellis, n m, enrejado

tremble, v, tembiar
trembling, n m, temblor
trial, n f, cata
trifle, n f, nonada
trimming, n f, randa
trinket, n f, chuchería
trinket, n m, dije
trip, n f, jira
troubadour, n m, trovador
trouble, n f, cuita
trouble, n m, enfado
troublesome, adj, engorroso, importuno
trousers, n f, calza
trout, n f, trucha
truck, n m, camión
true, adj, verdadero
trunk, n m, baúl, cofre, mastíl
trust fund, n f, fideicomiso
trust, v, fiar
trustee, n m, fideicomisario
trusting, adj, fiado
trustworthy, adj, fiable
truth, n f, verdad
truthful, adj, verídico
try again, v, recatar
try, v, procurar, tratar
tube, n m, caño
Tuesday, n m, martes
tumult, n m, alboroto
tune, n m, tañido
tune, v, entonar
turkey, n m, pavo
turn, n f, tanda
turn, n m, turno
turn, v, ladear, versar
turning, n m, borneo
turnip, n m, nabo
tweed, n m, cheviot
twenty, n f, veinte
twin, adj, gemelo
twine, v, enroscar
twist, v, torcer
twisted, adj, torcido
two months, adj, bimestre
two weeks (fortnight), n f, quincena

two years, n m, bienio
two, v, dos
type, n m, tipo
typewriting, n f, dactilografía
typhoon, n m, tifón
typist, n m, dactilógrafo
typographical, adj, tipográfico
tyrannical, adj, tirano
tyranny, n f, tiranía
tyrant, n m, tirano

U

ugliness, n f, fealdad
ugly, adj, feo
ulterior, adj, ulterior
ultimatum, n m, ultimátum
ultramarine, adj, ultramar, ultramarino
umbrella, n m, paraguas
unacceptable, adj, inaceptable
unadorned, adj, deslucido
unanimity, n f, unanimidad
unanimous, adj, unánime
unappealable, adj, inapelable
unbridle, v, desentrenar
unbridled, adj, desenfrenado
unbutton, v, desabotonar
uncertain, adj, incierto
unchain, v, desencadenar
unchanged, adj, inalterado
uncivil, adj, incivil
unclasp, v, desabrochar
uncle, n m, tío
uncommon, adj, descomunal
unconfessed, adj, inconfeso
unconnected, adj, inconexo
uncover, v, desabrrgar, descobijar, desencapotar
uncovered, adj, descubierto
unction, n f, unción
uncultivated, adj, baldío, inculto
undeceive, v, desengañar
undeceived, adj, desengañado
undeceiving, n m, desengaño
undecided, adj, indeciso

under stocking, n f, calceta
under, adv, abajo
underbrush, n m, matorral
undergrowth, n f, maleza
understand, v, entender
understanding, n m, entendimiento
undertake, v, emprender
undo, v, desandar, deshacer
undone, adj, deshecho
undress, v, desnudarse
undue, adj, indebido
undulate, v, ondear, ondular
unemployed, adj, desocupildo
unequal, adj, desigual, impar
unexpected, adj, impensado,
  improviso
unfailing, adj, indeficiente
unfavorable, adj, desfavorable
unfirm, adj, desazonado
unfit, v, desajustar
unfold, v, desenvolver
unforeseen, adj, imprevisto
unfortunate, adj, desafortunado,
  malhadado, malogrado
unfortunately, adv, desdichadamente
unfurnish, v, desamueblar
unfurnished, adj, desamueblado
ungrateful, adj, desagradecido,
  dosconocido
unguent, n m, ungüento
unhappy, adj, infeliz
unharness, v, desaparejar
unhealthy, adj, malsano
unheard of, adj, inaudito
unhurt, adj, ileso
uniform, adj, uniforme
uniform, n m, uniforme
uniformity, n f, uniformidad
unintelligible, adj, gringo
union, n f, ligazón, trabazón, unión
union, n m, ligamiento
United States, n, Estados Unidos
united, adj, unido
unity, n f, unidad
universal, adj, universal
universe, n m, universo
university, n f, universidad

unjustly, adv, indebidamente
unknown, adj, ignorado, incógnito
unlikely, adj, inverosímil
unlimited, adj, ilimitado
unloader, n f, descargador
unloading, n f, descarga
unnecessary, adj, innecesario
unpack, v, desembalar,
  desempacar, desempaquetar
unpardonable, adj, irremisible
unpopular, v, impopular
unpopularity, n f, impopularidad
unprepared, adj, desapercibido
unredeemable, adj, inamortizable
unskilfulness, n f, impericia
unskilled, adj, imperito
unsteady, adj, movedizo
untie, v, desamarrar, desanudar,
  desatar
until, adv, hasta
untune, v, desacordar
unusual, adj, desacostumbrado
upholster, v, tapizar
upholsterer, n m, tapicero
upset, adj, alborotado
upset, v, zozobrar
upstart, n m, advenedizo
urban, adj, urbano
urge, v, urgir
urgency, n f, urgencia
urgent, adj, apremiante, urgente
urinal, n m, orinal
urn, n f, urna
us, pro, nos
usage, n f, usanza
use, n m, uso, valimiento
use, v, usar
used, adj, usado
useful, adj, útil
uselessly, adv, inútilmente
usual, adj, usual
usurp, v, usurpar
utensil, n m, utensilio
utility, n f, utilidad
utilize, v, utilizar

V

vacancy, n f, vacancia
vacation, n f, vacación
vacillate, v, vacilar
vacillation, n f, vacilación
vagrant, adj, vago
vain, adj, vano
vainly, adv, vanamente
valiant, adj, guapo, valeroso
valid, adj, valedero, válido
validate, v, validar
valley, n m, valle
valor, n f, valentía
valuable, adj, valioso
valuation, n f, valuación
valuation, n m, evalúo
value, n f, valía
value, n m, valer
value, v, preciar, valuar
valued, adj, valorado
valve, n f, válvula
vanguard, n f, vanguardia
vanilla, n f, vainilla
vanity, n f, vanidad
vapor, n m, vapor
variable, adj, variable
variation, n f, variación
variegate, v, vetear
variegated, adj, abigarrado
variety, n f, variedad
various, adj, vario
varnish, n f, pega
varnish, n m, barniz, charol
varnish, v, barnizar, charolar,
  embarnizar
vary, v, variar
vast, adj, vasto
vegetable, adj, vegetal
vegetable, n f, legumbre
vegetable, n m, vegetal
vegetation, n f, vegetación
vehemence, n f, vehemencia
vehement, adj, vehemente
vehement, n m, anhelo
vehicle, n m, vehículo
veil, n m, velete, velo
vein, n f, vena

vein, n m, filón
velocity, n f, velocidad
velvet, n m, terciopelo
veneer, v, enchapar
venerate, v, venerar
vent, v, desfogar
ventilate, v, ventilar
ventilation, n f, ventilación
ventilator, n m, ventiladar
venture, n f, ancheta
veracious, adj, veraz
veracity, n f, veracidad
verbal, adj, verbal
verbally, adv, verbalmente
verdict, n m, veredicto
verification, n f, verficación
verify, v, verificar, comprobar
vermicelli, n m, fideos
vermilion, n m, bermellón
versatile, adj versátil
verse, n m, verso
version, n f, versión
vertical, adj vertical
very important, adj, importantísimo
very little, adj, pequeñito
very much, adj, muchísimo
very strong, adj, acérrimo
very, adv, muy
vesper, n f, víspera
vessel, n f, vasija, garrafa
vessel, n m, vaso, bajel
vest, n m, chaleco
vestibule, n f, vestíbulo
vestige, n m, vestigio
veteran, n m, veterano
veterinarian, n m, veterinario
veto, n m, veto
vex, v, vejar, enfadar, imapacientar
vexation, n f, vejación
vexatious, adj, enfadoso
viaduct, n f, m, viaducto
vibrate, v, vibrar
vice versa, adv, viceversa
vice, n m, vicio
vice-president, n m, vicepresdente
vicinity, n f, vecindad

vicious, adj, vicioso
victim, n f, víctima
victorious, adj, victorioso
victory, n f, victoria
victory, n m, vencimiento
vigil, n f, vigila
vigilance, n f, vigilancia
vigilant, adj, vigilante
vignette, n f, viñeta
vigor, n m, vigor
vigorous, adj, vigoroso, nervioso
vile, ad, bajuno
vilify, v, envilecer
village, n f, aldea
village, n m, villaje, pueblo, caserío
villager, n m, aldeano
villain, n m, villano
vindicate, v, vindicar
vindication, n f, vindicación
vine, n f, parra, vid
vinegar, n m, vinagre
vineyard, n f, viña
vintage, n f, vendimia
vintager, n m, viñero
vintner, n m, vinatero
violate, v, violar
violation, n f, violación
violet, adj, morado, violado
violet, n f, violeta
violin, n m, violín
virgin, adj, virgen
virtual, adj, virtual
virtue, n f, virtud,
virtuous, adj, virtuoso
visit, n f, visita
visit, v, visitar
vocabulary, n m, vocabulario
vocal, adj, vocal
voice, n f, voz
void, adj, vacío
void, n m, vacío
voter, n m vocal
vowel, n f, vocal

W

wade, v, vadear

wages, n f, mesada
wages, n m, alqiuler
wagon, n m, vagón
waist, n f, cintura
wait, n f, espera
waiter, n m, camarero, mozo
waitress, n f, camarera
wake up, v, despertar
walk, n f, caminata
walk, n m, paseo
walk, v, caminar
walking stick, n m, báculo
wall, n f, pared
walnut tree, n m, nogal
waltz, n m, vals
wander, v, desatinar, vagar
want, n m, apuro
wanting, adj, falto
war, n f, guerra
warble, v, gorjear
warehouse, n m, almacén
warehousing, n m, almacenaje
warlike, adj, bélico, belicoso
warm, adj, caliente
warm, v, acalorar, calentar
warning, n f, admonición
warp, v, alabearse, urdir
warping, n f, urdidura
warrior, n m, guerrero
wash, v, lavar
washable, adj, lavable
washer, n f, arandela
washing clothes, n f, colada
washing, n m, lavado
waste, adj, yermo
waste, n f, merma
waste, n m, derroche
waste, v, mermar, derrochar,
   desaprovechar
watch, n f, vela
watch, v, celar, velar, vigilar
watchman, n m, velador
water carrier, n m, aguador
water, n f, agua
water, n m, chorro
water, v, aguar, bañar, regar
watered, adj, aguado

watering place (cattle), n m, aguadero

watt (electrical unit), n m, vatio

wave, n f, onda

wax candle, n m, cirio

wax, n f, cera

wax, n m, lacre

way, n f, vía

waylaying, n m, acecho

we, adj, nosotros

weak, adj, débil, feble, flaco

weaken, v, enflaquecer

weakly, adv, débilmente

weakness, n f, languidez

weakness, n m, quebranto

wealthy, adj, adinerado

wear-and-tear, n m, desgaste

weariness, n f, lasitud

weariness, n m, aburrimiento, cansancio

weary, adj, aburrido, cansado

weary, v, aburrir, cansar

weather gauge, n m, barlovento

weave, v, tejer, tramar

weaver, n m, tejedor, tramador

wedge, n m, calce

Wednesday, n m, miércoles

week, n f, semana

weekly publication, n m, semanario

weekly, adj, semanal, hebdomadario

weep, v, llorar

weigh anchor, v, desanclar

weigh, v, pesar

weight, n f, pesa

weight, n m, peso

welcome, n f, bienvenida

well being, n m, bienestar

well, adv, bien

well, n m, pozo

West Indies, n fpl, Antillas

west, n m, oeste

whale, n f, ballena

whaler, n f, ballenera

wharf, n m, descargadero

what, pro, qué

wheel barrow, n f, carretilla

wheel, n m, torno

wheelwright, n m, aperador

when, adv, cuando

where, adv, adonde, dónde

whether, adv, sea que

whether, conj, ora

which, pro cual

while, adv, mientras

whim, n m, antojo

whip, n m, látigo

whirlwind, n m, remolino, torbellino

whistle, n f, chifla

whistle, n m, silbido

whistle, v, chiflar, silbar

white, adj, blanco

whiten, v, emblanquecer

whiteness, n f, candidez

whiteness, n m, albor, blancor

whitening, n f, blanqueadura

whitewash, n f, lechada

whitewash, n m, jalbegue

whitewash, v, enjalbegar, jalbegar

whitish, adj, blanquizco

who, pro, que, quien, quién

why, adv, porqué

wick, n f, torcida

wick, n m, pabilo

widen, v, ensanchar

widening, n m, ensanche

width, n f, anchura

width, n m, ancho

wife, n f, esposa

wild beast, n f, fiera

wild boar, n m, jabalí

will, v, testar

willow, n m, sauce

winch, n f, cabria

winch, n m, cigüeñal

wind, n m, viento

windfall, n f, chiripa

window, n f, ventana

windy, adj, ventoso

wine bag, n f, bota

wine press, n m, lagar

wine vault, n m, bodega

wine, n m, vino

wing, n f, ala
winter, n m, invierno
wintry, adj, inviernizo
wire, n m, alambre
wireless, adj, inalámbrico
wise, adj, sabio
wish, v, querer
with impunity, adv, impunemente
with me, prep, conmigo
with you, prep, contigo
with, prep, con
wither, v, marchitar
withered, adj, marchito
within, adv, adentro
within, prep, dentro
without merit, adj, demeritorio
without, adv, sin
witness, n m, deponente, testigo
witty, adj, chistoso, salado
woman, n f, mujer
wonder, n f, maravilla
wonder, n m, pasmo
wood, n f, leña, madera
wood, n m, bosque
woodcock, n f, becado
wooded, adj, arbolado
woodwork, n m, enmaderamiento
wool, n f, lana
woolly, adj, lanar, lanudo
word, n m, vocablo, palabro
work, n m, trabajo, obra
work, v, labrar, obrar, trabajar
workable, adj, gastado
worse, adj, peor
worship, v, adorar
worth, n, valor
worthy, adj, digno
wound, n f, herida, lesión, llaga
wound, v, herir, llagar
wounded, adj, herido
wrap up, v, envolver
write, v, escribir, redactar
writer, n m, escritor
written, adj, escrito
wrong, v, agraviar

X

X-ray, n m, rayos X
Xerox, n f, xerocopia
Xerox, v xerocopiar
xylophone, n m, xilófono

Y

yacht, n m, balandro, yate
yard (U.S. measurement), n f, yarda
yard, n m, patio
yardage, n m, yardaje
yarn, n m, meollar, hilaza
yawn, n m, bostezo
yawn, v, bostezar
year book, n m, anuario
year, n m, año
yeast, n m, jiste, levadura
yellow, adj, amarillo
yes, adv, sí
yesterday, adv, ayer
yet, adv, aún, todavía
yet, conj, empero
yield, v, darse
yoke, n m, yugo
yoke, v, uncir
you, pro, os, usted, vosotros
young lady, n f, señorita
young, adj, joven
your, adj, su, vuestro
yours, adj, suyo
youth, n m, joven, mocedad

Z

zeal, n m, celo
zebra, n f, cebra
zenith, n m, cenit
zephyr, n m, céfiro
zero, n m, cero
zigzag, n m, zigzag
zinc, n m, zinc
zone, n f, zona
zoological, adj, zoológico

Spanish to English Section

Abbreviation guide

adj	adjetivo	*f*	femenino	*pl*	plural
adv	adverbio	*int*	interjeción	*prep*	preposición
art	artículo	*m*	masculino	*pro*	pronombre
conj	conjunción	*n*	nombre	*v*	verbo

A

a, prep, in, to, at
ababa, n f, red poppy
abacá, n m, manilla hemp
abacería, n f, grocery
abacero, n m, grocer
ábaco, n m, abacus
abadejo, n m, codfish
abajo, adv, under, underneath, below
abalanzar, v, balance, dart, impel
abalorio, n m, glass bead
abandonado, adj, abandoned, given up
abandonamiento, n m, abandonment, cession
abandonar, v, abandon
abandono, n m, abandonment, cession
abanicar, v, fan
abanico, n m, fan
abaratamiento, n m, cheapening, making cheaper
abaratar, v, cheapen
abarcar, v, embrace, contain, undertake
abarrotamiento, n m, glut
abarrotar, v, tie down, stow cargo
abarrote, n m, broken stowage, small parcels
abastecedor, n m, supplier, provider
abastecer, v, provide, supply
abastecimiento, n m, provision, supply
abasto, n m, supply, provision
abatido, adj, dejected, depressed, dull
abatimiento, n m, depression, leeway
abatir, v, throw down, deject, depress
abdicar, v, abdicate
abecedario, n m, alphabet
abedul, n m, birch, birch wood
abeja, n f, bee
abertura, n f, chasm

abertura, n f, opening, aperture
abiertamente, adv, openly
abierto, adj, open, free
abigarrado, adj, variegated
abintestato, n m, interstate
abismo, n m, abyss, gulf
ablandar, v, soften, mellow
ablano, n m, hazel tree
abocar, v, meet
abogado, n m, lawyer
abogar, v, advocate, plead
abolición, n f, abolition
abolir, v, abolish
abolladura, n f, dent
abollar, v, emboss, dent
abominable, adj, adabominable
abonado, adj, respectable, rich
abonado, n m, subscriber
abonanzar, v, become calm, clear up
abonar, v, make good, allow, credit
abonaré, n f, promissory note
abono, n m, allowance, security
abordaje, n m, boarding a ship
abordar, board a ship
aborrecimiento, n m, abhorrence
abotonar, v, button
abrasar, v, burn
abrazar, v, cuddle
abrazar, v, embrace, comprise
abrazo, n m, embrace
abreviación, n f, abbreviation
abreviar, v, abbreviate, shorten
abrigado, adj, snug
abrigar, v, protect, shelter
abrigo, n m, shelter, protection
abril, n m, April
abrir, v, open
abrochar, v, button, fasten
abrogación, n f, abrogation
abrogar, v, annul, cancel
abrumado, adj, overwhelmed
abrumador, adj, overwhelming
abrumar, v, crush, overwhelm
absolutamente, adv, absolutely
absoluto, adj, absolute
absolver, v, absolve, acquit
absorber, v, absorb

absorto, adj, amazed, absorbed
abstenerse, v, abstain, refrain
abstinencia, n f, abstinence
abstraer, v, abstract
absurdo, adj, absurd
absurdo, n m, absurdity
abuela, n f, grandmother
abuelo, n m, grandfather
abultado, adj, bulky, large
abultar, v, increase, enlarge
abundancia, n f, abundance
abundante, adj, abundant
abundar, v, abound
aburrido, adj, weary, bored
aburrimiento, n m, weariness, boredom
aburrir, v, weary, hare
abusar, v, abuse
abuso, n m, abuse, breach
acá, adv, here, this way
acabado, adj, finished
acabado, n m, finish
acabamiento, n m, completion
acabar, v, finish, complete, end
academia, n f, academy
acaecer, v, happen, take place
acallar, v, silence
acalorar, v, warm, heat
acampamento, n, encampment
acampar, v, encamp
acanalar, v, channel
acanalar, v, make a groove, flute
acaparador, n m, monopolist
acaparamiento, n m, monopoly
acaparar, v, monopolize
acariciar, v, stroke
acarreador, n m, carrier, porter
acarrear, v, carry, convey
acarreo, n m, carriage, conveyance
acaso, adv, by chance, perhaps
acaso, n m, chance
acatar, v, respect, revere
acaudalado, adj, rich, wealthy
acceder, v, accede
acceder, v, comply
acceptador, n m, acceptor
acceso, n m, access, fit, seizure

accesorio, adj, accessory
accesorio, n m, acessory
accidente, n m, accident, attack
acción, n f, action, feat, stock
acechar, v, ambush lurk
acecho, n m, waylaying, lurking
aceite, n m, oil
aceitera, n f, oil can
aceitero, adj, oil
aceitero, n m, oil man
aceituna, n f, olive oil
acelerar, v, accelerate
acémila, n f, mule
acendrar, v, purify, refine
acento, n m, accent
acentuar, v, accentuate
acepción, n f, acceptation
acepilladura, n f, shaving
acepillar, v, plane
aceptable, adj, acceptable
aceptación, adj, acceptance
aceptar, v, accept
acequia, n f, canal, trench, drain
acera, n f, Sidewalk
acera, n f, sidewalk, footpath
acerbo, adj, rough, harsh
acerca, prep, about
acercar, v, approach, bring near
acerico, n m, small, pillow
acero, n m, steel
acérrimo, adj, very strong
acertado, adj, fit, proper
acertar, v, hit the mark
acetato, n m, acetate
achaque, n m, failing
achicar, v, diminish, lessen
achicar, v, scoop
aciago, adj, unfortunate
acicalar, v, pOlish, burnish
ácido, adj, acid, sour
ácido, n m, acid
acierto, n m, chance, dexterity, skill
acitrón, n m, lemon peel
aclamación, n f, acclamation
aclamación, n f, shout
aclamar, v, acclaim, applaud
aclamar, v, shout

aclaración, n f, explanation
aclarar, v, clear
aclarar, v, explain, clear up
aclimatar, v, acclimatize
acoger, v, admit, receive
acogida, n f, reception, welcome
acometer, v, attack, assault
acometida, n f, attack, assault
acomodado, adj, comfortable, convenient
acomodamiento, n m, accommodation, composition
acomodar, v, accommodate
acomodo, n m, accommodation
acompañar, v, accompany
acondicionado, adj, condition
acondicionar, v, dispose
aconsejar, v, advise
acontecer, v, happen
acontecimiento, n m, event
acopiamento, n m, monopoly
acopiar, v, gather
acopio, n m, gathering, buying
acoplar, v, join, couple
acorazado, n m, ironclad
acordar, v, resolve, arrange
acorde, adj, comfortable
acordonado, adj, corded
acordonar, v, cord, surround
acorralar, v, corral
acortar, v, shorten, lessen
acosar, v, pursue closely
acostar, v, lay down, put to bed
acostumbrar, v, accustom
acre, adj, sour, acrid
acrecentar, v, increase
acrecer, v, increase
acreditado, adj, established
acreditar, v, credit
acreedor, n m, creditor
acribillar, v, pierce, wound
acrisolar, v, refine, purify
acta, n f, act, record
actitud, n f, attitude
activar, v, hasten, push forward
actividad, n f, activity
activo, adj, active

acto, n m, act, action
actor, n m, actor
actriz, n f, actress
actuación, n f, actuation
actual, adj, actual, present
actualidad, n f, actuality
actualmente, adv, actually, now
actuar, v, act, put in action
acudir, v, assist, support
acuerdo, n m, agreement
acullá, adv, there
acumulación, n f, accumulation
acumulador, n m, accumulator
acumular, v, accumulate
acuñar, v, coin, mint
acusación, n m, charge
acusar, v, accuse, charge, show
acuse, n m, acknowledgement
adecuado, adj, adequate, fit
adelantado, adj, anticipated
adelantamiento, n m, progress
adelantar, v, advance
adelante, adv, forward
adelanto, n m, advance
adelgazar, v, attenuate, lessen
ademán, n m, gesture
además, adv, moreover
adentro, adv, within, inside
adepto, n m, adept
aderezar, v, dress, adorn
aderezo, n m, finery
adeudo, n m, charge, debit
adeudor, v, pay
adherir, v, adhere
adición, n f, addition
adicional, adj, additional
adinerado, adj, wealthy
adiós, int, good-bye
adivinar, v, foretell
adjunto, adj, enclosed
administración, n f, administration
administrador, n m, administrator
administrar, v, administer
administrativo, adj, administrative
admirable, adj, admirable
admiración, n f, admiration
admirar, v, admire

admisible, adj, admissible
admisión, n f, admission
admitir, v, admit
admonición, n f, warning
adobado, adj, pickled
adobar, v, dress, tan
adobo, n m, dressing
adolecer, v, suffer
adonde, adv, where
adopción, n f, adoption
adoptar, v, adopt
adorado, adj, adored
adorar, v, worship
adornar, v, adorn
adorno, n m, adorning
adquiridor, n m, acquirer
adquirir, v, acquire
adquisición, n f, acquisition
adrede, adv, knowingly
adredemente, adv, knowingly
aduana, n f, custom house
aduañarse, v, take possession
aducir, v, adduce
adulteración, n f, adulteration
adulto, adj, adult
advenedizo, adj, foreign
advenedizo, n m, upstart
adversario, n m, adversary
adverso, adj, adverse, opposite
advertencia, n f, advice
advertido, adj, noticed
advertir, v, notice, warn
adyacente, adj, adjacent
aeración, n f, aeration
aéreo, adj, aerial
aeronáutica, n f, aeronautics
aeroplano, n m, airplane
aeróstato, n m, airship
afabilidad, n f, affability
afable, adj, affable
afamado, adj, celebrated
afanar, v, toil
afanarse, v, toil
afanoso, adj, eager
afear, v, deform
afección, n f, affection
afectación, n f, affectation

afectado, n f, snob
afectar, v, affect
afecto, adj, affectionate
afeitar, v, shave
afeite, n m, rouge
afelpado, adj, plush
afelpado, adj, shaggy
aferrar, v, grapple
afianzador, n m, fastener
afianzar, v, guarantee, clinch
afición, n f, affection
aficionado, adj, fond
aficionado, n m, amateur, patron
aficionar, v, affect
afilado, adj, sharp
afilar, v, sharpen
afinar, v, complete
afirmar, v, affirm
afirmativo, adj, affirmative
aflicción, n f, affliction
afligir, v, afflict
aflojar, v, slacken
afluencia, n f, affluence
afluir, v, flow in
aforar, v, gauge
aforrar, v, line, sheath
aforro, n m, lining
afortunado, adj, fortunate
afrenta, n f, affront
afrentar, v, affront
afrontar, v, face
afuera, adv, abroad
afueras, n fpl, environs
agacharse, v, squat
agarradero, n f, anchoring ground
agarrar, v, grasp
agasajar, v, receive kindly
agasajo, n m, kind reception
ágata, n f, agate
agencia, n f, agency
agenciar, v, solicit
agenda, n f, agenda
agente, n m, agent
ágil, adj, agile
agio, n m, premium
agitación, n f, agitation
agitado, adj, agitated

agitar, v, agitate
agitar, v, stir
agitar, v, sway
aglomerar, v, heap up
agoblar, v, oppress
agolparse, v, crowd
agosto, n m, August, harvest
agotable, adj, exhaustible
agotar, v, exhaust
agraclar, v, adorn
agradable, adj, agreeable
agradar, v, please.
agradecer, v, thank
agradecido, adj, grateful
agradecimiento, n m, gratefulness
agrado, n m, liking
agrandar, v, enlarge
agravar, v, aggravate
agraviar, v, wrong
agravio, n m, offence
agredir, v, assault
agregado, n m, aggregate
agregar, v, aggregate
agriar, v, sour
agrícola, adj, agricultural
agrícola, n m, agriculturist
agricultor, n m, agriculturist
agricultura, n f, agriculture
agrimensor, n m, surveyor
agrimensura, n f, surveying
agrio, adj, sour
agrupar, v, group
aguacero, n m, heavy rain shower
aguachirle, n f, inferior wine
aguada, n f, water on board a ship, water color
aguadero, n m, watering place (cattle)
aguado, adj, watered
aguador, n m, water carrier
aguanieve, n f, sleet
aguantar, v, sustain
aguar, v, water
aguardar, v, expect
aguardiente, n m, brandy
aguarrás, n m, spirit of turpentine
agudamente, adv, sharply

agudeza, n f, acuteness
agudo, adj, pointed
agudo, adj, sharp
agudo, adj, shrill
agudo, adj, smart
ague, n f, water
aguijar, v, prick
aguijon, n m, sting
aguijón, n, sting
aguijonear, v, spur on
águila, n f, eagle
aguja, n f, needle
aguja, n f, switch
agujerear, v, pierce
agujero, n m, hole
aguzar, v, sharpen
ahi, adv, there
ahilarse, v, grow sour
ahínco, n m, earnestness
ahogado, adj, stifled
ahogar, v, smother
ahogar, v, stifle
ahogo, n m, affliction
ahora, adv, now
ahorcar, v, hang
ahorrar, v, economize
ahorrativo, adj, saving, thrifty
ahorro, n m, thrift
ahuecar, v, excavate
ahumado, adj, smoked
ahumar, v, smoke
ahuyentar, v, drive away
aire, n m, air
airoso, adj, airy
aislado, adj, isolated
aislador, n m, insulator
aislar, v, isolate
ajar, v, spoil
ajedrez, n m, chess
ajo, n m, garlic
ajuar, n m, furniture
ajustado, adj, exact
ajustar, v, adjust
ajustar, v, size
ajuste, n m, agreement
al, prep, to the, when
alabanza, n f, praise

alabar, v, praise
alabastro, n m, alabaster
alabearse, v, warp
alambicado, adj, distilled
alambique, n m, still
alambre, n m, wire
alameda, n f, grove
alarde, n m, review
alargar, v, lengthen
alarido, n m, shout
alarma, n f, alarm
alarmante, adj, alarming
alarmar, v, alarm
alba, n f, dawn
albañal, n m, sewer, sink
albañil, n m, mason
albañilería, n f, masonry
albaricoque, n m, apricot
albéitar, n f, veterinary
albérchiqo, n m, peach
albergar, v, lodge
albergue, n m, lodging
albor, n m, whiteness
alborotado, adj, upset
alborotar, v, disturb
alboroto, n m, tumult
alborozo, n m, merriment
albricias, n fpl, reward
alcabala, n f, excise
alcachofa, n f, artichoke
alcalde, n m, mayor
alcance, n m, balance
alcance, n m, scope
alcantarilla, n f, drawbridge
alcantarillado, n m, sewer
alcanzar, v, follow, reach
alcaravea, n f, caraway seed
alcázar, n m, castle
alcoba, n f, bedroom
alcohol, n m, alcohol
alcurnia, n f, family
aldea, n f, village
aldeano, n m, villager
ale, n f, wing
alegación, n f, allegation
alegar, v, allege
alegato, n m, allegation

alegrar, v, make merry
alegrarse, v, be glad
alegre, adj, cheerful
alegre, adj, merry
alegremente, adv, merrily
alegria, n f, mirth
alejar, v, remove
alemán, adj, German
Alemania, n f, Germany
alentado, adj, spirited
alentar, v, breathe
alerta, adj, alert
alfabético, adj, alphabetical
alfabeto, n m, alphabet
alfarería, n f, pottery
alfarero, n m, potter
alférez, n m, ensign
alfiler, n m, pin
alfiletero, n m, pin case
alfombra, n f, carpet
alfombrero, n m, carpet maker
alga, n f, seaweed
algo, adv, somewhat
algodón, n m, cotton
algodonal, n m, cotton plant
alguacil, n m, policeman
alguien, n f, somebody
algulen, pro, someone
algún tanto, adv, somewhat
alguna cosa, pro, something
algunas veces, adv, sometimes
alguno, adj, some, somebody
alhaja, n f, jewel
alianza, n f, alliance
alias, adv, alias
alicates, n mpl, pliers
aliciente, n m, attraction
aliento, n m, breath, spirit
aligerar, v, lighten
alijamiento, n m, jettison
alimentación, n f, feeding
alimentar, v, feed
alimenticio, adj, nutritious
alimento, n m, food
aliño, n m, dress
alisador, n m, polisher
alistado, adj, striped

aliviar, v, help
alivio, n m, alleviation
aljibe, n m, cistern
aljofaina, n f, earthen jug
allá, adv, there
allanar, v, level
allanar, v, smooth
allegar, v, collect
allende, adv, beyond
allí, adv, there
allsadura, n f, smoothing
allstar, v, get ready
alma, n f, soul, spirit
almacén, n m, warehouse
almacén, n mf, store
almacenaje, n m, storage
almacenaje, n m, warehousing
almacenar, v, store
almacenista, n m, store keeper
almadía, n f, canoe
almanaque, n m, almanac
almendra, n f, almond
almíbar, n m, syrup
almidón, n m, starch
almidonar, v, starch
almirantazgo, n m, admiralty
almirante, n m, admiral
almohada, n f, pillow
almohadilla, n f, pillow
almohadón, n m, large cushion
almoneda, n f, auction
almorzar, v, breakfast
almud, n m, measure of grain
almuerzo, n m, breakfast
aloe, n m, aloe
alojamiento, n m, lodging
alojar, v, lodge
alpaca, n f, alpaca
alpiste, n m, canary seed
alquería, n f, farm house
alquilar, v, let, hire, rent
alquiler, n m, wages, hiring
alquitrán, n m, tar
alquitranado, n m, tarpaulin
alquitranar, v, tar
alrededor, adv, around
alrededores, n mpl, environs

altamente, adv, highly
altanería, n f, haughtiness
altanero, adj, soaring
alteración, n f, alteration
alterar, v, change
altercación, n f, contest
alternar, v, alternate
alternativa, n f, alternative
alternativo, adj, alternate
alteza, n f, elevation
altitud, n f, altitude
altivo, adj, haughty
alto, adj, high
alto, adv, loud
alto, int, halt
alto, n m, height
altura, n f, height
alucinar, v, deceive
alud, n m, avalanche
aludir, v, allude
alumbrado, n m, lighting
alumbramiento, n m, child birth
alumbrar, v, light
aluminio, n m, aluminum
alumno, n f, pupil, disciple
alusión, n f, allusion
alza, n f, advance
alzada, n f, height
alzamiento, n m, raising
alzaprima, n f, lever
alzar, v, raise
ama, n f, landlady
amable, adj, nice
amado, adj, beloved
amaestrado, adj, taught
amaestrar, v, instruct
amaestrar, v, school
amainar, v, relax
amancillar, v, stain
amanecer, v, dawn
amansar, v, tame
amante, adv, lovingly
amante, n mf, lover
amanuense, n m, clerk
amar, v, love, like
amargar, v, make bitter
amargo, adj, bitter

amargura, n f, bitterness
amarillo, adj, yellow
amarra, n f, cable
amarradura, n f, moorings
amarrar, v, tie, fasten
amartillar, v, hammer
amasar, v, knead
amasijo, n m, dough
Amazona, n f, Amazon
Amazonas, n m, Amazon
ámbar, n m, amber
ambición, n f, ambition
ambicioso, adj, ambitious
ambigüedad, n f, ambiguity
ambiguo, adj, ambiguous
ambos, adj, both
amedrentar, v, frighten
amén, n m, amen
amenaza, n f, threat
amenazar, v, threaten
amenizar, v, agreeable
ameno, adj, pleasant
América, n, America
americano, adj, American
ametralladora, n f, machine gun
amianto, n m, asbestos
amigable, adj, amicable
amigo, n f, friend
amilanar, v, frighten
amillarar, v, assess a tax
aminorar, v, lessen
amistad, n f, amity
amistosamente, adv, amicably
amistoso, adj, friendly
amo, n m, master
amonedar, v, coin
amonestación, n f, advice
amonestar, v, advise
amontonar, accumulate
amor, n m, cupid
amor, n m, love
amoratado, adj, livid
amparar, v, shelter, help
amparo, n m, favor
ampliación, n f, enlargement
ampliamente, adv, largely
ampliar, v, amplify

amplificar, v, enlarge
amplio, adj, ample
amplitud, n f, extent
amueblar, v, furnish
ánade, n mf, duck
añadidura, n f, addition
añadir, v, add
añal, adj, annual
anana, n f, pineapple
anaquel, n m, shelf
ancheta, n f, venture
anchura, n f, width
ancia, n f, anchor
anciadero, n m, moorage
anciaje, n m, anchoring
anciano, adj, old
anciano, n m, old
anciar, v, anchor
andamio, n m, scaffold
andana, n f, row
andante, adj, going
andanza, n f, fortune
andar, n m, speed
andar, v, go, walk
andar, v, step
andén, n m, path
andrajo, n m, rag
anécdota, n f, anecdote
anegado, adj, overflowed
anejo, adj, annexed
añejo, adj, old, stale, musty
anexar, v, annex
angosto, adj, narrow
angostura, n f, narrowness
anguila, n f, í
ángulo, n f, corner
ángulo, n m, angle
anheloso, adj, anxious
añicos, n mpl, bits
anieblar, v, obscure
anillo, n m, finger, ring
animación, n f, animation
animado, adj, animated
animado, adj, spirited
animal, n m, animal
animar, v, animate
animo, n m, spirit, courage

animosidad, n f, animosity
animoso, adj, brave
aniversario, n m, anniversary
año, n m, year
anónimo, adj, anonymous
anormal, adj, abnormal
anotar, v, note
ansia, n f, eager
ansiedad, n f, anxiety
ansioso, adj, anxious
antaño, adv, formerly
antebrazo, n m, forearm
anteceder, v, precede
antedecir, v, predict
antepasados, n mpl, ancestors
anteponer, v, prefer
anterior, adv, previous, before
anteriormente, adv, previously
antes, adv, first, before
antes, prep, before
anticipación, n f, anticipation
anticipadamente, adv, in advance
anticipar, v, anticipate
anticipo, n m, advance
anticuado, adj, antiquated
antidoto, n m, antidote
Antillas, n fpl, West Indies
antojarse, v, long, desire
antojo, n m, whim
antorcha, n f, torch
anual, adj, annual
anualidad, n f, annuity
anualmente, adv, annually
anuario, n m, year book
anublado, adj, overcast
anublar, v, cloud
anudar, v, knot
anuencia, n f, compliance
anular, v, cancel
anunciar, v, announce
anuncio, n m, announcement
apacentar, v, graze
apacible, adj, affable
apaciguar, v, appease
apadrinar, v, support
apagador, n f, extinguisher
apagar, v, quench

apalabrar, v, appoint
apañar, v, grasp
aparador, n m, dresser
aparato, n m, apparatus
aparear, v, match
aparecer, v, appear
aparejado, adj, prepared
aparejar, v, prepare
aparejo, n m, preparation
aparentar, v, show
aparente, adj, apparent
apariencia, n f, appearance
apartadero, n f, rn, siding
apartado, adj, separated
apartado, n m, separate room
apartamiento, n m, seclusion
apartamiento, n m, separation
apartar, v, part
aparte, adv, apart
apatía, n f, apathy
apático, adj, apathetic
apeadero, n m, residence
apeador, n m, surveyor
apear, v, alight
apegar, v, adhere
apego, n m, attachment
apelación, n f, appeal
apelar, v, appeal
apellidado, adj, named
apellidar, v, name
apellido, n m, surname
apenado, adj, sorry
apenas, adv, scarcely
apéndice, n m, appendix
apeo, n m, survey
apercibido, adj, ready
apercibimiento, n m, providing
apercibir, v, prepare
apero, n m, tool
apertura, n f, opening
apesadumbrado, adj, concerned
apetecer, v, desire
apetecible, adj, desirable
apetencia, n f, appetite
apetito, n m, hunger
apiadarse, v, pity
apiñar, v, unite

apio, n m, celery
aplacable, adj, meek
aplacar, v, placate, pacify
aplanar, v, flatten
aplanchadora, n f, laundress
aplanchar, v, iron
aplastado, adj, caked
aplastar, v, flatten
aplastar, v, squash
aplaudir, v, applaud
aplauso, n m, applause
aplauso, n m, cheer
aplazar, v, adjourn
aplicable, adj, applicable
aplicación, n f, application
aplicado, adj, studious
aplicar, v, apply
apoderado, adj, proxy
apoderar, v, grant
apodo, n m, nickname
apologia, n f, excuse
aportar, v, bring
aposento, n m, room
aposesionar, v, possession
apostadero, n m, military station
apostar, v, bet, wager
apoyar, v, favor
apoyo, n m, support
apreciable, adj, respectable
apreciación, n f, appreciation
apreciador, n m, appraiser
apreciar, v, estimate
aprecio, n m, regard
aprehender, v, apprehend
aprehensión, n f, apprehension
aprehensivo, adj, apprehensive
apremiante, adj, urgent
apremiar, v, press
apremio, n m, pressure
aprender, v, learn
aprendiz, n m, apprentice
aprendizaje, n m, apprenticeship
aprensar, v, press, crush
aprensión, n f, apprehension
apresa, adv, in haste
apresamiento, n m, capture
apresar, v, seize

aprestador, n m, finisher
aprestar, v, prepare
apresto, n m, preparation
apresuradamente, adv, hastily
apresurado, adj, hasty
apresurar, v, hasten
apretadamente, adv, tightly
apretado, adj, mean
apretamiento, n m, crowd
apretar, v, squeeze
apretar, v, tighten
apretón, n m, pressure
apretura, n f, crowd
aprieto, n m, conflict
aprisa, adv, swiftly
aprisionar, v, imprison
aprobación, n f, approval
aprobar, v, approve
aprontar, v, prepare
apropiadamente, adv, conveniently
apropiado, adj, appropriate
apropiar, v, appropriate
aprovechado, adj, improved
aprovechamiento, n m, profit
aprovechar, v, make progress
aprovisionamiento, n m, supply
aproximación, n f, approximation
aproximadamente, adv, nearly
aproximado, adj, approximate
aproximar, v, approach
aproximativo, adj, approximate
aptamente, adv, aptly
aptitud, n f, aptitude
apto, adj, fit
apuesta, n f, bet, wager
apuesto, adj, elegant
apuntación, n f, annotation
apuntado, adj, pointed
apuntador, n m, observer
apuntamiento, n m, observation
apuntar, v, aim
apuradamente, adv, punctually
apurado, adj, poor
apurar, v, purify
apuro, n m, want
aquejar, v, complain
aquí, adv, here

aquietar, v, quiet
aquilatar, v, assay
araña, n f, spider
arañar, v, scratch
araño, n m, scratch
arbitrador, n m, umpire
arbitraje, n m, arbitration
arbitrar, v, arbitrate
arbitrariamente, adv, arbitrarily
árbitro, n m, referee
árbol de Navidad, n m, Christmas tree
árbol, n m, tree
arbolado, adj, wooded
arbolar, v, hoist
arboleda, n f, grove of trees
arboricultura, n f, cultivation of trees
arbusto, n m, shrub
arca, n f, chest
archiplelago, n m, archipelago
archivar, v, register
archivero, n m, recorder
archivo, n m, archives
arcilla, n f, clay
arco, n m, bow
arcón, n m, large chest, bin
arder, v, burn
ardilla, n f, squirrel
arena, n f, sand
argentino, n f, silver
aritmética, n f, arithmetic
armonía, n f, harmony
arranar, v, claw
arrancar, v, pull out, pick
arrastrar, v, sneak
arreglar, v, arrange, pack
arriero, n m, carrier
arrodillarse, v, kneel
arroz, n m, rice
arrugar, v, shrivel
arte, n f, skill
arte, n m, craft
arte, n mf, art
artículo, n m, article
asegurar, v, secure
así, adv, so
así, adv, so, thus

asiento, n m, seat
asir, v, seize
asqueroso, adj, sickening
astilla, n f, chip
astuto, adj, calculating
astuto, adj, shrewd
asunto, n m, subject
asustarse, v, startle
atajo, n m, short cut
atán, n m, anxiety
ataúd, n f, coffin
atención, n f, attention
Atlántico, n f, Atlantic
atornillar, v, screw
atravesar, v, cross
atreverse, v, dare
aturdir, v, stun
aula, n f, schoolroom
aún, adv, yet, still
aunque, adv, although
automóvil, n m, automobile
autor, n m, author
avenida, n f, avenue
aventura, n f, adventure
avergonzar, v, shame, embarrass
ay, int, oh
ayer, adv, yesterday
ayuda, n f, help
ayudar, v, help
azatrán, n m, saffron
azteca, n m, Aztec
azúcar, n m, sugar
azufre, n m, sulfur
azul, adj, blue

B

babucha, n f, slipper
bacalao, n m, codfish
bacín, n m, basin
báculo, n m, walking stick
bafiadoro, n m, bathing place
bafiarse, v, bathe
bagaje, n m, baggage
bahía, n f, bay
bailador, n m, dancer
bailar, v, dance

baile, n m, ball
baja, n f, fall
bajado, adj, descended
bajamar, n f, low tide
bajar, v, come down
bajel, n m, vessel
bajeza, n f, meanness
bajío, n m, shallow
bajo, adj, low, short
bajuno, adj, vile
bala, n f, ball
balance, n m, balance
balancear, v, balance, swing
balandra, n f, sloop
balandro, n m, yacht
balanza, n f, scale
balcón, n m, balcony
baldar, v, cripple
balde, n m, bucket
baldío, adj, uncultivated
baldosa, n f, slab
ballena, n f, whale
ballenera, n f, whaler
ballestero, n m, archer
balneario, adj, bathing
balompie, n m, football
balompié, n m, football
balón, n m, football
balsa, n f, pool
balsámico, adj, balmy
bálsamo, n m, balsam
balsarnico, adj, balmy
balsarno, n m, balsam
bamboleo, n m, reeling
bambú, n m, bamboo
bañadero, n m, bathing place
bañar, v, water, bathe
bañarse, v, bathe
banasta, n f, basket
banasto, n m, large basket
banca, n f, form, bench
bancario, adj, banking
bancarrota, n f, bankruptcy
bancaza, n f, bench
banco, n m, bench, bank
banda, n f, band, scarf
bandada, n f, covey

bandazo, n m, rolling
bandeja, n f, tray
bandera, n f, banner, flag
bandido, n m, bandit
bando, n m, proclamation
bandolero, n m, robber
banemérito, adj, meritorious
bañera, n f, bath, bath tub
baño, n m, bath, coat
banquero, n m, banker
banqueta, n f, stool
banquete, n m, banquet
bao, n m, beam
baqueta, n f, ramrod, switch
baraja, n f, cards
barajar, v, shuffle cards
baranda, n f, railing
barata, n f, barter, exchange
baratar, v, barter
baratear, v, cheapen
baratería, n f, fraud
baratillero, n m, peddler
baratillo, n m, cheap store
baratista, n m, barterer
barato, adj, cheap
baratura, n f, cheapness
baraúnda, n f, noise
barba, n f, beard, chin
barbaridad, n f, barbarity
barbarie, n f, barbarousness
bárbaro, adj, barbarous
barbecho, n m, fallow
barbero, n m, barber
barbilla, n f, chin
barca, n f, boat, bark
barcada, n f, boat load
barcaza, n f, barge
barco, n m, boat
bardana, n f, burr
barlovento, n m, weather gauge
barnbu, n m, bamboo
barniz, n m, varnish, polish
barnizar, v, varnish, gloss
barómetro, n m, barometer
barquero, n m, boatman
barqueta, n f, small boat
barra, n f, bar

barrena, n f, auger, bit
barrenar, v, bore, pierce
barrendero, n m, sweeper
barreno, n m, drill
barrer, v, sweep
barrera, n f, barrier
barriada, n f, suburb
barrica, n f,keg
barriga, n f, belly
barril, n m, barrel, jar
barrilla, n f, bar
barrio, n m, district
barriquita, n f, cask
barrizal, n m, mud hole
barro, n m, clay, mud
barrote, n m, iron bar
barruntar, v, conjecture
barrunto, n m, conjecture
basar, v, base
báscula, n f, lever, see-saw
base, n f, basis
basta, int, that is enough
bastante, adj, enough, rather
bastantemente, adv, sufficiently
bastar, v, enough
bastardilla, n f, italic type
bastidor, n m, frame, sash
bastilla, n f, hem
bastimento, n m, supply of
  provisions
bastión, n m, bastion
basto, n m, pack saddle
bastón, n m, cane
bastón, n m, staff
bastón, n m, stick
basura, n f, sweepings
basurero, n m, dust man
basurero, n m, scavenger
bata, n f, gown
batalla, n f, battle
batallar, v, battle
batallón, n m, battalion
batea, n f, tray
batería, n f, battery
batido, adj, beaten
batidor, n m, scout
batiente, n m, jamb

batir, v, beat
batista, n f, batiste, lawn
batuta, n f, conductor's baton
baúl, n m, trunk, chest
bautismo, n m, baptism
bautizar, v, baptize
baya, n f, berry
bayeta, n f, baize
bayetón, n m, baize, coating
bayo, adj, bay
bayoneta, n f, bayonet
baza, n f, card trick
bazar, n m, bazaar
bazo, adj, brown
beato, adj, happy, blessed
bebedero, adj, potable
bebedero, n m, drinking vessel,
  trough
bebedor, n m, drinker
beber, v, drink
bebida, n f, drink
beca, n f, tipper
becado, n f, woodcock
becerrillo, n m, calf leather
becerro, n m, yearling calf
bedel, n m, beadle
befa, n f, jeer
befar, v, mock, scoff
behetría, n f, confusion
beldad, n f, beauty
bélico, adj, warlike
belicoso, adj, warlike
beligerante, adj, belligerent
bellaco, n m, rogue, knave
belladama, n f, belladonna
bellaquería, n f, knavery
belleza, n f, beauty
bello, adj, beautiful
bellota, n f, acorn
bencina, n f, benzine
bendito, adj, blessed
beneficiar, v, benefit
beneficiario, n m, beneficiary
beneficio, n m, benefit
beneficioso, adj, beneficial
benevolencia, n f, benevolence
benévolo, adj, benevolent

bengala, n f, cane
benignidad, n f, kindness
benigno, adj, benign, kind
beodo, adj, drunk
berenjenal, n m, difficulty
bergantín, n m, brig
bermejizo, adj, reddish
bermejo, adj, bright reddish color
bermellón, n m, vermilion
berrinche, n m, anger
berro, n m, water cress
berza, n f, cabbage
besito, n m, little kiss
bestia, n f, beast
besugo, n m, fish
betún, n m, polish
biblia, n f, Bible
biblioteca, n f, library
bibliotecario, n m, librarian
bicarbonato, n m, bicarbonate
bicho, n m, insect, grub
bicicleta, n f, bicycle
biciclista, n m, cyclist
bien, adv, well, right, easily
bien, n m, goodness, utility, welfare
bienandanza, n f, prosperity
bienestar, n m, well being
bienhechor, n m, benefactor
bienio, n m, two years
bienvenida, n f, welcome
biftec, n m, beef steak
bifurcación, n f, branch
bifurcamiento, n m, branch
bifurcarse, v, branch off
bigornia, n f, anvil
bigote, n m, moustache
billete, n m, note, label, ticket
bimestre, adj, two months
binocular, adj, binocular
binóculo, n f, binoculars
biografía, n f, biography
biombo, n m, screen
bípedo, n m, biped
biplano, n m, biplane
birlocho, n m, open carriage
birrete, n m, cap
bisabuelo, n m, great grandfather

bisagra, n f, hinge
bisoño, adj, raw, undisciplined
bisturí, n m, surgical instrument
bisutería, n f, jewelry
bivalvo, adj, bivalve
bizarreía, n f, gallantry
bizarro, n m, gallant, brave
bizco, v, squint
bizcocho, n m, biscuit
biznieto, n m, great grandson
blanca, n f, copper coin, mite
blanco, adj, white
blanco, n m, target
blancor, n m, whiteness
blandamente, adv, softly, mildly
blandear, v, soften, brandish
blandir, v, brandish
blando, adj, soft
blandón, n m, taper
blandura, n f, softness
blanqueador, n m, bleacher
blanqueadura, n f, whitening
blanquear, v, bleach, whiten
blanqueo, n m, bleaching
blanquizco, adj, whitish
blasfemar, v, blaspheme
blasfemia, n f, blaspheming
blasón, n m, heraldry
blasonar, v, blazon, boast
bledo, n m, straw, rush
blindado, adj, iron clad, armored
blindaje, n m, blind, armor plate
blindar, v, armor
blonda, n f, lace curtain
blondo, adj, flaxen, fair
bloque, n m, block
bloquear, v, blockade
bloqueo, n m, blockade
blusa, n f, blouse
boato, n m, ostentation
bobamente, adv, foolishly
bobería, n f, foolish speech
bobina, n f, bobbin
bobo, n m, fool
boca, n f, mouth
bocado, n m, morsel
bocal, n m, pitcher

bocarte, n m, stamp
boceto, n m, sketch
bochorno, n m, hot weather
bochornoso, adj, shameful
bocina, n f, horn
bocoy, n m, hogshead
boda, n f, marriage, wedding
bode, n m, male goat
bodega, n m, wine vault, cellar
bodegón, n m, eating house
bodeguero, n m, butler
bofetada, n f, buffet, slap
boga, n f, rowing
bogotana, n f, shirting
boina, n f, cap
boj, n m, box tree, box wood
bola, n f, ball
boletín, n m, ticket
boleto, n m, ticket
bolillo, n m, jack, small ball
bolín, n m, jack, small ball
bolita, n, ball, spot
bollo, n m, small loaf, roll
bolo, n m, pin
bolsa, n f, purse
bolsillo, n m, purse, pocket
bolso, n m, money bag
bomba, n f, pump
bomba, n m, large drum
bombardear, v, bombard
bombardeo, n f, bombardment
bombero, n m, fireman
bombilla, n f, bulb, lamp
bonachón, adj, good natured
bonancible, adj, moderate
bonanza, n f, prosperity, success
bondad, n f, kindness
bondadoso, adj, kind, generous
boneplácito, n m, approbation
bonete, n m, bonnet
bonetería, n f, bonnet shop
bonico, adj, pretty good
bonificar, v, credit
bonito, adj, pretty good
bonlficación, n f, allowance
boquete, n m, gap, hole
boquilla, n f, little mouth

bórax, n m, borax
borbollar, v, bubble out, gush
borbollón, n m, bubbling
borceguí, n m, laced shoe
bordada, n f, tack
bordado, n m, embroidery
bordador, n f, embroiderer
bordadura, n f, embroidery
bordar, v, embroider
borde, n m, border, edge
bordo, n m, board, ship
borgoña, n f, Burgundy
borla, n f, tassel
bornear, v, bend
borneo, n m, turning
borra, n f, yearling ewe
borracha, n m, leather wine bag
borrachera, n f, drunkenness
borracho, adj, drunk
borrador, n m, rough draft
borraj, n m, borax
borrar, v, erase
borrasca, n f, storm
borrascoso, adj, stormy
borrego, n m, lamb
borrico, n m,ass
borrón, n m, blot, blur
borroso, adj, blotted, blotchy
bosque, n m, wood, forest
bosquejar, v, sketch
bosquejo, n m, sketch
bostezar, v, yawn
bostezo, n m, yawn
bota, n f, wine bag
botador, n m, driver
botadura, n f, launching
botánico, adj, botanic
botar, v, throw
bote, n m, boat ò
botella, n f, bottle
Brasil, n f, Brazil
brazo, n m, arm
breve, adv, short
brillo, n m, shine
brinco, n m, spring
brotar, v, spring, shoot
brusco, adj, sturdy

bueno, adj, good, kind, nice
buey, n m, ox
bufón, n m, clown
buque, n m, ship
burla, n f, skit
burro, n m, donkey
busca, n f, search
buscar, v, search, seek, look for
butaca, n f, stall

C

cabal, adj, just, exact
cabalgadura, n f, horse
cabalgar, v, ride, mount
caballería, n f, chivalry
caballeriza, n f, stable
caballero, n m, squire
caballerosidad, n f, nobleness
caballeroso, adj, noble
caballete, n m, ridge
caballo, n m, horse
cabalmente, adv, exactly
cabaña, n f, cabin, cottage, shanty
cabecear, v, nod from sleep
cabecera, n f, head
cabecilla, n f, ringleader
cabellera, n f, long hair
cabello, n m, hair
caber, v, be right
cabestrillo, n m, arm sling
cabestro, n m, halter
cabeza, n f, head
cabezada, n f, headshake
cabida, n f, space, room
cabilla, n f, dowel
cabizbajo, adj, down-hearted
cable, n m, cable
cablear, v, cable
cablegrafiar, v, cable
cablegrama, n m, cablegram
cabo, n m, end
cabotaje, n m, coasting
cabra, n f, goat
cabria, n f, crane
cabrío, adj, male goat
cabrio, n m, rafter

cabriola, n f, jump
cabritilla, n f, kidskin
cabrón, n m, male goat
cabullería, n f, ship's chandlery
cabullero, n m, ship chandler
cacao, n m, cocoa
cacareo, n m, cackle
cacería, n f, hunting party
cacerola, n f, saucepan
cacha, n f, razor handle
cachalote, n m, sperm whale
cacharro, n m, earthen pot
cachaza, n f, tardiness
cachazudo, adj, cool, calm
cachemira, n f, cashmere
cachimba, n f, pipe
cachiporra, n f, club
cachivache, n m, rubbish
cacho, n m, slice, piece
cachorrillo, n m, small cub
cachorro, n m, puppy, kitten
cacique, n m, principal inhabitant
cacto, n m, cactus
cada, pro, every, each
cadalso, n m, scaffold
cadarzo, n m, coarse silk
cadáver, n m, corpse
cadena, n f, chain, link
cadencia, n f, cadence, measure
cadeneta, n f, chain stitch
cadenilla, n f, small chain
cadera, n f, hip
cadete, n m, cadet
caducar, v, be worn out
caduco, adj, senile
caer, v, fall
cafÄína, n f, caffeine
café, n m, coffee, caf$
cafetal, n m, coffee plantation
cafetera, n f, coffee pot
cafetero, n m, coffee tree
cafeto, n m, coffee tree
cafre, n m, savage
caída, n f, fall
caimán, n m, alligator
caja para té, n f, caddy
caja, n f, case, chest

cajero, n m, cashier
cajista, n m, compositor
cajita, n f, casket, little box, box
cajón, n m, drawer, box
cal, n f, lime
cala, n f, creek
calabaza, n f, pumpkin
calabazada, n f, bump
calabozo, n m, dungeon, prison
calabrote, n m, cable
calado, adj, open worked
calafate, n m, calker
calafatear, v, calk
calafateo, n m, calking
calambre, n m, cramp, spasm
calamidad, n f, calamity
calamina, n f, calamine
calamitoso, adj, calamitous
calaña, n f, character
calar, v, penetrate
calavera, n f, skull
calaverada, n f, foolish
calcañar, n m, heel bone
calcar, v, trace
calce, n m, wedge
calceta, n f, under stocking
calcetín, n m, sock, stocking
calco, n m, tracing
calculación, n f, calculation
calculador, n m, calculator
calcular, v, calculate
cálculo, n m, calculation
caldarón, n m, copper
caldear, v, iron, heat
caldera, n f, caldron
calderilla, n f, brass money
caldo, n m, broth
calefacción, n f, heating
calendario, n m, calendar
calentador, n m, warming pan
calentar, v, warm, heat
calentura, n f, fever
calesa, n f, calash, gig
calibre, n m, calibre, sort
calicó, n m, calico
calidad, n f, quality
cálido, adj, hot, piquant

caliente, adj, warm, hot
calificación, n f, qualification
calificar, v, qualify
caligrafía, n f, caligraphy
calígrafo, n m, pen man
cáliz, n m, chalice
callada, n f, silence
calladamente, adv, silently
callado, adj, silent
callar, v, be silent
calle, n f, street
callejero, adj, loitering
callejón, n f, lane
callejuela, n f, slum, lane
callo, n m, foot corn
calma, n f, calm
calmar, v, soothe, still
caló, n m, cant, jargon, slang
calofrío, n m, shivering fit
calor, n m, heat
calorífero, n m, furnace
calumnia, n f, slander
calumniar, v, slander
calumnioso, adj, calumnious
caluroso, adj, sultry, warm
calvario, n m, calvary
calvicie, n f, baldness
calvo, adj, bald, barren
calza, n f, trousers
calzada, n f, causeway
calzado, n, footwear
calzador, n m, shoehorn
calzar, v, put on shoes
calzo, n m, block, wedge, shoe
calzón, n mpl, breeches
calzoncillos, n mpl, pants
cama, n f, couch, bed, layer
camafeo, n m, cameo
cámara, n f, chamber, camera
camarada, n m, comrade
camarera, n f, waitress
camarero, n m, waiter, steward
camarón, n m, shrimp
camarote, n m, berth, cabin
cambalache, n m, barter
cambial, n m, bill of exchange
cambiamano, n f, railroad switch

cambiamiento, n m, change ò
cambiante, adj, bartering
cambiar, v, change
cambio, n m, exchange
cambista, n m, broker
cambray, n m, fine linen
camello, n m, camel
camilla, n f, small bed, cot
caminante, n m, traveller
caminar, v, walk
caminata, n f, walk
camino, n m, road
camión, n m, truck
camionaje, n m, cartage
camisa, n f, shirt, smock
camiseta, n f, shirt
camisola, n f, ruffled shirt
camorra, n f, quarrel
campamento, n m,encampment
campana, n f, bell
campaña, n f, campaign
campanada, n f, sound of bell
campanario, n m, steeple
campanilla, n f, small bell
campanudo, adj, bell shaped
campar, v, encamp
campear, v, excel
campeón, n m, champion
campeonato, n m, championship
campesino, adj, rural
campiña, n f, land, field
campo, n m, camp, country
camuesa, n f, pippin, apple
can, n m, dog
caña, n f, chase, cane
cana, n f, grey hair
cañada, n f, glen, shade
cañafístula, n f, cassia
canal, n m, channel, canal
canalete, n m, paddle
canalla, n f, mob
canalón, n m, gutter, spout
cañamazo, n m, canvas
cáñamo, n m, hemp
cañamón, n m, hemp seed
canapé, n m,couch, settee
canario, n m, canary

canasta, n f, basket
canastero, n m, basket maker
canastilla, n f, small basket, trousseau
canasto, n m, basket
cancelación, n f, cancellation
cancelar, v, cancel
cáncer, n m, cancer
canceroso, adj, cancerous
canciller, n m, chancellor
canción, n f, song
candado, n m, padlock
cande, adj, sugar candy
candela, n f, candle
candelabro, n m, candlestick
candelaria, n f, Candlemas
candelero, n m, candlestick, chandelier
candente, adj, incandescent
candidato, n, candidate
candidez, n f, whiteness, candor
cándido, adj, candid, white
candil, n m, lamp
candilejas, n f, fpl, footlights
candonga, n f, trick
candor, n m, candor
canela, n f, cinnamon
cañería, n f, pipe, piping
cangilón, n m, earthen jar, pitcher
cangrejo, n m, crab
caníbal, n f, cannibal
canilla, n f, bone, reel, faucet
canino, adj, canine
canje, n m, exchange
caño, n m, tube, pipe
canoa, n f, canoe
cañón, n m, cannon, tube
cañonazo, n m, cannon shot
cañonera, n f, gun port
cañonero, n m, gun boat
canoso, adj, hoary, old
cansado, adj, weary, tired
cansancio, n m, weariness
cansar, v, weary, tire
cantar, n m, song
cantar, v, chant, sing
cántara, n f, pitcher

cantárida, n f, Spanish fly, blister
cantarina, n f, singer
cántaro, n m, pitcher, vessel
cantera, n f, quarry
cantero, n m, stone cutter
cantidad, n f, quantity
cantina, n f, canteen
cantinela, n f, ballad
canto, n m, chant, song, stone
cantor, n m, singer
cañutillo, n m, small tube, bugle
cañuto, n m, pipe, cylinder
caoba, n f, mahogany
caos, n m, chaos
capa, n f, cape
capacidad, n f, capacity
caparrosa, n f, copper
capataz, n m, overseer
capaz, adj, capable
caperuza, n f, hood
capilla, n f, chapel
capirote, n m, hood, cap
capitación, n f, poll tax
capital, adj, capital
capital, n f, capital, money
capitalista, n m, capitalist
capitalizar, v, capitalize
capitán, n m, captain
capitel, n m, capital
capitolio, n m, capitol
capitulación, n f, capitulation
capitular, v, capitulate
capítulo, n m, chapter
capón, n m, capon
caporal, n m, corporal
capota, n f, bonnet
capote, n m, cloak
capricho, n m, caprice, whim
caprichoso, adj, capricious
cápsula, n f, capsule, cartridge
captar, v, captivate
captura, v, capture
capucha, n f, cowl, hood
capucho, n m, hood
capullo, n m, cocoon, bud
caqui, adj, khaki
cara, n f, face

carabela, n f, caravel
carabina, n f, carbine
caracol, n m, snail
carácter, n m, character
característica, n f, characteristic
característico, adj, characteristic
característico, n m, characteristic
caramba, int, good gracious
caramelo, n m, candy, caramel
caramillo, n m, flageolet, small flute
carátula, n f, mask, title page
caravana, n f, caravan
carbón de leña, n m, charcoal
carbón, n m, carbon, coal
carbonada, n f, broiled steak,
  pancake
carbonato, n m, carbonate
carbonería, n f, coal yard
carbonero, n m, charcoal maker,
  miner
carbónico, adj, carbonic
carbonífero, adj, coal
carbonizar, v, char
carburador, n m, carburetor
carcajada, n f, loud laughter
cárcel, n f, prison
carcelería, n f, imprisonment
carcelero, n m, jailer
carcoma, n f, wood house
carcomer, v, gnaw, corrode
carcomido, adj, worm-eaten,
  decayed
cardar, v, card wool
cardenal, adj, red color
cardenal, n m, cardinal
cardero, n m, card maker
cardillo, n m, thistle
cardinal, adj, principal, cardinal
cardinal, n m, cardinal
cardo, n m, thistle
carear, v, compare
carecer, v, lack
carena, n f, repairing a ship
carencia, n f, lack, want
careo, n m, confrontation,
  comparison
carestía, n f, scarcity

careta, n f, mask
carey, n m, tortoise shell
carga, n f, cargo ò
cargado, adj, loaded
cargador, n m, loader
cargamento, n m, cargo
cargar, v, load, charge
cargo, n m, burden, load
carguío, n m, cargo, load
caricatura, n f, caricature
caricia, n f, caress
caridad, n f, charity
carillón, n m, chime
cariño, n m, affection, love
cariñoso, adj, affectionate, kind
carita, n f, little face
caritativo, adj, charitable
cariz, n m, face, aspect
carmelita, n f, carmelite, brown color
carmesí, adj, crimson
carmín, n m, carmine
carnaleón, n f, rn, chameleon
carnaval, n m, carnival
carne, n f, meat
carnero, n m, sheep
carnicería, n f, carnage
carnicero, n m, butcher
carnívoro, adj, carnivorous
carnoso, adj, fleshy
caro, adj, dear, expensive
caro, adv, dearly
carpa, n f, carp
carpeta, n f, portfolio
carpintería, n f, carpentry
carpintero, n m, carpenter
carraspera, n f, hoarseness
carrera, n f, career
carreta, n f, cart
carretada, n f, cart load
carrete, n m, spool, bobbin
carretera, n f, highway
carretero, n m, carter, cartwright
carretilla, n f, wheel barrow
carretón, n m, small cart
carril, n m, rut, rail
carrillo, n m, cheek
carrito, n m, small carriage

carro, n f, carriage, cart
carroza, n f, large coach
carruaje, n m, carriage
carta, n f, card, chart, letter
cartearse, v, correspond
cartel, n m, placard, poster
cartera, n f, portfolio
cartero, n m, mailman
cartilla, n f, small letter, primer
cartón, n m, cardboard
cartuchera, n f, cartridge box, pouch
cartucho, n m, cartridge
cartulina, n f, cardboard
casa, n f, house, firm
casaca, n f, coat
casación, n f, abrogation
casamiento, n m, marriage
casar, v, marry
casarse, v, marry
casca, n f, grape skin
cascabel, n m, animal bell, rattlesnake
cascada, n f, cascade
cascado, adj, broken, infirm
cascajo, n m, gravel
cascanueces, n m, nutcracker
cascar, v, crack
cáscara, n f, rind peel
cascarón, n m, egg shell
cascarrón, edj, rough, harsh
casco, n m, skull, helmet
cascote, n m, rubbish
casería, n f, country house
caserío, n m, village
casero, adj, domestic
casero, n m, landlord
caserón, n m, large house
casi, adv, almost
casilla, n f, ticket office
casillero, n m, pigeon holes
casino, n m, casino, club
caso, n m, event, case
casquete, n m, casque, helmet
casquillo, n m, cap, socket
casquivano, adj, inconsiderate
casta, n f, caste, race
castaña, n f, chestnut

castañeta, n f, castanet
castaño, adj, brown, chestnut
castaño, n m, chestnut tree
castañuela, n f, castanet
castellano, adj, Castilian, Spanish
castidad, n f, chastity
castigar, v, chastise
castigo, n m, punishment
castillo, n m, castle
castizo, adj, pure blooded, chaste
casto, adj, pure, chaste
castor, n m, castor, beaver
casual, adj, casual, accidental
casualidad, n f, casualty
casualmente, adv, casually
casucha, n f, hut, hovel
cata, n f, trial, taste, proof
cataclismo, n m, cataclysm
catacumbas, n f, fpl, catacombs
catador, n m, taster
catálogo, n f, rn, catalog
catapulta, n f, catapult
catar, v, taste, try
catarata, n f, cataract, waterfall
catarro, n m, cold
catástrofe, catastrophe
catedral, n f, cathedral
categoría, n f, category
categórico, adj, categorical
católico, edj, catholic
catorce, n f, fourteen
catre, n m, bed
cauce, n m, riverbed
caudal, n m, fortune, stock
caudaloso, adj, flowing
causa, n f, cause, sake
causante, adj, causing
causar, v, cause
cáustico, adj, caustic
cautamente, adv, cautiously
cautela, n f, caution
cauterizar, v, cauterize
cautivar, v, capture
cautivo, n m, captive
cauto, adj, cautious
cava, n f, cellar
cavar, v, dig

caverna, n f, cavern
cavidad, n f, cavity
caza, n f, chase
cazador, n m, hunter
cazar, v, hunt, chase
cazuela, n f, saucepan
cebada, n f, barley
cebar, v, feed, fatten
cebellina, n f, sable
cebo, n m, food, fodder
cebolla, n f, onion
cebra, n f, zebra
cedazo, n m, sieve
ceder, v, cede, grant
cedro, n m, cedar
cédula, n f, schedule
céfiro, n m, zephyr
cegar, v, make blind, darken
cegarrita, ad, blindly
ceguera, n f, blindness
ceja, n f, eyebrow
cejar, v, relax
celada, n f, helm, ambush
celador, n m, curator, overseer
celar, v, watch
celda, n f, cell
celebración, n f, celebration
celebrar, v, celebrate
célebre, adj, celebrated
celebro, n m, brain
celeste, adj, celestial, sky blue
cellosía, n f, Venetian blind
celo, n m, zeal
celoso, adj, jealous, zealous
Celta, n m, Celt
cementerio, n m, cemetery
cemento, n m, cement
cena, n f, supper
cenagal, n m, quagmire
cenar, v, have supper
cenefa, adj, border, fringe
ceniciento, adj, ash colored
ceñir, v, gird, reduce
cenit, n m, zenith
ceniza, n f, ashes
ceño, n m, frown
censo, n m, census

censura, n f, censure, reproach
censurar, v, censure, blame
centavo, n m, cent
centella, n f, spark, flash
centellar, v, sparkle
centelleo, n m, spark, scintillation
centena, n f, hundred
centeno, n m, rye
céntimo, n m, centime
centinela, n mf, sentry
central, adj, central
céntrico, adj, central
centrífugo, adj, centrifugal
centro, n m, center
centuria, n f, century
ceñudo, adj, frowning, grim
cepa, n f, root, foundation
cepillo, n m, brush
cepo, n m, block, reel
cera, n f, wax, bees' wax
cerámico, adj, ceramic
cerca, adj, near, about
cerca, adv, near
cerca, n f, enclosure, fence
cercanía, n f, neighborhood
cercar, v, enclose
cerciorar, v, assure, affirm
cerco, n m, hoop, ring, circle
cerdo, n m, pig
cerdoso, adj, bristly
cereal, adj, cereal
cereales, n mpl, cereals
cerebro, n m, brain
ceremonia, n f, ceremony
cereza, n f, cherry
cerezal, n m, cherry orchard
cerezo, n m, cherry tree, wood
cerner, v, sift, shut, close
cerñido, adj, moderate
cero, n m, zero, cypher
cerquita, adv, near
cerradero, n m, staple
cerrado, adj, close, reserved
cerradura, n f, lock
cerrajero, n m, locksmith
cerrar, v, close, lock
cerrazón, n f, darkness

cerril, adj, mountainous
cerro, n m, hill, mountain
cerrojo, n m, bolt
certamen, n f, controversy
certero, n m, sharpshooter
certeza, n f, certainly
certidumbre, n f, certainty
certificación, n f, certificate, certification
certificado, adj, certified, registered
certificado, n m, certificate
certificar, v, certify
cervato, n m, fawn
cervecería, n f, brewery
cerveza, n f, beer, ale
cerviz, n f, nape of neck
cesacíon, n f, cessation
cesante, n m, retired official
cesantía, n f, pension
cesar, v, cease
cesión, n f, cession, transfer
césped, n m, sod
cesto, n m, basket
cetro, n m, scepter
chacota, n f, noisy mirth, fun
chafar, v, crush, crease
chal, n m, shawl
chalán, n m, hawker, huckster
chaleco, n m, vest
chalina, n f, cravat, scarf
chamorro, adj, shorn, bald
champaña, n f, champagne
champú, n m, shampoo
chamuscar, v, singe
chancear, v, jest, joke
chancero, adj, jesting
chancleta, n f, slipper
chanclo, n m, clog
chanza, n f, jest, joke
chaparrón, n m, hard rain
chapear, v, plate
chapotear, v, splash
chapucear, v, botch, bungle
chapurrar, v, speak gibberish
chaqueta, n f, jacket
charco, n m, pool
charla, n f, chat, smalltalk

charlar, v, chat
charlatán, n m, charlatan
charnela, n f, hinge
charol, n m, varnish
charolar, v, varnish
charque, n m, salt beef
charretera, n f, epaulette
charro, adj, gaudy, tawdry
chasco, n m, joke, fun
chasquear, v, crack, snap, fool
chato, adj, flat
cheviot, n m, tweed
chica, n f, little girl, girl
chico, adj, little, small
chico, n m,boy
chifla, n f, whistle
chiflado, adj, silly, crazy
chifladura, n f, hobby
chiflar, v, whistle, mock
chillar, v, scream, squeak
chillido, n m, scream, shriek
chimenea, n f, hearth, fireplace
china, n f, china, porcelain
chinche, n f,bug
chinchilla, n f, chinchilla
chinela, n f, slipper
chinesco, adj, Chinese
chino, n m, Chinaman
chiquito, adj, little
chiripa, n f, windfall
chirriar, v, hiss, creak
chirrido, n m, chirp
chismear, v, tattle
chispa, n f, spark
chispear, v, sparkle
chisporrotear, v, sputter
chistar, v, mutter, mumble
chiste, n m, joke, jest
chistoso, adj, witty, lively
chito, int, silence
chivo emisario, n m, scapegoat
chivo, n m, fraud
chocar, v, collide
chocolate, n m, chocolate
chofeta, n f, chafing dish
choque, n m, shock
chorizo, n m, pork sausage

chorrear, v, gush, outpour
chorrillo, n m, outpour
chorro, n m, water, gush
chova, n f, chough
choza, n f, hut
chuchería, n f, trinket
chucho, n m, owl
chufa, n f, boast
chufleta, n f, jeer
chuleta, n f, chop, cutlet
chulo, n m, punster, assistant
chumbro, n m, Indian fig
chunga, n f, jest, joke
chupar, v, suck
churla, n f, bag, bale
chusco, adj, pleasant, droll
chuzo, n m, pike
cibar, v, screen
cicatriz, n f, scar
cicatrizar, v, heal
cicio, n m, cycle
ciclismo, n m, cycling
ciclista, n m, cyclist
cidra, n f, citron
cidro, n m, citron tree
ciegamente, adv, blindly
ciego, adj, blind
cielo, n m,sky
cien, adj, one hundred
ciénaga, n f, marsh
ciencia, n f, science
cieno, n m, mud, mire
científico, adj, scientific
ciento, n m, cent, one hundred
cierre, n m, closing, closure
ciertamente, adv, certainly
cierto, adj, certain, true
ciervo, n m, deer
cifra, n f, cipher
cifrar, v, cipher
cigüeña, adj, crank
cigüeñal, n m, winch, crank
cigarrera, n f, cigar case
cigarrero, n m, cigar seller
cigarrillo, n m, cigarette
cigarro, n m, cigar
cilindrar, v, cylinder, roll

cilíndrico, adj, cylindrical
cilindro, n m, cylinder
cima, n f, summit
címbalo, n m, cymbal
cimentar, v, found
cimento, n m, cement
cimiento, n m, foundation
cinabrio, n m, cinnabar, vermilion
cincel, n m, chisel
cincelador, n m, engraver, sculptor
cincelar, v, chisel, engrave
cincha, n f, girth
cinchar, v, gird
cincho, n m, belt, girdle
cinco, n f, five
cincuenta, n f, fifty
cine, n m, movie
cine, n m, zinc
cinematógrafo, n m, cinematograph
cínico, adj, cynical
cínico, n m, cynic
cinta, n f, sash, ribbon
cintillo, n m, hat band
cinto, n m, belt, girdle
cintura, n f, waist
cinturón, n m, belt
ciprés, n m, cypress tree
circo, n m, circus
circuito, n m, circuit
circulación, n f, circulation
circulante, adj, circulating
circular, adj, circular
circular, v, circle
círculo, n m, circle, compass
circundar, v, surround
circunferencia, n f, circumference
circunnavegar, v, circumnavigate
circunscribir, v, circumscribe
circunspecto, adj, circumspect,
   cautious
circunstancia, n f, circumstance
circunstanciado, adj, circumstantial
circunvecino, adj, neighboring
cirial, n m, candlestick
cirio, n m, wax candle
ciruela, n f, plum, prune
ciruelo, n m, plum tree

cirugía, n f, surgery
cirujano, n m, surgeon
cisne, n m, swan
cisterna, n f, cistern
cita, n f, appointment, citation
citación, n f, citation
citar, v, quote, cite
citrato, n m, citrate
ciudad, n f, city
ciudadanía, n f, citizenship
ciudadano, n m, citizen
ciudadela, n f, citadel
civil, adj, civil
civilidad, n f, civility, politeness
civilización, n f, civilization
civilizado, adj, civilized
civilizar, v, civilize
civilmente, adv, civilly
cizalla, n f, filings
cizaña, n f, discord
clamar, v, cry out
clamor, n m, clamour
clamorear, v, clamour
clamoroso, adj, clamorous
clandestino, adj, clandestine
claraboya, n f, sky light, bull's eye
claramente, adv, clearly
clarear, v, grow light
clarete, n m, claret
claridad, n f, clearness
clarificar, v, clarify
clarín, n m, clarion, trumpet
clarinete, n m, clarinet
clarión, n m, crayon
claro, adj, clear, evident, of course
claro, n m, clearness
clase, n f, class, classroom, kind
clásico, adj, classical
clasificación, n f, classification
clasificar, v, class, sort
claustro, n m, cloister
cláusula, n f, clause
clausura, n f, cloister
clavar, v, nail, stick in
clave, n f, key
clavel, n m, carnation, pink
clavete, n m, tack

clavija, n f, pin
clavillo, n m, small nail, rivet
clavito, n m, tack
clavo, n m, stud, nail, clove
clemencia, n f, clemency
clerical, adj, clerical
clérigo, n m, clergyman, cleric
clero, n m, clergy
cliente, n m, client, customer
clientela, n f, clientele
clima, n m, climate
clímax, n m, climax
clínica, n f, clinic
clínico, adj, clinical
clisé, n m, matrix
cloaca, n f, sewer
clorato, n m, chlorate
clorhidrato, n m, hydrochlorate
clorhídrico, n m, hydrochloric
clórico, adj, chloric
cloro, n m, chlorine
cloroformo, n m, chloroform
cloruro, n m, chloride
coacción, n f, coercion
coactivo, adj, compulsory
coadjutor, n m, coadjutor, assistant
coadyuvar, v, help, assist
coartada, n f, alibi
coartar, v, restrict, limit
cobalto, n m, cobalt
cobarde, adj, cowardly
cobarde, n mf, coward
cobardía, n f, cowardice
cobertizo, n m, shelter
cobertor, n m, coverlet, quilt
cobertura, n f, cover
cobija, n f, gutter tile, blanket
cobijar, v, cover, shelter
cobradero, adj, recoverable
cobrado, adj, recovered, received
cobrador, n m, collector, receiver
cobranza, n f, collection, recovery
cobrar, v, collect, recover
cobre, n m, copper
cobro, n m, collection, payment
cocear, v, kick
cocer, v, stew, boil, bake

coche, n m, carriage, coach
cochera, n f, coach house
cochero, n m, coachman
cochina, n f, sow
cochino, n m, pig
cocido, adj, boiled, baked, experienced
cocina, n f, kitchen
cocinar, v, cook
cocinera, n f, cook
cocinero, n m, cook
coco, adj, cocoa
coco, n m, coconut, coconut oil
cocodrilo, n m, crocodile
codear, v, elbow
codicia, n f, covetousness
codiciar, v, covet
codicioso, adj, greedy, covetous
código, n m, code
codo, n m, elbow
codorniz, n f, quail
coetáneo, adj, contemporary
cofre, n m, trunk, chest
cofrero, n m, trunk maker
coger, v, catch, gather, take
cogida, n f, catching, gathering
cogucho, n m, raw sugar
cohechar, v, bribe
cohecho, n m, bribery
coheredero, n m, joint heir
cohesivo, adj, cohesive
cohete, n m, rocket
cohombro, n m, cucumber
coincidir, v, coincide
cojín, n m, cushion
cojinete, n m, cushion, bearing
cojo, adj, lame
col, n f, cabbage
cola, n f, tail, train, glue
colaboración, n f, collaboration
colaborador, n m, collaborator
colación, n f, collation, repast
colada, n f, washing clothes
coladero, n m, colander, strainer
colapso, n m, collapse
colar, v, strain
colateral, adj, collateral

colcha, n f, coverlet, quilt
colchar, v, quilt
colchón, n m, mattress
colección, n mf, collection
colectivo, adj, collective
colega, n m, colleague ò
colegial, adj, collegial
colegio, n m, college
colegir, v, gather, deduce
cólera, n f, anger, fury
colérico, adj, angry, choleric
coleto, n m, doublet, jacket
colgadizo, adj, pendant, suspended
colgado, adj, suspended, hung
colgadura, n f, tapestry
colgante, adj, hanging
colgar, v, hang up
coliflor, n f, cauliflower
colilla, n f, cigarette butt
colina, n f, hill
colindante, adj, contiguous
colindar, v, be contiguous
coliseo, n m, coliseum
collar, n m, necklace, collar
collera, n f, collar, horse collar
collsión, n f, collision
colmar, v, heap up
colmena, n f, bee hive
colmenar, n m, apiary
colmillo, n m, canine tooth, fang
colmo, n m, heap
colocación, n f, placement
colocar, v, place, station
colón, n m, opint, colon
colonia, n f, settlement, colony
colono, n m, colonist, settler
coloquio, n m, colloquy, talk
color, n m, color
colorado, adj, colored red
colorar, v, color
colosal, adj, colossal, large
columbrar, v, discern
columna, n f, column
columpiar, v, swing
columpio, n m, swing
colusión, n f, collusion
colza, n f, colza, rape, rapeseed

coma, n f, comma
comandancia, n f, command
comandante, n m, commander
comandar, v, command
comarca, n f, district
comba, n f, bend
combar, v, bend
combate, n m, combat
combatir, v, combat
combinación, n f, combination
combinar, v, combine
comedero, adj, edible
comedero, n m, dining room
comedia, n f, comedy
comedido, adj, civil, polite
comedor, n m, dining room
comentar, v, comment
comentario, n m, commentary
comento, n m, comment
comenzar, v, begin
comer, v, eat, dine
comercial, adj, commercial
comerciar, v, trade
comercio, n m, commerce, business
comestible, adj, edible
cometa, n f, kite
cometa, n m, comet
cometer, v, commit
cometido, n m, commission
cómico, adj, comical
cómico, n m, actor, comedian
comida, n f, food, dinner, meal
comienzo, n m, beginning
comino, n m, cumin plant, seed
comisar, v, confiscate
comisaría, n f, police station
comisión, n f, commission
comisionar, v, commission
comité, n m, committee
comitente, n constituent, client
comitiva, n f, suite, retinue
cómo, adv, how
como, prep, as, like
cómoda, n f, chest of drawers
cómodamente, adv, conveniently
comodidad, n f, commodity
cómodo, adj, comfortable,

convenient
cómodo, n m, profit, convenience
compacto, adj, compact
compadecerse, v, pity
compadre, n m, godfather, protector
compaginar, v, join, unite
compañero, n m, companion
compañía, n f, company
comparable, adj, comparable
comparar, v, collate, compare
compartir, v, divide, share
compasión, n f, compassion
compasivo, adj, compassionate
compatibilidad, n f, compatibility
compeler, v, compel
compendiar, v, abridge, shorten
compensar, v, compensate
competente, adj, competent
competir, v, compete
compilar, v, compile
complacer, v, please, oblige
complejo, adj, complex
completar, v, complete
completo, adj, complete, self-
  contained
complexo, adj, complex
complicado, adj, complicated
complicar, v, complicate
cómplice, n mf, accomplice
complicidad, n f, complicity
complot, n m, plot, conspiracy
componedor, n m, composer
componer, v, compose
comportamiento, n m, behavior
comportarse, v, behave oneself
composición, n f, composition
compota, n f, jam
compra, n f, purchase
comprar, v, buy
comprender, v, comprehend,
  understand
comprensión, comprehension
comprobar, v, verify, prove
comprometer, v, compromise
compromisario, n m, arbitrator
compromiso, n f, compromise
compuesto, n m, compound

computar, v, compute
computista, n m, computer
comunicación, n f, communication
comunicar, v, communicate
comunidad, n f, community
comunión, n f, communion
comúnmente, adv, commonly
con, prep, with, by
conato, n m, endeavor
cóncavo, adj, concave
concebible, adj, conceivable
concebir, v, conceive
conceder, v, concede
concentrar, concentrate
concha, n f, shell
conciencia, n f, conscience
concienzudo, adj, conscientious
concierto, n m, concert
conciso, adj, concise
concluir, conclude
concreto, adj, concrete
concurrencia, n f, competition
concurrir, v, compete, concur
conde, n m, count
condenar, v, condemn
condensación, n f, condensation
condición, n f, condition
condicional, adj, conditional
condimento, n m, seasoning
conducir, v, conduct, take
conducta, n f, conduct
conexión, n f, connection
conferencia, n f, conference
conferir, v, confer
confesar, v, confess
confesión, n m, confession
confianza, n f, confidence
confirmar, v, confirm
confiscar, v, confiscate
confitería, n f, candy store
conformar, v, comform
confortación, n f, comfort
confrontar, v, confront
congestión, n f, congestion
conjurar, v, conjure
conmigo, prep, with me
conmutar, v, commute

cono, n m, cone
conocer, v, know a person
conquista, n f, conquest
conquistador, n m, conqueror
conquistar, v, conquer
consecutivo, adj, serial
consentimiento, n m, consent
consentir, v, consent
conservación, n f, conservation
conservar, v, conserve, preserve
considerado, adj, considerate
consignar, v, consign
consistente, adj, consistent
consistir, v, consist
considerar, v, consider
conspicuo, adj, conspicuous
conspiración, n f, conspiracy
conspirar, v, conspire
constancia, n f, constancy
constante, adj, changeless, constant
constreñimiento, n m, constraint
constreñir, v, constrain
construcción, n f, construction
construir, v, build, construct
consultar, v, consult
contacto, n m, contact
contar, v, count, tell, relate
contener, v, contain
contenido, n m, contents
contento, adj, content, happy
contestación, n f, answer
contestar, v, answer
contexto, n m, context
contigo, prep, with you
continente, n m, continent
continuo, adj, continual
contorno, n m, contour
contrabando, n m, smuggling
contrapunto, n m, counterpoint
contrario, adj, contrary
contraste, n m, contrast
contrato, n m, contract
convaleciente, adj, convalescent
conveniente, adj, convenient
convergir, v, converge
conversación, n f, conversation
converso, v, converse

convertir, v, convert
cooperar, v, cooperate
copa, n f, cup
copete, n m, crest tuft
copia, n f, copy
copiador, n m, copier
copiar, v, copy
copioso, adj, copious
copista, n m, copyist
copo, n m, flake, bundle
copra, n f, coconut fiber
coquina, n f, shell fish, cockle
coral, n m, coral
corambre, n f, pelts
corazón, n m, heart
corbata, n f, necktie, tie
corcel, n m, horse, steed
corchete, n m, clasp
corcho, n m, cork
corcova, n f, hump
cordel, n m, cord, rope
cordial, adj, cordial
cormún, adj, common
corona, n f, crown
coronel, n m, colonel
correa, n f, strap
correcto, adj, correct
corredor, n m, corridor
corregir, v, correct
correo, n m, post office, mail
correr, v, scamper, stream, run
corresponder, v, correspond
corrida de toros, n f, bullfight
corrida, n f, course, race
corriente, n f, stream
corroer, v, corrode
corrupto, adj, corrupt
corsé, n m, corset
corso, n m, cruise
cortaplumas, n m, penknife
cortar, v, cut, slash, stump
cortarse, v, cut oneself
corte, n f, court
corte, n m, court, cut
cortedad, n f, smallness, shortness
cortejo, n m, court
cortés, adj, courteous

cortina, n f, curtain
corto, adj, short
corva, n f, curve
corvo, adj, bent
cosa, n f, thing
coser, v, sew, stitch
costa, n f, coast, shore
costado, n m, side flank
costoso, adv, costly
costumbre, n f, custom
costura, n f, seam
cotón, n m, cotton
cráneo, n m, skull
crear, v, create
crecer, v, increase
crédito, n m, credit
creer, v, believe
creíble, adj, credible
cresta, n f, crest
criada, n f, servant maid
criado, n m, servant
criarse, v, be brought up, grow
criatura, n f, creature
criba, n f, sieve
cripta, n f, crypt
crisantemo, n m, chrysanthemum
cristal, n m, crystal
cristiano, n m, Christian
Cristo, n m, Christ
Crónico, adj, chronic
crucifijo, n m, crucifix
crudo, adj, crude
cruel, adj, cruel
cruz, n f, cross
cruzada, n f, crusade
cruzar, v, cross
cuaderno, n m, notebook
cuadra, n f, stable
cuadrado, n m, square
cuadro, n m, picture
cual, pro, which
cuando, adv, when
cuánto, adv, how much, how many
cuarenta, n f, forty
cuarto, n m, room, quarter
cuatro, n f, four
cubierta, n f, cover

cubierto, adj, cover
cubo, n m, cube
cubrir, v, cover
cucú, n m, cuckoo
cuchara, n f, spoon
cucharita, n f, teaspoon
cucharón, n m, scoop
cuchillo, n m, knife
cuello, n m, neck, collar
cuenco, n m, bowl
cuenta, n f, account, bill
cuento, n m, story
cuerda, n f, string
cuero, n m, hide, pelt
cuerpo, n m, corps, body
cuerva, n f, crow, rook
cuervo, n m, crow
cuestión, n f, question
cuestionar, v, question
cueva, n f, cave
cuidado, n m, care
cuidadosamente, adv, carefully
cuidadoso, adj, careful
cuita, n f, trouble, care, grief
culebra, n f, snake
culpa, n f, fault, blame
culpar, v, blame
cultivar, v, cultivate, raise
culto, n m, cult
cultura, n f, culture
cumbre, n f, summit, top
cumpleaños, n m, birthday
cumplir, v, keep
cuota, n f, quota
cura, n f, cure
curar, v, cure
curia, n f, court, tribunal
curiosidad, n f, curiosity
curioso, adj, curious
cursar, v, frequent
curso, n m, course
cutis, n m, skin
czar, n m, czar

D

dable, adj, easy, possible

dactilógrafa, n f, lady typist
dactilografía, n f, typewriting
dactilógrafo, n m, typist
dádiva, n f, gift, present
dadivoso, adj, generous, liberal
dado, n m, die
dador, n m, bearer
daga, n f, dagger
dama, n f, lady, dame
damasco, n m, damask
dañar, v, hurt, harm
dañino, adj, hurtful, harmful
daño, n m, harm, damage
dañoso, adj, harmful
danza, n f, dance
danzante, n mf, dancer
danzar, v, dance
dar, v, give, hit, beat
dardo, n m, dart
darse, v, yield, give in
dársena, n f, dock, basin
dasagüe, n m, drain, drainage
dasmán, n m, misfortune
data, n f, date
datar, v, date
dátil, n m, date (fruit)
dato, n m, datum
datos, n mpl, data, information
datrás, adv, behind, after
de, prep, of, from, about
de algún modo, adv, somehow
de lado, adj, sideways
de pronto, adj, sudden
de veras, adv, seriously
debajo, prep, below, underneath
debate, n m, debate, discussion
debatir, v, debate, discuss
debe, n m, debtor, debit
deber, n m, duty
deber, v, owe, must
debidamente, adv, duly
debido, adj, due, owing
debiente, n m, debtor
débil, adj, weak, feeble
debilidad, n f, debility, weakness
debilitación, n f, debilitation
debilitar, v, debilitate

débito, n m, debit, debt
débllrnente, adv, weakly
década, n f, decade
decadencia, n f, decay, decline
decadente, adj, declining
decaer, v, decay, decline
decagramo, n m, decagram
decámetro, n m, decameter
decampar, v, decamp
decantar, v, decant, exaggerate
decencia, n f, decency
decentar, v, commence, tap
decente, adj, decent
decentemente, adv, decently
decepcíon, n f, deception
dechado, n m, sample
decible, adj, expressible
decidir, decide
decigramo, n m, decigram
decilitro, n m, deciliter
decimal, adj, decimal
decímetro, n m, decimeter
decir, n m, saying
decir, v, say, tell
decisiín, n f, decision
decisivo, adj, decisive, final
declamar, v, declaim, harangue
declaración, n f, declaration
declarado, adj, declared
declarante, n m, declarer
declarar, v, declare
declarnación, n f, declamation,
  discourse
declinacíon, n f, declination, descent
declinar, v, decline
declive, n m, slope, slant
decolorar, v, discolor
decomisar, v, confiscate
decoración, n f, decoration
decorador, n m, decorator
decorar, decorate
decoro, n m, decorum
decoroso, adj, decorous, decent
decrecer, v, decrease
decremento, n m, decrement
decréplto, adj, decrepit
decretar, v, decree

decreto, n m, decree
dedal, n m, thimble
dedicación, n f, dedication
dedicar, v, dedicate, devote
dedicatoria, n f, dedicatior
dedillo, n m, little finger
dedo, n m, finger
deducción, n f, deduction
deducir, v, deduce, deduct
defecto, n m, defect
defectuoso, adj, defective
defender, v, defend, protect
defendible, adj, defensible
defensa propia, n f, self-defense
defensa, n f, defense
defensable, adj, defensible
defensiva, n f, defensive
defensivo, adj, defensive
defensor, n m, defender
deferencia, n f, deference
deferente, adj, deferent
deferir, v, defer
deficiencia, n f, deficiency
deficiente, adj, deficient
déficit, n m, deficit
definición, n f, definition
definido, adj, definite
definir, v, define, describe
definitivamente, adv, definitively
definitivo, adj, definite
deformar, v, deform
deforme, adj, deformed, shapeless
defraudación, n f, fraud
defraudador, n m, defrauder
defraudar, v, defraud, cheat
defunción, n f, death
degenerar, v, degenerate
degollar, v, behead
degradación, n f, degradation
degradar, v, degrade
dehesa, n f, pasture
dejación, n f, resignation, giving up
dejar, v, leave, let, allow
dejo, n m, end, taste, result
del, prep, of the, from the
delación, n f, accusation
delantal, n m, apron

delante, prep, in front of
delantera, n f, front, advantage
delantero, adj, foremost, first
delatable, adj, blamable
delatante, n m, accuser
delatar, v, accuse, denounce
delator, n m, accuser, informer
delegación, n f, delegation
delegado, n f, delegate, deputy
delegar, v, depute, delegate
deleitable, adj, delightful
deleitar, v, delight
deleite, n m, delight
deleitoso, adj, delightful
deletrear, v, spell
deletreo, n m, spelling
deleznable, adj, brittle, fragile
delgadez, n f, thinness, slenderness
delgado, adj, slender
deliberación, n f, deliberation
deliberar, v, deliberate
delicadez, n f, delicacy, tenderness
delicadeza, n f, delicateness
delicado, adj, delicate
delicia, n f, delight
delicioso, adj, delightful
delincuente, n m, delinquent
delinear, v, delineate
delinquir, v, offend
delirar, v, rave
delirio, n m, delirium
delito, n m, fault, crime
delusivo, adj, delusive
delusorio, adj, deceitful
demagogo, n m, demagogue
demanda, n f, demand
demandado, n m, defendant
demandante, n mf, claimant
demandar, v, demand, ask
demarcar, v, demarcate
demás, adj, the rest, the others
demasía, adv, too
demasía, n f, excess, abundance
demasiadamente, adv, excessively
demasiado, adj, excessive
demencia, n f, dementia
demente, adj, mad, frantic

demérito, n m, demerit
demeritorio, adj, without merit
democracia, n f, democracy
demócrata, n m, democrat
democrático, adj, democratic
demoler, v, demolish
demolición, n f, demolition
demonio, n m, demon
demora, n f, delay
demorar, v, delay
demostrable, adj, demonstrable
demostración, n f, demonstration
demostrar, v, demonstrate
demostrativo, adj, demonstrative
denario, adj, tenth
denegación, n f, denial, refusal
denegar, v, deny, refuse
denegrecer, v, blacken, darken
denigrar, v, blacken
denodadamente, adv, boldly
denodado, adj, bold
denominación, n f, denomination
denominar, v, denominate
denostar, v, insult
denotar, v, denote
densamente, adv, densely
densidad, n f, density
denso, adj, dense
dentado, adj, serrated
dentadura, n f, set of teeth
dentadura, v, snag
dentellado, adj, dented
dentera, n f, tooth pain
dentífrico, n m, dentifrice
dentista, n m, dentist
dentro, prep, within
denuesto, n m, insult
denuncia, n f, denunciation
denunciación, n f, denunciation
denunciar, v, denounce
deparar, v, offer
departamento, n m, department
departir, v, divide
dependencia, n f, dependence
depender, v, depend
dependiente, adj, dependent
dependiente, n m, clerk

deplorable, adj, deplorable
deplorar, v, deplore
deponente, n m, witness
deponer, v, depose, declare
deportación, n f, deportation
deportar, v, transport
deporte, n m, diversion
deposición, n f, deposition
depositador, n m depositor
depositante, adj, depositing
depositante, n m, depositor
depositaría, n f, depository
depósito, n m, deposit, depository
deprecar, v, deprecate
deprecativo, adj, deprecatory
depreciación, n f, depreciation
depresión, n f, depression
depresivo, adj, depressive
deprimir, v, depress
depuración, n f, purification
depurar, v, cleanse, purify
derecha, n f, right hand, right side
derechamente, adv, rightly
derecho, adj, right, straight
derecho, n m, right, justice, law
derechura, n f, rectitude
deriva, n f, ship's course
derivación, n f, derivation
derivar, v, derive
derogar, v, derogate, annul, reform
derogatorio, adj, derogatory
derramamiento, n f, effusion, waste
derramar, v, leak, waste
derrame, n m, leakage
derredor, n f, circumference
derretimiento, n m, thaw, melting
derretir, v, liquefy, melt
derribar, v, demolish
derrochador, n m, spendthrift
derrochar, v, waste, squander
derroche, n m, waste
derrota, n f, ship's course, defeat
derrotar, v, rout, defeat
derrotero, n m, ship's course,
  conduct
derruir, v, demolish
derrumbamiento, n m, precipitation

derrumbar, v, precipitate
desabono, n f, prejudice, injury
desabor, n m, insipidity, dejection
desabotonar, v, unbutton
desabrido, edj, tasteless, bleak
desabrigar, v, uncover
desabrigo, n destitution, nakedness
desabrimiento, n m, insipidity, severity
desabrochar, v, unclasp, unbutton
desacato, n m, disrespect
desacertado, adj, inconsiderate
desacertar, v, make a mistake, err
desacierto, n m, mistake, error
desacomodado, adj, destitute, unemployed
desacomodar, v, molest
desacordar, v, untune
desacordarse, v, be forgetful, disagree
desacorde, adj, discordant
desacostumbrado, adj, unusual
desacreditar, v, discredit
desacuerdo, n m, disagreement
desafecto, adj, disaffected
desaferrar, v, raise
desafiar, v, defy, dare
desaficción, n f, disaffection
desafío, n m, challenge, duel
desaforado, adj, disorderly, impudent
desaforar, v, deprive of one's rights
desafortunado, adj, unfortunate
desafuero, n m, excess
desagradable, adj, disagreeable
desagradar, v, displease
desagradecido, adj, ungrateful
desagrado, n m, discord, displeasure
desagraviar, v, give satisfaction
desagravio, n m, relief, satisfaction
desagregar, v, separate
desaguadero, n m, channel, drain
desaguador, n m, channel, conduit
desaguar, v, drain
desahogado, adj, free, easy
desahogar, v, ease pain
desahogo, n m, ease, freedom

desahuciar, v, despair
desahucio, n m, eviction
desairado, adj, disregarded
desairar, v, slight, disrespect
desaire, n m, slight, rebuff
desajustar, v, unfit
desajuste, n m, disagreement
desalentar, v, discourage
desaliento, n m, discouragement
desaliñar, v, disarrange
desaliño, n m, carelessness
desalmado, adj, inhuman
desalojar, v, dislodge
desamarrar, v, untie
desamparar, v, abandon
desamparo, n m, abandonment
desamueblado, adj, unfurnished
desamueblar, v, unfurnish
desanclar, v, weigh anchor
desandar, v, undo
desanimado, adj, dull, flat
desanimar, v, discourage, dampen
desanudar, v, untie, loosen
desapacible, adj, sharp, rough
desaparecer, v, disappear
desaparejar, v, unharness
desaparición, n f, disappearance
desapego, n m, coolness, indifference
desapercibido, adj, unprepared
desapiadado, adj, merciless
desapreciar, v, depreciate
desaprobar, v, disapprove
desapropiación, n f, alienation
desapropiar, v, deprive
desapropio, n m, alienation
desaprovechar, v, waste
desarmamiento, n m, disarmament
desarmar, v, disarm
desarraigar, v, eradicate
desarraigo, n m, eradication
desarreglado, adj, immoderate, extravagant
desarreglo, n m, disorder
desarrollar, v, develop
desarrollo, n m, development
desasir, v, loosen, give up

desasosegar, v, disquiet, disturb
desasosiego, n m, restlessness
desastre, n m, disaster, misfortune
desatado, adj, loose, untied
desatar, v, untie, loosen
desatender, v, disregard
desatentado, adj, inconsiderate
desatento, adj, inattentive
desatinadamente, adv,
  inconsiderately
desatinar, v, wander
desatino, n m, extravagance
desavenencia, n f, discord
desavenir, v, disconcert
desaventajado, adj,
  disadvantageous
desayunarse, v, breakfast
desayuno, n m, breakfast
desazón, n m, insipidity, disgust
desazonado, adj, unfit, peevish
desazonar, v, disgust
desbancar, v, dircumvent, supplant
desbarajuste, n m, derangement
desbaratar, v, defeat, break
desbastar, v, plane, smooth
desbordar, v, overflow
descabalgar, v, dismount
descabellado, adj, dishevelled, wild
descabezado, adj, beheaded,
  lightheaded
descabezar, v, behead, surmount
descalabrado, adj, injured
descalabrar, v, hurt, disable
descalabro, n m, misfortune
descalzo, adj, barefoot
descaminado, adj, misguided
descaminar, v, mislead
descamino, n m, error
descansadamente, adv, easily
descansado, adj, quiet, easy
descansar, v, rest, repose, sleep
descanso, n m, rest, repose, quiet
descaradamente, adv, boldly
descarado, adj, bold, impudent
descarga, n f, unloading
descargadero, n m, wharf
descargador, n m, unloader

descargar, v, discharge
descargo, n m, discharge
descaro, n m, impudence
descarriar, v, mislead
descarrilar, v, derail
descartar, v, discard, dismiss
descendencia, n f, descent
descendente, adj, descending
descender, v, descend
descendiente, n m, descendant
descensión, n f, descent
descenso, n m, descent
descerrajar, v, discharge (firearm)
descifrar, v, decipher, unravel
descobijar, v, uncover
descolgar, v, take down
descollar, v, excel, exceed
descolorar, v, discolor
descomedido, adj, rude, haughty
descomedirse, v, be rude,
  disrespectful
descomodidad, n f, inconvenience
descómodo, adj, inconvenient
descompasado, adj, excessive
descomponer, v, decompose, be
  indisposed
descomposición, n f, decomposition
descompostura, n f, discomposure,
  confusion
descompuesto, adj, audacious
descomunal, adj, uncommon
desconcertado, adj, disorderly
desconcertar, v, discompose,
  disagree
desconcierto, n m, disorder
desconcordar, v, discord, disagree
desconfiado, adj, distrustful
desconfianza, n f, distrust
desconfiar, v, distrust, doubt
desconformar, v, dissent, differ
desconforme, adj, disagreeing
desconformidad, n f, disagreement
desconocer, v, disown
desconocido, adj, ungrateful
desconocido, n m, stranger
desconsiderado, adj, inconsiderate
desconsolado, adj, disconsolate

desconsolar, v, afflict
desconsuelo, n m, affliction
descontar, v, discount
descontentadizo, adj, particular, discontented
descontentar, v, discontent, displease
descontento, adj, discontent
descontinuar, discontinue
desconvenir, v, disagree
descortés, adj, impolite
descortesía, n f, discourtesy
descoyuntamiento, n m, dislocation
descoyuntar, v, dislocate
descrédito, n m, discredit
descreer, v, disbelieve
describir, v, describe
descripción, n f, description
descriptivo, adj, descriptive
descuajar, v, dissolve, frighten
descuajo, n f, eradication
descuartizar, v, quarter
descubierta, n f, recognition
descubierto, adj, uncovered
descubridor, n m, discoverer
descubrimiento, n m, discovery
descubrir, v, discover
descuello, n m, excessive height, superiority
descuento, n m, discount
descuidadamente, adv, carelessly
descuidado, adj, careless
descuidar, v, neglect, overlook
descuido, n m, carelessness
desde, prep, from, since, after
desde que, adv, since
desdecir, v, differ, disagree
desdén, n m, disdain
desdeñar, v, disdain, scorn
desdeñoso, adj, disdainful
desdicha, n f, misfortune
desdichadamente, adv, unfortunately
desdichado, adj, unfortunate
desdorar, v, sully, tarnish
desdoro, n m, dishonor, blemish
deseable, adj, desirable
desear, v, desire, want

desecar, v, dry
desechado, adj, refused, rejected
desechar, v, refuse, reject
desecho, n m, residue
desembalar, v, unpack
desembarazar, v, free, disengage
desembarazo, n m, freedom
desembarcación, n f, disembarkation, landing
desembarcadero, n m, quay
desembarcar, v, disembark, land
desembarco, n m, landing
desembarque, n m, landing, clearing
desembocadero, n m, mouth of river
desembocar, v, flow into, enter
desembolsar, v, disburse
desembolso, n m, expenditure
desemejante, adj, dissimilar
desemejanza, n f, difference
desemejar, v, be dissimilar
desempacar, v, unpack
desempaquetar, v, unpack
desemparejar, v, part, be separated
desempeñado, adj, debt free
desempeñar, v, redeem, perform
desempeño, n m, performance, function
desencadenar, v, unchain, break loose
desencajar, v, disjoint, disfigure
desencapotar, v, uncover, make clear
desenfadado, adj, free, spacious
desenfado, n m, ease
desenfrenado, adj, unbridled, ungoverned
desenfrenar, v, unbridle, be wild
desengañado, adj, undeceived
desengañar, v, undeceive, disabuse
desengaño, n m, undeceiving, censure
desenlace, n m, conclusion, end
desenredar, v, disentangle
desenredo, n m, disentanglement
desentendido, adj, ignorant, unaware
desentrañar, v, penetrate
desenvoltura, n f, cheerfulness,

effrontery

desenvolver, v, unfold, unravel

desenvolvimiento, n m, development

deseo, n m, desire, wish

deseoso, adj, desirous

deserción, n f, desertion

desertar, v, desert

desesperación, n f, despair, desperation

desesperado, edj, desperate

desesperar, v, despair

desestimación, n f, disrespect

desestimar, v, disregard

esfachatez, n f, impudence

desfallecer, v, fall away, faint

desfallecimiento, n m, fainting, decline

desfavor, n m, disfavor

desfavorable, adj, unfavorable

desfavorecer, v, disfavor

desfigurar, v, disfigure

desfilar, v, defile

desfogar, v, vent

desgarrar, v, rend, tear

desgarro, n m, rent, looseness

desgastar, v, consume, waste

desgaste, n m, wear-and-tear

desgobernar, v, disturb

desgobierno, n m, misgovernment

desgracia, n f, misfortune

desgraciado, adj, unfortunate

desguarnecer, v, strip, deprive

deshacer, v, undo, break

deshecho, adj, undone

deshelar, v, thaw, melt

deshonestidad, n f, immodesty

deshonor, n m, dishonor

deshonrar, v, dishonor

deshonroso, adj, dishonorable

deshora, n f, inconvenient time

desierto, adj, deserted

desierto, n m, desert

designación, n f, designation

designar, v, design, appoint

designio, n m, design, purpose

desigual, adj, unequal

desigualdad, n f, inequality

desinteresado, adj, disinterested

desistir, v, desist

desleal, adj, disloyal

deslealtad, n f, disloyalty

desligar, v, loosen

deslindar, v, survey

deslinde, n m, demarcation, boundaries

desliz, n m, slip, lapse

deslizar, v, slip, slide

deslucido, adj, unadorned, useless

deslucir, v, tarnish

deslumbramiento, n m, glare

deslumbrar, v, dazzle, glare

deslustre, n m, spot, stain

desmaña, n f, awkwardness

desmantelar, v, dismantle

desmayado, adj, pale, faint

desmayar, v, dismay

desmayo, n m, swoon, dismay

desmedrar, v, decay

desmentir, v, deny

desmenuzar, v, crumble

desmesurar, v, discompose

desmontar, v, remove

desmoralizar, v, demoralize

desmoronar, v, destroy

desnudarse, v, undress

desnudez, n f, nudity

desnudo, adj, naked, bare

desobedecer, v, disobey

desocupación, n f, leisure

desocupado, adj, unemployed

desocupar, v, quit, empty

desolación, n f, desolation

desolado, adj, desolate

desolar, v, desolate

desorden, n m, disorder

desordenar, v, disorder

despachar, v, dispatch

despacio, adv, slowly, gently

desparecer, v, disappear

despecho, n m, spite, defiance

despedirse, v, take leave of

despender, v, spend, expend

desperdiciar, v, squander

desperfecto, n m, deterioration
despertador, n m, alarm clock
despertar, v, wake up
despoblar, v, depopulate
desposeer, v, dispossess
despótico, adj, despotic
despotismo, n m, despotism
despreciable, adj, contemptible
despreciar, v, depreciate
despropósito, n m, absurdity
desprovisto, adj, bare
después, adv, afterwards, then, later
despuntar, v, advance, dawn
desquitar, v, retrieve
desquite, n m, recovery
destinado, adj, extravagant
destrozar, v, destroy
destruir, v, destroy
detallar, v, detail
detalle, n m, detail
detallista, n m, retailer
detencíon, n f, detention
detenerse, v, stop
deterioracíon, n f, deterioration
deteriorar, deteriorate
determinación, n f, determination
determinado, adj, determinate
detestar, v, detest
deuda, n f, debt
deudo, n m, parent, kin
deudor, n m, debtor
devocíon, n f, devotion
dia, n m, day
diamante, n m, diamond
diariamente, adv, daily
diario, n m, journal, diary, newspaper
dibujar, v, draw, design
diccionario, n m, dictionary
dicha, n f, happiness
dicho, n m, saying
diciembre, n m, December
dictar, v, dictate
diente, n m, tooth
diestra, n f, right hand, favor
dieta, n f, diet
diez, n f, ten

diezmar, v, tithe
difamatorio, adj, defamatory
diferencia, n f, difference
diferente, adj, different
difícil, adj, difficult
dificultad, n f, difficulty
digerir, v, digest
dignidad, n f, dignity
digno, adj, worthy
dije, n m, trinket
diligente, adj, industrious
dinero, n m, cash
dinero, n m, money
Dios, n m, God
direcciún, n f, address
director, n m, principal
dirigir, v, direct
discípulo, n m, pupil
disco, n m, disk, record
discurso, n m, speech
disipar, v, scatter
dislocación, n f, sprain
dispensar, v, excuse
dispuesto, adj, ready
distancia, n f, distance
distinto, adj, different
distribuir, v, share
distrito, n m, county
diverso, adj, several
divertir, v, amuse
dividir, v, divide
docena, n f, dozen
doctor, n m, doctor
dogal, n m, rope
dólar, n m, dollar
doler, v, feel pain
doloroso, adj, sore
domar, v, tame
doméstico, adj, domestic
domicilio, n m, domicile
dominante, adj, dominant
dominar, v, rule
domingo, n m, Sunday
dominio, n m, dominion
don, n m, don (title), gift
donoso, adj, gay, witty
dóonde, adv, where

dorado, adj, golden
dormir, v, sleep
dormitar, v, snooze
dormitorio, n m, bedroom
dorso, n m, back
dos, n, two
dosel, n m, canopy
dosis, n f, dose
dote, n mf, dowry
dote, n mpl, gifts, talents
dragar, v, dredge
droga, n f, drug
droguero, n m, druggist
ducho, adj, dexterous
duda, n f, doubt
dudar, v, doubt
duelo, n m, duel, sorrow
dueña, n f, owner, proprietress
duende, n m, fairy, ghost
dueño, n m, owner, master
dulce, adj, sweet
dulces, n mpl, candies, cakes
dulcificar, v, sweeten
dulzura, n f, sweetness
duplicar, v, duplicate
duplicidad, n f, duplicity, deceit
duplo, n m, double
duque, n m, duke
durante, adv, during
durar, v, last, endure
dureza, n f, hardness
durmiente, adj, sleeping
duro, adj, hard
duro, n m, dollar

E

ancía, n f, gum
ascénico, adj, scenic
ascéptico, n mf, skeptic
ascudriñar, v, scan, scrutinize
e, conj, and
ébano, n m, ebony
ebrio, adj, inebriated
echar, v, throw, cast, pour
echazón, n f, jettison
eclipsar, v, eclipse

eclipse, n m, eclipse
eco, n m, echo
economía, n f, economics, saving
económico, adj, economical
economista, n m, economist
economizar, v, economize, save
ecuador, n m, equator
edad, n f, age
edecán, n m, aide-de-camp
edición, n f, edition
edicto, n m, edict
edificación, n f, edification
edificar, v, edify, build
edificio, n m, edifice, building
editor, n m, publisher, editor
editorial, adj, editorial
editorial, n m, editorial
edredón, n m, eider down
educación, n f, education
educador, n m, instructor
educar, v, educate
efectivamente, adv, effectively, certainly
efectivo, adj, effective, cash
efecto, n m, effect
efecto, n mpl, effects, assets, goods
efectualmente, adv, ettectuallv
efectuar, v, effect
efervescencia, n f, effervescence
eficacia, n f, efficacy
eficaz, adj, efficacious
eficazmente, adv, efficaciously
eficiencia, n f, efficiency
eficiente, adj, efficient
efigie, n f, effigy
efugio, n m, subterfuge, evasion
efusión, n f, effusion
egoísmo, n f, selfishness
egoísta, adj, selfish
egoísta, n m, egoist, selfish person
egregio, adj, egregious, eminent
éica, n f, ethics
eje, n m, axis, axle
ejecución, n f, execution
ejecutable, adj, executable, practicable
ejecutar, v, execute

ejecutivo, adj, executive
ejecutor, n m, executor
ejecutoria, n f, execution decree, executorship
ejecutorio, adj, executory
ejemplar, adj, exemplary
ejemplar, n m, example
ejemplo, n m, example
ejercer, v, exercise
ejercicio, n m, exercise, practice
ejercitar, v, exercise
ejército, n m, army
el, art, the
él, pro, he
elaboración, n f, elaboration
elaborado, adj, elaborate
elaborar, v, elaborate
elástica, adj, elastic
elasticidad, n f, elasticity
elección, n f, election
electo, adj, elect, chosen
elector, n m, elector
electorado, n m, electorate
electricidad, n f, electricity
electricista, n m, electrician
eléctrico, adj, electric
electrizar, v, electrify
electroimán, n m, electromagnet
elefante, n mf, elephant
elegancia, n f, elegance
elegante, adj, elegant
elegible, adj, eligible
elegir, v, elect, choose
elemental, adj, elementary
elemento, n m, element
elenco, n m, table, index
elevación, n f, elevation, promotion
elevado, adj, high
elevador, n m, elevator
elevar, v, elevate
eliminar, v, eliminate
ella, pro, she
ello, pro, it
elocución, n f, elocution
elocuencia, n f, eloquence
elocuente, adj, eloquent
elogiar, v, praise, eulogize

elogio, n m, praise, eulogy
eludir, v, elude
emanar, v, emanate
emancipar, v, emancipate
embajada, n f, embassy
embajador, n m, ambassador
embalador, n m, packer
embalaje, n m, packing
embalar, v, pack
embarazoso, adawkward, embarrassing
embarcación, n f, embarkation
embarcadero, n m, quay, wharf
embarcar, v, ship, embark
embargar, v, seize, attach
embargo, n m, embargo
embarnizar, v, varnish
embarque, n m, shipment
embarrar, v, daub, plaster
embastar, v, baste, sew loosely
embate, n m, beating of waves
embaucar, v, deceive
embebecer, v, amuse, entertain
embeber, v, imbibe
embelesar, v, astonish
embeleso, n m, amazement
embellecer, v, embellish
embellecimiento, n m, embellishment
embestida, n f, attack
embestir, v, attack
emblandecer, v, moisten
emblanquecer, v, whiten
emblema, n m, emblem
embobar, v, amuse, amaze
embobecer, v, stupefy
embocadero, n m, river's mouth
embocadura, n f, mouthpiece
embocar, v, cram
émbolo, n m, piston, plunger
embolsar, v, reimburse
emborrachar, v, intoxicate
emborrar, v, stuff
emborronar, v, scribble
emboscada, n f, ambush
emboscar, v, ambush, emboss
embotado, adj, dull, blunt

embotamiento, n m, bluntness
embotar, v, blunt
embotellar, v, bottle
embotijar, v, fill jars
embozar, v, cover one's face, muzzle
embozo, n m, muffling, disguise
embravecer, v, enrage
embreado, n m, tarpaulin
embrear, v, tar, pitch
embriagado, adj, intoxicated
embriagar, v, intoxicate
embriaguez, n f, intoxication
embridar, v, bridle
embrión, n m, embryo, beginning
embrollar, v, embroil, entangle
embrollo, n m, fraud, deception
embrollón, n m, imposter
embromar, v, cajole, wheedle
embrutecer, v, stupefy
embuchado, n m, sausage
embudo, n m, funnel, fraud
embuste, n m, fraud, imposition
embustero, n m, impostor, cheat
embutido, n m, inlay, insertion
embutir, v, inlay, cram
emergencia, n f, emergency, accident
emético, adj, emetic
emigración, n f, emigration
emigrado, n m, emigrant, immigrant
emigrante, n m, emigrant
emigrar, v, emigrate, immigrate
eminencia, n f, eminence, height
eminente, adj, eminent
emisario, n m, emissary
emisión, n f, emission, vent
emitir, v, emit, issue
emoción, n f, emotion
emolumento, n m, emolument, fee, profit
empacar, v, pack
empachado, adj, timid, overloaded
empachar, v, impede, embarrass
empacho, n m, timidity, embarrassment
empadronamiento, n m, list, register

empalar, v, empale
empalizada, n f, palisade
empalmar, v, dovetail
empalme, n m, joining, splice
empalmo, n m, shank
empanada, n f, meat pie
empañar, v, swaddle, tarnish
empapar, v, imbibe, soak
empapelar, v, wrap in paper
empaque, n m, packing
empaquetado, n m, packing
empaquetar, v, pack
emparedado, n m, sandwich
emparedar, v, enclose between walls
emparejar, v, level, match
emparentado, adj, related by marriage
emparrado, n m, arbor
empastar, v, paste, bind books
empaste, n m, paste, binding
empatar, v, equal, tie
empate, n m, equality
empedernir, v, harden
empedrado, n m, pavement
empedrar, v, pave
empeine, n m, groin, instep, hoof
empellón, n m, push
empeñar, v, pawn, engage
empeño, n m, obligation
empeorar, v, impair
emperador, n m, emperor
emperatriz, n f, empress
empero, conj, yet, however
empezar, v, begin
empinar, v, raise
empírico, adj, empirical
empírico, n m, quack
emplastar, v, plaster
emplasto, n m, plaster
emplazamiento, n m, summons
emplazar, v, summon, convene
empleado, adj, employed
empleado, n m, employee, clerk
emplear, v, employ
empleo, n m, employment
empobrecer, v, impoverish

empobrecimiento, n m, impoverishment
empodrecer, v, corrupt
empollar, v, hatch
emponzoñar, v, poison
emporcar, v, soil, dirty
emporio, n m, emporium
emprendedor, adj, enterprising
emprendedor, n m, enterpriser
emprender, v, undertake, attempt
empresa, n f, enterprise
empresario, n m, theater manager, undertaker
empréstito, n m, lending, loan
empujar, v, push
empuñar, v, grasp, clutch
emulación, n f, emulation
emular, v, emulate
emulsión, n f, emulsion
en alguna parte, adv, somewhere
en, prep, in, on, at
enaguas, n f, fpl, petticoat
enajenable, adj, alienable
enajenación, n f, alienation
enajenar, v, alienate, transfer
enamorado, adj, in love
enamorado, n mf, sweetheart, lover
enano, n m, dwarf
enarbolar, v, raise
enardecer, v, kindle
enarenar, v, sand
encabezar, v, register
encadenar, v, chain
encajar, v, drive in, enclose
encaje, n m, encasing, inlay
encajero, n m, lace maker
encajonar, v, box
encallar, v, run aground
encallecido, adj, hardened
encalmado, adj, quiet, calm
encalmarse, v, becalmed
encaminar, v, guide, direct
encandilar, v, dazzle
encanecer, v, grow grey
encantado, adj, enchanted
encantador, adj, charming
encantador, n m, enchanter

encantar, v, captivate, charm
encanto, n m, charm, spell
encapado, adj, cloaked
encapotar, v, cloak, cover
encapuchar, v, cover with hood
encara, v, face
encarado, adj, faced
encarcelación, n f, imprisonment
encarcelar, v, imprison, cage
encarecer, v, raise price, overrate
encarecidamente, adv, exceedingly
encarecimiento, n m, enhancement
encargar, v, recommend
encargo, n m, charge, command
encarnado, adj, incarnate, red
encarnar, v, incarnate, entice
encarnizar, v, provoke, be furious
encender, v, kindle, enrage
encendido, adj, inflamed
encendimiento, n m, inflammation
encerado, n m, oil cloth, tarpaulin
encerrar, v, close in
enchapar, v, veneer, inlay
enciclopedia, n f, encyclopedia
encierro, n f, enclosure, prison
encima, adv, above, on top, on
encina, n f, evergreen oak
enclavar, v, nail, spike
encoger, v, shrink, contract
encogimiento, n m, shrug, contraction
encolar, v, glue
encolerizar, v, anger, irritate
encomendar, v, recommend, commend
encomienda, n f, commission
encomio, n m, praise, eulogy
enconar, v, inflame
encono, n m, malevolence
encontrar, v, meet, find
encorajar, v, animate, inflame
encordonar, v, lace
encorvar, v, curve
encorvarse, v, slouch
encrespador, n m, curling iron
encrespar, v, curl, frizzle
encrucijada, n f, crossroads

encuadernación, n f, binding
encubiertamente, adv, secretly
encubrimiento, n m, concealment
encubrir, v, conceal, hide
encuentro, n m, meeting, encounter
encumbrado, adj, high, lofty
encumbrar, v, raise, elevate
encurtido, adj, pickled
encurtidos, n mpl, pickles
encurtir, v, pickle
endeble, adj, feeble
enderezar, v, guide
endibia, n f, endive
endosar, v, endorse
endulzar, v, sweeten
endurecer, v, harden
endurecido, adj, hard
endurecimiento, n m, hardness, obstinacy
enebro, n m, juniper
enemigo, n m, enemy
enemistad, n f, enmity
enemistar, v, make an enemy
energía, n f, energy
enérglco, adj, energetic
enero, n m, January
enfadadizo, adj, irritable
enfadar, v, vex, annoy
enfadarse, v, be annoyed
enfado, n m, trouble
enfadoso, edj, vexatious, troublesome
enfardar, v, pack
énfasis, n m, emphasis
enfático, adj, emphatic
enfermar, v, fall ill, weaken
enfermedad, n f, sickness
enfermera, n f, nurse
enfermería, n f, infirmary
enfermizo, adj, sickly
enfermo, adj, ill, sick
enfervorizar, v, inflame
enflaquecer, v, weaken
enfocar, v, focus
enfrenar, v, bridle, restrain
enfrente, adj, opposite
enfriador, n f, refrigerator

enfriamiento, n m, refrigeration
enfriar, v, cool
enfurecer, v, irritate
engalanar, v, adorn
engañadizo, adj, easily deceived
engañado, adj, mistaken
engañador, n m, impostor, cheat
engañar, v, deceive, cheat
enganchar, v, hook
enganche, n m, enlistment
engaño, n m, mistake, deception
engarce, n m, link
engarzar, v, link
engastar, v, encase
engendrar, v, engender, beget
englobar, v, comprise
engomado, adj, gummed, stiff
engordar, v, fatten
engorro, n m, embarrassment
engorroso, adj, troublesome
engranaje, n m, gear
engranar, v, gear, connect
engrandecer, v, augment
engrandecimiento, n m, increase
engrasar, v, grease
engreimiento, n m, elation, vanity
engreir, v, lift, make proud
engrosar, v, make fat
engrudo, n m, paste
engullir, v, gobble
enhebra-cartas, n m, letter file
enhebrar, v, link, unite
enhiesto, adj, erect, upright
enhorabuena, n f, congratulation, welcome
enigma, n m, enigma, riddle
enigmático, adj, enigmatical
enjabonar, v, soap
enjalbegar, v, whitewash
enjambrar, v, swarm
enjambre, n m, swarm, crowd
enjaular, v, cage
enjuagar, v, cleanse
enjugar, v, dry, wipe off
enjuiciar, v, pass judgment
enjuto, adj, dried, sparing
enlace, n m, connection, link

enladrillado, n m, brickwork
enlazar, v, join, bind
enloquecer, v, enrage, madden
enmaderamiento, n m, woodwork
enmarañar, v, snare
enmendación, n f, correction
enmendar, v, correct, reform
enmienda, n f, correction, amendment
enmohecer, v, mold
enmohecido, adj, musty, moldy
enmollecer, v, soften
enmudecer, v, be silent
ennegrecer, v, blacken
ennoblecer, v, ennoble
enojadizo, adj, angry, freliul
enojar, v, vex, irritate
enojo, n m, anger, passion
enojoso, adj, offensive
enorme, adj, enormous
enormemente, adv, enormously
enormidad, n f, enormity
enranciarse, v, grow rancid
enrasar, v, smooth
enredado, adj, entangled
enredar, v, entangle
enredo, n m, snarl
enrejado, n m, trellis, grate
enriquecer, v, enrich
enriscado, adj, mountainous
enrojecer, v, make red
enroscar, v, twine, twist
ensalada, n f, salad
ensaladera, n f, salad bowl
ensalzar, v, exalt
ensanchar, v, widen
ensanche, n m, widening
ensayar, v, assay, instruct
ensayo, n m, assay, trial
ensebar, v, grease
enseña, n f, standard
ensenada, n f, creek
enseñanza, n f, teaching, instruction
enseñar, v, coach, teach, show
enseñorear, v, lord, domineer
enseres, n mpl, chattels, fixtures
ensillar, v, saddle

ensimismado, adj, selfish
ensordecer, v, deafen
ensordecimiento, n m, deafness
ensuciar, v, dirty, soil
entablar, v, plank, claim
entallador, n m, engraver
entallar, v, engrave
entarimado, n m, inlaid floor
ente, n m, entity, being
entenada, n f, step-daughter
entenado, n m, step-son
entender, v, understand
entendido, adj, learned, knowing
entendimiento, n m, understanding
enteramente, adv, entirely, fully
enterar, v, inform, acquaint
entereza, n f, entirety, integrity
enternecer, v, soften
entero, adj, entire
enterrador, n m, gravedigger
enterrar, v, bury
entibiar, v, cool, moderate
entidad, n f, entity
entintar, v, ink
entoldado, n m, awning
entonado, adj, haughty, harmonized
entonar, v, tune, tone
entonces, adv, then
entorpecer, v, stupefy, hinder
entrada, n f, entrance
entrambos, pro, both
entraña, n f, entrail
entrañable, adj, intimate
entrante, adj, entering
entrar, v, enter
entre, prep, between, among
entredicho, n m, interdiction
entrefino, adj, middling
entrega, n f, delivery
entregar, v, deliver
entrelistado, adj, striped
entremetido, n m, busybody
entremetimiento, n m, interference
entrenar, v, train
entrepaño, n m, panel
entreponer, v, interpose
entretanto, adv, meanwhile

entretener, v, entertain, put off
entretenimiento, n m, entertainment
entrevista, n f, interview
entristecer, v, sadden
entumecer, v, swell
enturbiar, v, muddle
entusiasmar, v, transport
entusiasmo, n m, enthusiasm
entusiasta, adj, enthusiastic
enumerar, v, enumerate
enunciar, v, enunciate
envainar, v, sheathe
envanecer, v, make vain
envasador, n m, filter
envejecer, v, make old
envejecido, adj, looking old
envenenar, v, poison
envestir, v, invest
enviado, n m, envoy
enviar, v, send
envidar, v, stake
envidia, n f, envy
envidiable, adj, enviable
envidiar, v, envy
envidioso, adj, envious
envilecer, v, vilify
envío, n m, sending, consignment
envoltorio, n m, bundle
envolver, v, wrap up
envolvimiento, n m, envelopment
envuelto, adj, involved
epidemia, n f, epidemic
epidémico, adj, epidemic
epidermis, n f, epidermis
epílogo, n m, epilogue
episodio, n m, episode
epitafio, n m, epitaph
epoca, n f, epoch, period
equidad, n f, equity
equilátero, adj, equilateral
equilibrar, equilibrate
equilibrio, n f, equilibrium
equipaje, n m, baggage
equipar, v, equip
equitación, n f, horsemanship
equitativo, adj, equitable
equivalencia, n f, equivalence

equivaler, v, be equal
equivocación, n f, mistake, error
equivocar, v, mistake
era, n f, era
erección, n f, erection
erguir, v, erect
erigir, v, erect
ermita, n f, hermitage
ermitaño, n m, hermit
erogar, v, distribute, divide
erradamente, adv, erroneously
erradicación, n f, eradication
errado, adj, mistaken, wrong
errante, adj, errant
errar, v, err, wander
errata, n f, error
errático, adj, erratic
erróneamente, adv, erroneously
erróneo, adj, erroneous
error, n m, error
erudición, n f, erudition, learning
erudito, adj, scholarly
erupción, n f, eruption
esa, pro, that
esbelto, adj, tall, genteel
esbirro, n m, bailiff
esbozo, n m, sketch, rough draft
escabechar, v, pickle
escabeche, n m, pickle
escabel, n m, footstool
escabroso, adj, rough, uneven
escala, n f, ladder, scale
escalafón, n m, list
escalar, v, scale
escaldar, v, scald
escalera, n f, staircase
escalfar, v, poach eggs
escalón, n m, step of stair
escalpelo, n m, scalpel
escama, n f, scale
escamar, v, scale
escandalizar, v, shock
escándalo, n m, scandal
escaparate, n m, show window
escaramuza, n f, skirmish
escarpado, adj, steep
escaso, adj, scant

escaso, adj, scarce
escena, n f, scene
escepticismo, n m, skepticism
escéptico, adj, skeptical
esclavo, n m, slave
escoger, v, choose, select
escolar, n m, scholar
escolástico, adj, scholastic
esconder, v, hide
escoplear, v, score
escoria, n f, slag
escorpión, n m, scorpion
escotar, v, cut out, hollow
escribano, n m, notary, writer
escribir, v, write
escrito, adj, written
escrito, n m, communication
escritor, n m, Writer
escrupuloso, adj, scrupulous
escrutinio, n m, scrutiny
escuadra, n f, squadron
escuadrar, v, square
escuchar, v, listen, hear
escudar, v, shield
escudo, n m, shield
escuela, n f, school
esculpir, v, sculpt
escultor, n m, sculptor
escultura, n f, sculpture
escupir, v, Spit
esencia, n f, essence
esfera, n f, sphere
esfinga, n f, sphinx
esfuerzo, n m, strain, effort
eso, adj, that
espacio, n m, space
espacioso, adj, spacious
espada, n f, sword
espalda, n f, shoulder
España, n, Spain
español, adj, Spanish
español, n, Spanish (language)
espantajo, n m, scarecrow
espantar, v, scare
espanto, n m, scare
espasmo, n m, spasm
especial, adj, special

especiar, v, spice
especias, n fpl spices
especie, n f, spice
especificar, v, specify
espectáculo, n m, show, spectacle
espectador, n mf, spectator
espectro solar, n, spectrum
especular, v, speculate
espera, n f, wait
esperar, v, hope, wait, expect
espeso, adj, thick
espía, n mf, spy
espiar, v, spy
espina, adj, thorn
espina, n f, spine
espinacas, n fpl, spinach
espiral, n f, spiral
espíritu, n m, spirit
esplendente, adj, resplendent
espléndido, adj, splendid
esplendor, n, splendor
esponja, n f, sponge
esponjar, v, sponge
esponjoso, adj, spongy
espontáneo, adj, spontaneous
esposa, n f, Wife
esposo, n mf, spouse
espuerta, n f, frail, basket
espuma, n f, scum spray
esqueleto, n m, skeleton
esquiciar, v, sketch
esquicio, n, sketch
esquife, n m, skiff
esquivar, v, shirk
estable, adj, stable, steadfast
establecer, v, state, establish
estaca, n f, stake
estación, n f, station, season
estacional, adj, seasonable
estado, n m, state
Estados Unidos, n, United States
estallar, v, snap
estallido, n m, crash
estancado, adj, stagnant
estar, v, be
estatua, n f, statue
estatura, n f, stature

estatuto, n m, statute
este, n m, east
este, pro, this
estereotipar, v, stereotype
estéril, adj, sterile
esterilidad, n f, sterility
estilo, n m, style
estimular, v, stimulate
esto, adj, this
estofado, n mf, stew
estómago, n m, stomach
estornino, n m, starling
estornudar, v, sneeze
estornudo, n m, sneeze
estos, adj, these
estrangular, v, strangle
estrechar, v, shrink
estrella, n f, star
estrellado, adj, starry
estremecerse, v, shudder
estuco, n m, stucco
estudiante, n m, student
estudiar, v, study
estudio, n m, study
estudioso, adj, studious
estufa, n f, stove
estupidez, n f, stupidity
estúpido, adj, stupid
eternal, adj, eternal
eternidad, n f, eternity
eterno, adj, eternal
ético, adj, ethical
etiqueta, n f, etiquette, ticket
Europa, n, Europe
europeo, adj, European
evacuar, v, evacuate
evadir, v, evade
evaluar, v, appraise, value
evalúo, n m, valuation, appraisement
evaporación, n f, evaporation
evaporar, v, evaporate
evasión, n f, evasion, escape
evasivo, adj, evasive, elusive
evento, n m, event
eventual, adj, eventual
evicción, n f, eviction

evitable, adj, avoidable
evitar, v, avoid
evocar, v, call out, invoke
examen, n m, examination
examinar, v, survey
exánime, adj, spiritless, weak
exasperado, adj, exasperated
exasperar, v, exasperate
excavar, v, excavate
excedente, adj, exceeding
excepto, adv, except
exceptuar, v, except, exempt
exceso, n m, surplus
excitar, v, excite
exclamar, v, exclaim
excluir, v, exclude
excusa, n f, excuse, apology
existir, v, exist
éxito, n m, end, termination
expedición, n f, expedition
expedir, v, speed
experimentar, v, experience
experto, adj, expert
expirar, v, expire
explicación, n f, explanation
explicar, v, explain
explorador, n m, explorer
explorar, v, explore
exponer, v, expose
exportación, n f, exportation
exportar, v, export
exposición, n f, statement
expreso, n m, express
expulsar, v, drive out
exquisito, adj, delicious
extender, v, spread
extenderse, v, stretch
externo, adj, external
extranjero, adj, foreign
extranjero, n m, stranger
extraño, adj, strange
extravagancia, n f, extravagance
extravagante, adj, extravagant
extraviar, v, mislead
extremidad, n f, extremity, end
extremo, adj, extreme
extremo, n m, extreme

F

fábrica, n f, fabrication, fabric, factory
fabricación, n f, fabrication
fabricador, n m, inventor
fabricante, n m, maker, manufacturer
fabricar, v, fabricate, manufacture
fábula, n f, fable
fabuloso, adj, fabulous, fictitious
faca, n f, knife
facción, n f, action, faction, feature
facha, n f, aspect, look
fachada, n f, face, fa|ade
fácil, adj, easy
facilidad, n f, facility, ease
facilitar, v, make easy
fácilmente, adv, easily
facistol, n m, reading desk
facsímile, n m, facsimile
factible, adj, feasible
factor, n m, factor
factoría, n f, factory
factura, n f, invoice
facturar, v, invoice, note
facultad, n f, faculty, privilege
facultar, v, authorize
facultativamente, adv, optionally
faena, n f, task, work, labor
faisán, n, pheasant
faja, n f, band, bandage
fajo, n m, bundle
fajuela, n f, bandage, roller
falange, n f, phalanx
falbalá, n m, flounce
falda, n f, skirt, train
falla, n f, defect
fallar, v, judge, be deficient
fallecer, v, die
fallecido, adj, deceased
fallecimiento, n m, decease, death
fallido, adj, disappointed, bankrupt
fallo, n m, judgment, decision
falsamente, adv, falsely
falsear, v, falsify
falsedad, n f, falsehood

falsificación, n f, falsification
falsificador, n m, forger, counterfeiter
falsificar, v, falsify, forge, counterfeit
falso, adj, false
falta, n f, mistake
faltar, v, be wanting, fail
falto, adj, wanting, lacking, short
faltriquera, n f, pocket
falucho, n m, small boat
fama, n f, fame, rumor
familia, n f, family
familiar, adj, familiar
familiar, n m, domestic, intimate
familiaridad, n f, familiarity
familiarizar, v, familiarize
familiarmente, adv, familiarly
famoso, adj, famous
fanal, n m, lantern, lighthouse
fanático, adj, fanatical
fanatismo, n f, fanaticism
fanfarrón, n m, bully
fango, n m, mire, mud
fangoso, adj, muddy
fantasear, v, fancy, imagine
fantasía, n f, fancy, imagination
fantasma, n m, phantom
fantástico, adj, fantastic
fardel, n m, bag, knapsack
fardo, n m, bale, package
farfalá, n f, flounce
farmacéutico, n m, apothecary, chemist
farmacia, n f, pharmacy
faro, n m, lighthouse
farol, n m, lantern, lamp
farolero, n m, lamp lighter
farsa, n f, farce
fascinación, n f, fascination
fascinador, adj, fascinating
fascinar, v, fascinate
fastidiar, v, annoy, bore
fastidio, n m, distaste, boredom
fastidioso, adj, squeamish, tedious
fasto, n m, pride, splendour
fatal, adj, fatal
fatalidad, n f, fatality

fatídico, adj, prophetic
fatiga, n f, fatigue, labor
fatigar, v, fatigue
fatuo, adj, fatuous, foolish
fausto, adj, happy
fausto, n m, splendour
favor, n m, favor
favorable, adj, favorable
favorecedor, n m, favorer, friend, patron
favorecer, v, favor, patronize
favorito, adj, favorite
favorito, n m, favorite
faz, n f, face
fe, n f, faith
fealdad, n f, ugliness
feble, adj, weak, feeble
febrero, n m, February
fecha, n f, date
fechar, v, date
fechoría, n f, action, deed
fécula, n f, starch
fecundidad, n f, fecundity, fertility
federación, n f, federation
federal, adj, federal
fehaciente, adj, authentic
felicidad, n f, happiness, felicity
felicitación, n f, congratulation
felicitar, v, congratulate, compliment
feligrés, n mf, parishioner
feliz, adj, happy
felizmente, adv, happily
felonía, n f, treachery
felpado, adj, shaggy
felpudo, adj, downy
felpudo, n m, doormat
femenino, adj, feminine
fenecer, v, terminate
fenecimiento, n m, close, finish
feo, adj, ugly, plain
feracidad, n f, fruitfulness, fertility
feraz, adj, fertile, fruitful
féretro, n m, bier, coffin, hearse
feria, n f, fair
fermentar, v, ferment
fermento, n m, ferment, leaven
ferocidad, n f, ferocity

feroz, adj, ferocious, fierce
férreo, adj, ferrous, of iron
ferretería, n f, hardware store
ferrocarril, n m, railroad
férvido, adj, fervent, ardent
fervor, n m, fervor, warmth
festejar, v, feast, entertain
festín, n m, feast, banquet
festividad, n f, festivity
festivo, adj, festive
fétido, adj, fetid, stinking
fiable, adj, trustworthy
fiado, adj, trusting
fiador, n m, guarantor
fiambre, adj, cold
fiambre, n m, cold meat
fianza, n f, guarantee
fiar, v, trust, confide
fiasco, n m, failure
fibra, n f, fiber, staple
fibroso, adj, fibrous
ficción, n f, fiction
ficticio, adj, fictitious
fideicomisario, n m, trustee
fideicomiso, n m, trust fund
fidelidad, n f, fidelity
fideos, n m, vermicelli
fiebre, n f, fever
fiel, adj, faithful
fielmente, adv, faithfully
fieltro, n m, felt
fiera, n f, wild beast
fiereza, n f, fierceness
fiero, adj, fierce
fierro, n m, iron
fiesta, n f, feast, entertainment
figura, n f, figure, shape, face
figurar, v, figure
figurativo, adj, figurative
figurín, n m, model
fijación, n f, fixation
fijamente, adv, fixedly
fijar, v, fix, fasten
fijo, adj, fixed, firm
fila, n f, row
filamento, n m, filament
filete, n m, fillet, hem, grain

filigrana, n f, filigree
Filipinas, n fpl, Philippines
filón, n m, vein, lode
filosofía, n f, philosophy
filósofo, n m, sage, philosopher
filtrar, v, filter
filtro, n m, filter
fin, n m, end
finado, adj, dead
final, adj, final
finalizar, v, finalize
finalmente, adv, finally
finar, v, die, end
finca, n f, estate, property
fineza, n f, fineness
fingido, adj, feigned
fingimiento, n m, sham
fingir, v, feign
fino, adj, fine, perfect, nice
firma, n f, signature
firmar, v, sign
firme, adj, steady
fiscal, adj, fiscal
fisga, n f, sneer
fisgar, v, mock, scoff
física, n f, physics
físico, adj, physical
físico, n m, physician, physique
flaco, adj, weak
flagrante, adj, flagrant
flamante, adj, flaming, bright
flanco, n m, flank, side
flaquear, v, grow feeble
flecha, n f, shaft
fleje, n m, hoop
fletador, n m, freighter
flete, n m, freight
flexible, adj, flexible
flojamente, adv, slowly
flojear, v, slacken
flojo, adj, lax, slack
flor, n f, flower, blossom
floreado, adj, flowered
florecer, v, flourish
floreciente, adj, flourishing, blossoming
florero, n m, flower pot

florescencia, n f, florescence
floresta, n f, forest
Florida, n, Florida
florido, adj, flowery, elegant
florista, n m, florist
flota, n f, fleet
flotante, adj, floating
flotar, v, float
fluente, adj, fluent
fluido, n m, fluid
fluir, v, flow
foca, n m, seal (animal)
fofo, adj, soft, spongy
fogón, n m, hearth, furnace
fogoso, adj, fiery, ardent
folío, n m, folio, leaf
follaje, n m, foliage
fonda, n f, inn, hotel
fondo, n m, bottom
fondos, n mpl, funds
fonógrafo, n m, phonograph
forastero, n m, stranger
forma, n f, shape
formar, v, form
fórmula, n f, formula
fornido, adj, furnished
forro, n m, lining
fortaleza, n f, fortitude, strength
fortificar, v, strengthen
fortuna, n f, fortune, chance
fósforo, n m, match
fotografía, n f, photograph
fracaso, v, crash
fraile, n m, friar
francés, adj, French
francés, n, French (language)
Francia, n, France
frase, n f, sentence
fregar, v, scour
fresa, n f, strawberry
fresco, adj, fresh
friega, n f, friction
frío, adj, cold
frío, n m, chill
frisar, v, frizzle
frito, adj, fried
frontera, n f, frontier, border

frotar, v, scrub, rub
fruta, n f, fruit
fuego, n m, fire
fuente, n f, fountain
fuerte, adj, strong, severe
fuerte, n m, fort
fuerza, n f, force, strength
fugarse, v, escape
fumador, n f, smoker
fumarada, n f, smoke
fumosos, adj, smoky
fundamento, n f, foundation
fundar, v, found
furia, n f, fury, rage
furtivo, adj, furtive
fusil, n m, gun
fútil, adj, futile

G

gabarra, n f, lighter
gabinete, n m, cabinet, closet
gaceta, n f, gazette
gafa, n f, hook
gafete, n m, clasp
gaitero, n m, piper
gaje, n m, salary
gala, n f, gala, parade
galán, edj, gallant
galán, n m, gallant, courtier
galantería, n f, gallantry
galápago, n m, freshwater tortoise
galeón, n m, galleon
galería subterránea, n f, subway
galería, n f, gallery
galerna, n f, stormy NW wind
galgo, n m, greyhound
gallardo, adj, gay, graceful
gallina, n f, hen, fowl
gallo, n m, cock
galocha, n f, galosh, clog
galopar, v, gallop
galope, n m, gallop
galvanizar, v, galvanize
gama, n f, gamut, doe
gamarra, n f, martingale
gamuza, n f, chamois

gana, n f, appetite, desire
ganado, n m, cattle
gañán, n m, servant, day laborer
ganancia, n f, gain, profit
ganancioso, adj, lucrative
ganapán, n m, scamp
ganar, v, gain, win, earn
gancho, n m, hook, crook
ganga, n f, grouse, bargain
ganoso, adj, desirous
ganso, n m, gander, goose
garabatear, v, hook, scrawl
garante, n m, guarantee
garantir, v, guarantee
garapiñar, v, ice
garapiñera, n f, cooler
garbanzo, n m, pea
garbo, n m, gracefulness
garboso, adj, genteel
garfa, n f, claw
garfio, n m, hook
garganta, n f, throat, instep of foot
gargantilla, n f, necklace
garlito, n m, snare, trap
garra, n f, claw, talon
garrafa, n f, vessel, decanter
garrote, n m, cudgel
garrucha, n f, pulley
garrulo, adj, garrulous
gas, n m, gas
gasa, n f, gauze
gaseoso, adj, gaseous
gastado, adj, worn out
gastador, n f, spendthrift
gastar, v, spend
gasto, n m, expense
gatillo, n m, kitten, trigger
gato, n m, cat, jack
gaveta, n f, drawer
gaviota, n f, seagull
gazmoñería, n f, hypocrisy
gazmoño, adj, hypocritical
gaznate, n m, throttle, windpipe
gelatinoso, adj, gelatinous
gema, n f, cut, gem, bud
gemelo, adj, twin
gemido, n m, groan, moan

gemir, v, groan, moan

genealogía, n f, genealogy

general, adj, general

generalidad, n f, generality

generalizar, v, generalize

generalmente, adv, generally

género, n m, kind, class, manner

generosidad, n f, generosity

generoso, adj, generous

genio, n m, genius, temper

gente, n f, people, folk

gentil, adj, genteel, nice

gentileza, n f, gentility

gentío, n f, rabble, mob

gentío, n m, crowd

genuino, adj, genuine

geografía, n f, geography

geología, n f, geology

geometría, n f, geometry

geranio, n m, geranium

gerente, n m, manager

germen, n m, germ, bud, shoot

germinar, v, germinate

geroglífico, adj, hieroglyphic

geroglífico, n m, hieroglyphic

gerundio, n m, gerund

gesticulación, n f, gesticulation

gestión, n f, conduct

gestionar, v, manage

gesto, n m, face

gestor, n m, superintendent

gigante, adj, gigantic

gigante, n m, giant

gigote, n m, minced meat

gimnasio, n m, gymnasium, school

gimnasta, n mf, gymnast

girador, n m, drawer

girar, v, revolve

girasol, n m, sunflower

giratorio, adj, rotary

giro, n m, circumference

gitano, n m, gypsy

glándula, n f, gland

globo, n m, globe

gloria, n f, glory

glorieta, n f, summer house

glorificar, v, glorify

glorioso, adj, glorious

glosario, n m, glossary

glucosa, n f, glucose

gobenación, n f, government

gobernador, n m, governor

gobernalle, n m, rudder

gobernar, v, govern

gobierno, n m, control, government

goce, n m, enjoyment

gola, n f, gullet

golfo, n m, gulf

golondrina, n f, swallow (bird)

golondro, n m, desire

golpe, n m, blow, stroke

golpear, v, strike

goma, n f, gum, rubber

gordo, adj, fat, rich

gordura, n f, grease, fat

gorjear, v, warble

gorra, n f, cap

gorrión, n m, sparrow

gota, n f, drop

gotear, v, drop

gotera, n f, gutter

gótico, adj, gothic

gozar, v, enjoy

goze, n m, joy

gozne, n m, hinge

gozoso, adj, joyful, glad

grabar, v, engrave

gracia, n f, grace, gentility

gracias, n f, fpl, thanks

gracioso, adj, graceful

grada, n f, stair step

gradación, n f, gradation

grado, n m, step, grade

graduación, n f, graduation

graduado, adj, graduated

gradual, adj, gradual

gradualmente, adv, gradually

graduar, v, measure

gráfico, adj, graphic

gramática, n f, grammar

gramatical, adj, grammatical

gran, adj, great, famous

grana, n f, grain, dye

granada, n f, pomegranate, grenade

granado, adj, large, principal
granado, n m, pomegranate tree
granar, v, seed, grain
granate, adj, dark red
granate, n m, garnet
grande, adj, large, great
grandemente, adv, greatly
grandeza, n f, greatness
grandioso, adj, grand, great
grandor, n m, size, magnitude
grandura, n f, greatness
granero, n m, granary
granizar, v, hail
granizo, n m, hail
granja, n f, grange, farm
granjear, v, gain, get
granjeo, n m, gain
granjería, n f, farming, gain
granjero, n m, farmer
grano, n m, corn, grain
granoso, adj, grainy
granulación, n f, granulation
granular, v, granulate
grao, n m, strand, shore
grasa, n f, grease, fat
grasiento, adj, greasy, grimy
graso, n m, fat, grease
gratamente, adv, graciously
gratificación, n f, gratification, gratuity
gratificar, v, gratify
gratis, adv, free
gratitud, n f, gratitude
grato, adj, graceful
gratuitamente, adv, gratuitously
gravamen, n m, charge
gravar, v, burden, oppress
grave, adj, grave, heavy
gravedad, n f, gravity, seriousness
gravitación, n f, gravitation
gravoso, adj, grievous
greda, n f, chalk
gremio, n m, lap
grey, n f, flock
grieta, n f, crevice, crack
grifado, adj, italic
grifo, n m, tap, cock

grillo, n m, cricket
gringo, adj, unintelligible
gringo, n m, foreigner
gris, adj, gray
gritar, v, cry, shriek, shout
grito, n m, squall, cry
grosella, n f, currant
grosería, n f, grossness, coarseness
grosero, adj, gross, coarse
grosor, n m, thickness
grosura, n f, fat
grúa, n f, crane
grueso, adj, fat, heavy
gruñir, v, snarl, grunt, growl
grupo, n m, group
gruta, n f, cavern, grotto
guadaña, n f, scythe
guadañar, v, mow
guano, n m, guano
guante, n m, glove
guantelete, n m, gauntlet
guapeza, n f, bravery
guapo, adj, valiant
guarda, n f, guard, border
guardar, v, keep, guard
guasa, n f, jest
guerra, n f, war
guerrero, n m, warrior
guía, n m, guide
guiar, v, guide, drive
guijarro, n m, pebble
guisante, n m, pea
guisar, v, cook
guitarra, n f, guitar
gula, n f, gullet, gluttony
gusano, n m, maggot, worm
gustar, v, please
gusto, n m, pleasure
gustoso, adj, tasty, cheerful, glad

H

haba, n f, bean
habano, adj, Havana tobacco
habano, n m, Havana cigar
haber, v, have, possess
habichuela, n f, kidney bean

hábil, adj, clever
habilidad, n f, ability, cleverness
hábilmente, adv, ably
habilitación, n f, habilitation, qualification
habilitado, adj, qualified
habilitar, v, qualify, enable
habitación, n f, habitation, room
habitante, n m, inhabitant
habitar, v, inhabit, live
hábito, n m, coat, dress, habit
habitual, adj, habitual
habituar, v, habituate, accustom
habitud, n f, habitude
habla, n f, speech, language
hablador, adj, talkative
habladuría, n f, gossip, chatter
hablar, v, speak, talk
hablilla, n f, rumor
haca, n f, pony
hacedero, adj, feasible
hacendado, adj, landed, rich
hacendado, n m, land owner
hacendoso, adj, assiduous
hacer, v, make, do, pack
hacerse, v, become
hacha, n f, axe, hatchet
hacia, adv, toward, to
hacienda, n f, land, estate
hacinar, v, hoard
hada, n f, fairy
hadado, adj, fortunate, lucky
hado, n m, fate, destiny
halagüeño, adj, encouraging, attractive
halagar, v, please, flatter
halago, n m, flattery
halcón, n m, falcon
hálito, n m, breath
hallar, v, find
hamaca, n f, hammock
hambre, n f, hunger
hambriento, adj, hungry
haragán, n m, idler
haraganear, v, idle, lounge
harapo, n m, rag
harina, n f, flour

hartar, v, stuff, cloy
harto, adj, satiated, full
hasta, adv, until, up to, as far as
hastío, n m, loathing, disgust
hato, n m, herd of cattle
hay, adv, there is, there are
haz, n m, fagot, bundle
hazaña, n f, exploit, deed
hebdomadario, adj, weekly
hebilla, n f, buckle, clasp
hebra, n f, fiber, thread
hechicero, n m, sorcerer
hechizar, v, bewitch, charm
hecho, adj, made, done
hecho, n m, fact
hectárea, n f, hectare
hectogramo, n m, hectogram
hectolitro, n m, hectoliter
hectómetro, n m, hectometer
heder, v, stink
hedor, n m, stench, stink
helada, n f, frost, nip
helado, adj, frozen, frigid
helado, n m, ice cream
helar, v, congeal, freeze
hembra, n f, female
hemisferio, n m, hemisphere
henchimiento, n m, abundance
henchir, v, fill up
hender, v, crack
hendir, v, split
heñir, v, knead, dough
heno, n m, hay
heraldo, n m, herald
heredar, v, inherit
heredero, n m, heir
hereditario, adj, hereditary
herencia, n f, inheritance
herida, n f, wound
herido, adj, wounded
herir, v, wound
hermana, n f, sister
hermanar, v, match
hermandad, n f, brotherhood
hermanita, n f, little sister
hermanito, n m, little brother
hermano, n m, brother

hermosear, v, beautify
hermoso, adj, beautiful
hermosura, n f, beauty
héroe, n m, hero
heroico, adj, heroic
herrador, n m, farrier
herradura, n f, shoe
herramienta, n f, tool, instrument
herrería, n f, forge
herrero, n m, smith
hervir, v, boil, seethe
hesitar, v, hesitate
hidalgo, n m, nobleman
hidalguía, n f, nobility
hidráulica, n f, hydraulics
hidrógeno, n m, hydrogen
hiel, n f, gall, bile
hielo, n m, frost, ice cream
hiena, n f, hyena
hierba, n f, herb, grass
hierbabuena, n f, mint
hierro, n m, iron
hígado, n m, liver
higiene, n f, hygiene
higo, n m, fig
hija, n f, daughter
hijo, n m, child, son
hila, n f, row, line
hilar, v, spin
hilaza, n f, yarn
hilo, n m, thread, wire
himno, n m, hymn
hinchado, adj, swollen, vain
hinchar, v, inflate, swell
hinchazón, n f, swelling
hipil, n m, chemise
hipocresía, n f, hypocrisy
hipoteca, n f, mortgage
hirviente, adj, boiling
hispano, adj, Spanish
historia, n f, history, story
historiador, n m, historian
histórico, adj, historic
hito, n m, landmark, object
hocico, n m, shout
hogaño, adv, this year
hogar, n m, hearth

hoguera, n f, bonfire
hoja, n f, leaf
hojalata, n f, tin
holgado, adj, loose, easy
holgar, v, rest
holgazán, adj, idle, lazy
holgura, n f, ease, repose
hollar, v, trample on
hollín, n m, soot
hombre, n m, man
hombrera, n f, pad
hombro, n m, shoulder
homicidio, n m, murder, homicide
honor, n m, honor
honrado, adj, honorable
honrar, v, honor
hora, n f, hour, time
horquilla, n f, hairpin
hositación, n f, hesitation
hospital, n m, hospital
hotel, n m, hotel
hoy, adv, today
hueste, n m, host, army
huevo, n m, egg
humano, adj, human
humear, v, smoke
humo, n m, smoke
humor, n m, humor
humoso, adj, smoky
hundir, v, sink
huracán, n m, hurricane
huraño, adj, shy
hurtador, n m, robber, thief
hurtar, v, steal
hurto, n m, theft, robbery
husmear, v, sniff
husmo, n m, smell (bad)

I

ibero, n m, Iberian
ida, n f, departure
idea, n f, idea
ideal, adj, ideal
ideal, n m, ideal
idear, v, form an idea, think
idem, pro, the same, ditto

idénticamente, adv, identically
idéntico, adj, same
identidad, n f, identity
identificar, v, identify
idioma, n m, idiom, language
idiosincrasia, n f, idiosyncrasy
idiota, adj, idiot
idiotismo, n m, idiom, idiocy
idoneidad, n f, aptitude
idóneo, adj, fit, capable
iglesia, n f, church
ignición, n f, ignition
ignominia, n f, ignominy
ignominioso, adj, ignominious
ignorado, adj, unknown
ignorancia, n f, ignorance
ignorante, adj, ignorant
ignorar, v, be ignorant of
igual, adj, equal
igual, n m, equal
iguala, n f, agreement, level
igualación, n f, equalization
igualada, n f, tie, draw
igualar, v, equalize
igualdad, n f, equality
igualmente, adv, equally
ijada, n f, flank
ijar, n m, flank
ilegal, adj, illegal
ilegalidad, n f, illegality
ilegible, adj, illegible
ilegítimo, adj, illegal, illegitimate
ileso, adj, unhurt
ilícito, adj, illicit
ilimitado, adj, unlimited
iliterato, adj, illiterate
ilógico, adj, illogical
iluminación, n f, illumination
iluminado, adj, illuminated
iluminar, v, illuminate
iluminativo, adj, illuminative
ilusión, n l, self-deception
ilusivo, adj, illusive
iluso, adj, deluded
ilusorio, adj, illusory
ilustración, n f, illustration
ilustrador, n m, illustrator

ilustrar, v, illustrate
ilustre, adj, illustrious
imagen, n f, image
imaginable, adj, imaginable
imaginación, n f, imagination
imaginar, v, imagine
imaginario, adj, imaginary
imaginativo, adj, imaginative
imán, n m, magnet
imanar, v, magnetize
imbécil, adj, weak, imbecile
imbecilidad, n f, imbecility
imitable, adj, imitable
imitación, n f, imitation
imitado, adj, imitated
imitar, v, imitate
impaciencia, n f, impatience
impacientar, v, vex, become
 impatient
impaciente, adj, impatient
impacto, adj, impacted
impar, adj, unequal, odd
imparcial, adj, impartial
imparcialidad, n f, impartiality
imparcialmente, adv, impartially
impartible, adj, indivisible
impartir, v, grant, impart
impasibilidad, n f, impassibility
impasible, adj, impassible
impavidez, n f, intrepidity
impávido, adj, dauntless
impecable, adj, impeccable
impedimento, n m, impediment
impedir, v, impede
impelente, adj, forcing
impeler, v, impel, incite
impenetrable, adj, impenetrable
impenitencia, n f, impenitence
impenitente, adj, impenitent
impensado, adj, unexpected
imperar, v, command
imperativo, adj, imperative
imperceptible, adj, imperceptible
imperdible, adj, indestructible
imperdible, n m, safety pin
imperfección, n f, imperfection
imperfecto, adj, imperfect

imperial, adj, imperial
imperial, n m, carriage roof
impericia, n f, unskillfulness
imperio, n m, empire
imperioso, adj, imperious
imperito, adj, unskilled
impermeable, adj, impermeable
impermeable, n m, raincoat
impersonal, adj, impersonal
impertinencia, n f, impertinence
impertinente, adj, impertinent
ímpetu, n m, impetus, impulse
impetuoso, adj, impetuous
implicación, n f, implication
implicado, adj, implicated
implicar, v, implicate
implícito, adj, implicit
implorar, v, implore
impolítico, adj, impolitic, impolite
imponente, adj, imposing, stately
imponer, v, lay put
impopular, v, unpopular
impopularidad, n f, unpopularity
importación, n f, importation
importador, n m, importer
importancia, n f, importance
importante, adj, important
importantísimo, adj, very important
importar, v, import, matter
importe, n m, amount, value
importunar, v, importune, vex
importuno, adj, troublesome
imposibilidad, n f, impossibility
imposibilitar, v, make impossible
imposible, adj, impossible
imposición, n f, imposition
impostor, n m, impostor
impostura, n f, imposture
impotencia, n f, impotence
impotente, adj, impotent
impracticable, adj, impracticable
imprecar, v, imprecate, curse
impregnar, v, impregnate
imprenta, n f, printing
imprescindible, adj, indispensable
impresión, n f, impression, print
impresionar, v, impress

impreso, adj, printed
impreso, n m, pamphlet
impresor, n m, printer
imprevisión, n f, imprevision
imprevisto, adj, unforeseen
imprimir, v, print
improbabilidad, n f, improbability
improbable, adj, improbable
ímprobo, adj, corrupt
impropiedad, n f, impropriety
impropio, adj, improper
impróvido, adj, improvident
improviso, adj, unexpected
imprudencia, n f, imprudence
imprudente, adj, imprudent
impudencia, n f, impudence
impudente, adj, impudent
impuesto, adj, imposed
impuesto, n m, duty, tax
impugnar, v, impugn
impulsar, v, impel
impulsión, n f, impulsion
impulsivo, adj, impulsive
impulso, n m, impulse
impulsor, n m, impeller
impune, adj, exempt from
  punishment
impunemente, adv, with impunity
impunidad, n f, impunity
impureza, n f, impurity
impuro, adj, impure
imputable, adj, imputable,
  chargeable
imputación, n f, imputation
imputar, v, impute, attribute
inacabable, adj, interminable
inaccesible, edj, inaccessible
inacción, n f, inaction
inaceptable, adj, unacceptable
inactividad, n f, inactivity
inactivo, adj, inactive
inadaptable, adj, not adaptable
inadecuado, adj, inadequate
inadmisible, adj, inadmissible
inadvertencia, n f, inadvertence
inadvertido, adj, inadvertent
inagotable, adj, inexhaustible

inaguantable, adj, insupportable
inalámbrico, adj, wireless
inalterado, adj, unchanged
inamortizable, adj, unredeemable
inanición, n f, starvation
inapelable, adj, unappealable
inaplicable, adj, inapplicable
inaudito, adj, unheard of
inauguración, n f, inauguration
inaugurar, v, inaugurate
inca, n m, Inca
incalculable, adj, incalculable
incandescencia, n f, incandescence
incandescente, adj, incandescent
incansable, adj, indefatigable
incapacidad, n f, incapacity
incapaz, adj, incapable
incautamente, adj, incautiously
incautarse, v, take possession of
incauto, adj, incautious
incendiar, v, inflame
incendiario, n m, incendiary
incendio, n m, fire
incentivo, n m, incentive
incertidumbre, n f, incertitude
incesante, adj, incessant
incidencia, n f, incidence
incidental, adj, incidental
incidente, adj, incidental
incidente, n m, incident, accident
incierto, adj, uncertain
incipiente, adj, beginning
incisión, n f, incision
incitar, v, incite
incivil, adj, uncivil
incivilidad, n f, incivility
inclemencia, n f, inclemency
inclemente, adj, inclement
inclinación, n f, inclination
inclinado, adj, inclined
inclinado, n f, shelving
inclinar, v, incline, shelve
incluir, v, include
inclusión, n f, inclusion
inclusive, adv, inclusively
inclusivo, adj, inclusive
incluso, adj, enclosed

incluso, adv, including
incoar, v, begin, commence
incobrable, adj, irrecoverable
incógnito, adj, unknown
incoloro, adj, colorless
incombustible, adj, incombustible
incomodidad, n f, inconvenience
incómodo, adj, inconvenient
incomparable, adj, incomparable
incompatibilidad, n f, incompatibility
incompatible, adj, incompatible
incompetencia, n f, incompetency
incompetente, adj, incompetent
incompleto, adj, incomplete
incomprensibilidad, n f,
  incomprehensibility
incomprensible, adj,
  incomprehensible
inconcebible, adj, inconceivable
inconcuso, adj, incontestable
inconexión, n f, incoherency
inconexo, adj, unconnected
inconfeso, adj, unconfessed
inconfidencia, n f, distrust
incongruencia, n f, incongruity
incongruo, adj, incongruous
inconsecuencia, n f, inconsequence
inconsecuente, adj, inconsequent
inconsidaración, n f, inconsideration
inconsiderable, adj, inconsiderable
inconsiderado, adj, inconsiderate
inconsiguiente, adj, inconsequent
inconsistencia, n f, inconsistency
inconsistente, adj, inconsistent
inconsolable, adj, inconsolable
inconstancia, n f, inconstancy
inconstante, adj, inconstant
incontestable, adj, incontestable
incontrastable, adj, insurmountable
incontrovertible, adj, incontrovertible
inconvenible, adj, inconsistent
inconveniencia, n f, inconvenience
inconveniente, adj, inconvenient
inconveniente, n m, difficulty
incorporación, n f, incorporation
incorporar, v, incorporate
incorrecto, adj, incorrect

incorregible, adj, incorrigible
incredibilidad, n f, incredibility
incredulidad, n f, incredulity
incrédulo, adj, incredulous
increíble, adj, incredible
incremento, n m, increment
increpar, v, reproach
incriminar, v, incriminate
incubadora, n f, incubator
inculcar, v, inculcate
inculpable, adj, inculpable
inculpar, v, accuse
inculto, adj, uncultivated
incumbencia, n f, incumbency
incuria, n f, negligence
incurrir, v, incur
indagación, n f, inquiry
indagar, v, investigate
indebidamente, adv, unjustly
indebido, adj, undue, illegal
indecencia, n f, indecency
indecente, adj, indecent
indecible, adj, inexpressible
indecisión, n f, indecision
indeciso, adj, undecided
indecoroso, adj, indecorous
indefensible, adj, indefensible
indefenso, adj, defenseless
indeficiente, adj, unfailing
indefinido, adj, indefinite
indeleble, adj, indelible
indemnidad, n f, indemnity
independencia, n f, independence
independiente, adj, independent
indicar, v, indicate
indio, n m, Indian
infeliz, adj, unhappy
inflar, v, swell
informe, n m, report
Inglaterra, n f, England
inglés, adj, English
inglés, n, English (language)
ingrato, adj, thankless
innecesario, adj, unnecessary
inocente, adj, innocent
inodoro, adj, scentless
insensible, adj, senseless

inseparable, adj, inseparable
insignia, n f, badge
insignificación, n f, insignificance
insistir, v, insist
insolente, adj, insolent
inspirar, v, inspire
instancia, n f, instance
instar, v, press, urge
instigación, n f, instigation
instinto, n m, instinct
instruir, v, instruct
instrumento, n m, instrument
insuficiente, adj, insufficient
insultar, v, insult
integridad, n f, integrity
intelecto, n m, intellect
intelectual, adj, intellectual
inteligente, adj, intelligent
intencional, adj, intentional
intensidad, n f, intensity
intento, n m, intent
interceder, v, intercede
interceptar, v, intercept
interdicto, n f, prohibition
interés, n m, interest
interesado, adj, selfish
interesante, adj, interesting
interesar, v, interest
intermitente, adj, intermittent
internacional, adj, international
interno, adj, internal
interpelar, v, appeal
interponer, v, interpose
interpretación, n f, interpretation
interpretar, v, interpret
interrogación, n f, interrogation
interrogativo, adj, interrogative
interrumpir, v, interrupt
intersección, n f, intersection
intervenir, v, intervene
intimidad, n f, intimacy
intimidar, v, intimidate
intimo, adj, intimate
intolerable, adj, intolerable
intolerante, adj, intolerant
intrigar, v, intrigue
intrincar, v, perplex

intrínseco, adj, intrinsic
introducción, n f, introduction
introducir, v, introduce
inútilmente, adv, uselessly
invadir, v, invade
inválido, adj, invalid
invariable, adj, invariable
invencible, adj, invincible
inventario, n m, inventory
inventor, n m, inventor
invernizo, adj, wintry
inverosímil, adj, unlikely
inverso, adj, inverse
invertir, v, invert
investigación, n f, investigation
investigar, v, investigate
investir, v, invest
invierno, n m, winter
invisible, adj, invisible
invitar, v, invite
invltación, n f, invitation
invocar, v, invoke
involuntario, adj, involuntary
inyectar, v, inject
iodo, n m, iodine
ir, v, go, be going, be
ira, n f, ire, anger
iris, n m, iris
irlandés, adj, Irish
irlandés, n, Irish (language)
ironía, n f, irony
irónico, adj, ironic
irreflexivo, adj, inconsiderate
irregular, adj, irregular
irremisible, adj, unpardonabie
irreparable, adj, irreparable
irresistible, adj, irresistible
irresoluto, adj, irresolute
irresponsabilidad, n f, irresponsibility
irrevocable, adj, irrevocable
irrisorio, adj, derisive
irritable, adj, irritable
irritación, n f, irritation
irritar, v, irritate
irrogar, v, cause
isla, n f, island
Islandia, n f, Iceland

isleta, n f, islet
istmo, n m, isthmus
italiano, adj, Italian
italiano, n, Italian (language)
iterar, v, iterate, repeat
itinerario, n m, itinerary
izar, v, hoist
izquierdo, adj, left, left-handed

J

jaba, n f, crate
jabalí, n m, wild boar
jabón, n m, soap
jabonar, v, soap
jacinto, n m, hyacinth
jactancia, n f, boasting, arrogance
jactarse, v, boast, brag
jaez, n m, harness
jalbegar, v, whitewash
jalbegue, n m, whitewash
jalea, n f, jelly
jaletina, n f, gelatine
jamás, adv, never
jamón, n m, ham
Japón, n f, Japan
japonés, adj, Japanese
japonés, n, Japanese (language)
jaque, n m, braggart
jaqueca, n f, headache
jaquel, n m, chessboard
jaqueta, n f, jacket
jarabe, n m, syrup
jarcia, n f, fishing tackle
jardín, n m, garden
jardinería, n f, gardening
jardinero, n m, gardener
jarra, n f, jug, jar, pitcher
jarrete, n m, ham
jarro, n m, can, jar
jaula, n f, cage, crate
jefe, n m, chief, head
jengibre, n m, ginger
jerarquía, n f, hierarchy
jerga, n f, slang, jargon
jergón, n m, mattress
jerigonza, n f, gibberish

jeringa, n f, syringe
jeroglífico, adj, hieroglyphic
jeroglífico, n m, hieroglyphs
jira, n f, trip, excursion
jirón, n m, strip, rag
jiste, n m, yeast
jofaina, n f, basin, bowl
jornada, n f, journey
joven, adj, young
joven, n m, youth
joya, n f, jewel
joyería, n f, jewelry
joyero, n m, jeweler
jubileo, n m, jubilee
júbilo, n m, glee, joy
jubón, n m, jacket
judía, n f, kidney bean
judicial, adj, judicial
juego, n m, game, sport
jueves, n m, Thursday
juez, n m, judge
jugada, n f, play, trick
jugador, n m, player, gambler
jugar, v, play, gamble
jugo, n m, sap, juice, marrow
jugoso, adj, juicy, succulent
juguete, n m, toy, plaything
juicio, n m, judgement, opinion,
  wisdom
juicioso, adj, judicious, prudent
julio, n m, July
junio, n m, June
junto, adj, together
jurar, v, swear
justicia, n f, justice
justo, adj, just
juzgar, v, judge

K

aki, adj, khaki
kilo, n m, kilogram (abbr.)
kilogramo, n m, kilogram
kilolitro, n m, kiloliter
kilómetro, n m, kilometer
kilovatio, n m, kilowatt
kiosco, n m, kiosk, newsstand

L

la, art, the, that
la, pro, her, it
laberinto, n f, labyrinth, maze
labio, n m, lip
labor, n f, labor
laborable, adj, workable
laborativo, adj, workable
laborear, v, cultivate
laboreo, n m, labor, cultivation
laborioso, adj, laborious, industrious
labrador, n m, farmer, laborer
labrante, n m, sculptor, stone
labrar, v, work, labor, cultivate
laca, n f, laquer
lacayo, n m, footman, lackey,
  servant
lacear, v, lace
lacerar, v, lacerate, mangle
lacìnico, adj, brief
lacre, n m, wax
lácteo, adj, milky
ladear, v, turn, incline
ladino, adj, cunning, crafty
lado, n m, side
ladrar, v, bark, howl
ladrido, n m, barking
ladrillo, n m, brick
ladrìn, n m, thief, robber
lagar, n m, wine press
lagarto, n m, lizard
lago, n m, lake
lágrima, n f, tear
laguna, n f, pond lake, marsh
lama, n f, mud, slime
lamentable, adj, lamentable
lamentar, v, lament, bemoan, regret
lamento, n m, lamentation, lament
lamer, v, lick
lámina, n f, plate (of metal), sheet
  (of metal)
laminar, v, roll
lámpara, n f, lamp
lamparilla, n f, nightlight
lana, n f, wool

lanar, adj, woolly, woolen
lance, n m, accident, chance, affair
lanceta, n f, lancet
lancha, n f, launch, boat
lanchìn, n m, lighter
langosta, n f, locust, also lobster
languidez, n f, weakness
lánguido, adj, languid, weak
lanudo, adj, woolly
lanza, n f, lance, spear
lanzar, v, start, throw
lapicero, n m, pencilcase
lápiz, n m, crayon, pencil
lapso, n m, lapse
lardo, n m, lard
lardoso, adj, greasy
larga, n f, delay, procrastination
largamente, adv, largely
largar, v, loosen, slacken
largo, adj, long, large
largor, n m, length
largueza, n f, length, largeness
largura, n f, length, extent
las, art, these, those
las, pro, them
lasitud, n f, weariness
laso, adj, weary, lax
lástima, n f, pity, grief
lastimar, v, hurt, wound, pity
lastimero, adj, sad, mournful
lata, n f, can
latente, adj, latent, hidden
lateral, adj, lateral, sideways
látigo, n m, whip
latin, n m, brass
latir, v, beat (as a heart)
latitud, n f, latitude, width
lato, adj, large, extensive
latrocinio, n m, robbery, theft
laudable, adj, laudable
lavable, adj, washable
lavadero, n m, laundry
lavado, n m, washing
lavandera, n f, laundress
lavar, v, wash
lavatorio, n m, lavatory
laxitud, n f, laxity

laxo, adj, lax
lazo, n m, bow, lasso
lazo, n m, snare
le, art, to him, to her, to it
le, pro, him, her
leal, adj, loyal
lealtad, n f, loyalty
lebrel, n m, greyhound
lección, n f, lesson
lechada, n f, whitewash
leche, n f, milk
lechìn, n m, pig
lecho, n m, bed, couch
lechuga, n f, lettuce
lechuza, n f, owl
lector, n m, reader, lecturer
lectura, n f, reading, lecture
leer, v, read
legado, n m, legacy
legajo, n m, file
legal, adj, legal, lawful
legalidad, n f, legality, lawfulness
legalizar, v, legalize
legalmente, adv, legally
legación, n f, embassy
legalización, n f, legalization
legar, v, bequeath
legible, adj, legible
legislación, n f, legislation
legislador, n m, legislator
legislar, v, legislate
legislativo, adj, legislative
legislatura, n f, legislature
legitimidad, n f, legitimacy, authenticity
legítimo, adj, legitimate, legal, authentic
legón, n m, shovel
legua, n f, league
legumbre, n f, vegetable
leíble, adj, legible, readable
lejanía, n f, distance
lejano, adj, distant, far, remote
lejos, adv, far, distant
lema, n m, motto
leña, n f, wood
leñador, n m, lumberjack

eñero, n m, lumber yard

engua, n f, tongue, language

enguaje, n m, language, speech, style

enguaraz, adj, fluent, talkative, chatty

enidad, n f, leniency

eño, n m, log

ente, n mf, lens

enteja, n f, lentil

entitud, n f, slowness

ento, adj, slow

eón, n m, lion

erdamente, adv, slowly, heavily

erdo, adj, slow, heavy

es, art, to them, to you

esión, n f, wound, lesion, injury

lesionar, v, hurt, wound, injure

leso, adj, hurt, wounded

letra, n f, letter, type, handwriting

letrado, n m, lawyer

letrero, n m, inscription, lettering

letrina, n f, latrine, bathroom

leva, n f, impose, levy (a tax)

levadura, n f, yeast, leavening

levantamiento, n m, lifting, uprising, rebellion

levantar, v, raise, lift

leve, adj, light

levedad, n f, levity

levemente, adv, lightly, gently

levita, n f, coat

ley, n f, law

leyenda, n f, legend

liaga, n f, wound

liagar, v, wound, injure, hurt

liar, v, tie, bind

libar, v, taste, sip

libelar, v, petition, sue

libelo, n m, libel

liberación, n f, liberation, freedom

liberal, adj, liberal, free

liberalidad, n f, liberality

libertad, n f, liberty

libertar, v, liberate, free

libra, n f, pound

librar, v, free, deliver

libre, adj, open, free

libremente, adv, freely

librería, n f, library

librero, n m, book-seller

libro de pólizas, n m, checkbook

libro, n m, book

licencia, n f, license, permission

licenciar, v, permit, license, allow

liceo, n m, public school

lícito, adj, lawful

licor, n m, liquor

lid, n f, conflict, fight

lidiar, v, fight

lienza, n f, tape

lienzo, n m, linen

ligado, adj, bound, tied

ligamento, n m, ligament

ligamiento, n m, union

ligar, v, tie, bind, fasten

ligazón, n f, union, connection

ligeramente, adv, swiftly, lightly

ligereza, n f, lightness, agility

ligero, adj, light, slight

lila, n f, lilac

lima, n f, lime

limar, v, file, polish

limitación, n f, limitation, restriction

limitado, adj, limited

limitar, v, confine

límite, n m, limit, border

limón, n m, lemon, lemon tree

limonada, n f, lemonade

limonado, adj, lemon

limoso, adj, muddy, slimy

limpiar, v, clean, cleanse

límpido, adj, transparent

limpieza, n f, cleanliness

limpio, adj, clean, neat

linaje, n m, lineage, family

lince, adj, acute

lindamente, adv, neatly

linde, n m, landmark, boundary

lindero, adj, contiguous

lindeza, n f, neatness

lindo, adj, pretty, neat

línea, n f, line

lineal, adj, lineal

lineamiento, n m, feature
linear, v, line
lingual, adj, lingual
lingüista, n m, linguist
lingüistico, adj, linguistic
lino, n m, linen
linóleo, n m, linoleum
linón, n m, lawn
linterna, n f, lantern
lío, n m, parcel, package
liquidar, v, liquidate
líquido, adj, liquid
lirio, n m, lily
lirondo, adj, pure, clean
lisamente, adv, smoothly
liso, adj, smooth
lisonja, n f, flattery
lisonjear, v, flatter
lisonjero, adj, flattering
lisonjero, n m, flatterer
lista, n f, strip, stripe
listado, adj, striped
listo, adj, ready, clever
listón, n m, ribbon, tape
litera, n f, litter
literal, adj, literal
literario, adj, literary
literato, adj, literate
literatura, n f, literature
litigar, v, litigate, dispute
litigio, n m, lawsuit, litigation, dispute
litio, n m, lithium
litro, n m, liter
liviandad, n f, levity
liviano, adj, light
lívido, adj, livid
llama, n m, llama
llamada, n f, call
llamar, v, call, knock
llamativo, adj, attractive
llano, adj, plain, smooth
llave, n f, key
llavero, n m, keyring
llegar, v, arrive, come
llenar, v, fill, stuff
lleno, adj, full
llevar, v, carry, wear, take

llorar, v, weep, cry
llover, v, rain, shower
lluvia, n f, rain, shower
lo, art, the
lo, pro, him, it
loco, adj, crazy
los, art, them, those
los, pro, them, you
lotería, n f, lottery
lucha, n f, struggle
luchar, v, fight, struggle
lucir, v, shine
luego, adv, shortly, by-and-by
lugar, v, spot
luminoso, adj, shiny
luna, n f, moon
lunes, n m, Monday
luz, n f, light

M

música, n f, music
macarrón, n m, macaroni
macear, v, hammer
maceta, n f, mallet
machacar, v, crunch, pound
machado, n m, hatchet
machar, v, pound
machete, n m, machete
macho, adj, masculine, male
machón, n m, buttress
macilento, adj, lean
macizo, adj, massive
madera, n f, wood, lumber
madero, n m, beam of wood
madre, n f, mother
madreselva, n f, honeysuckle
madrugada, n f, dawn
madtastra, n f, stepmother
maduración, n f, maturation
madurar, v, mature, ripen
madurez, n f, maturity, ripeness
maduro, adj, mature, ripe, advanced
maestra, n f, teacher, mistress
maestría, n f, mastery, wisdom
maestro, n m, teacher, expert
magia, n f, magic

mágico, adj, magic, magical
mágico, n m, magician
magín, n m, imagination
magisterio, n m, mastery
magistrado, n magistrate, court
magistral, adj, masterly
magnate, n m, magnate
magnético, adj, magnetic
magnetismo, n m, magnetism
magnificencia, n f, magnificence
magnífico, adj, magnificent
magnitud, n f, magnitude
magno, adj, great
mago, n m, magician
magro, adj, meager, thin
magullamiento, n m, bruise
magullar, v, bruise
maíz, n f, corn
maizal, n m, corn field
maizena, n f, cornmeal
majadería, n f, nonsense
majadero, adj, foolish
majar, v, beat, pound
majestad, n f, majesty
majestuoso, adj, majestic
majoría, n f, improvement
majuela, n f, shoelaces
mal, adv, badly, ill
mal, n m, evil, illness, harm
mala, n f, mail
malamente, adv, badly
malaventura, misfortune
malaventurado, adj, unfortunate
malbaratar, v, spoil
malcontento, adj, discontented
malcriado, adj, rude, crude, ill-
mannered
maldad, n f, badness
maldecir, v, curse
maldición, n f, curse
maldito, adj, cursed, accursed
maleable, adj, malleable
malear, v, injure, malign
malecìn, n m, levee, jetty
maledicencia, n f, slander
malestar, n m, misery
maleta, n f, suitcase

malevolencia, n f, malevolence
malévolo, adj, malevolent
maleza, n f, undergrowth
malgastar, v, waste
malhadado, adj, unfortunate
malhecho, adj, misshapen
malhechor, n m, malefactor
malhumorado, adj, sullen
malicia, n f, malice
malicioso, adj, malicious
maligno, adj, malignant
malla, n f, mesh
malo, adj, bad, poor, wretched
malogrado, adj, unfortunate
malograr, v, disappoint
malogro, n m, disappointment
malquerencia, n f, hatred
malquerer, v, hate
malquisto, adj, hated
malsano, adj, unhealthy
maltratar, v, abuse
maltrato, n m, abuse
malvado, adj, malicious
mamá, n f, mamma, mother
mamar, v, suck
maña, n f, skill
manada, n f, flock, herd
mañana, n f, morning, tomorrow
manantial, n m, source, spring
mancar, v, maim, wound
mancebo, n m, adolescent
mancha, n f, smear, spot, stain
manchar, v, smear, stain
mancilla, n f, blemish
mancillar, v, blemish
manco, adj, maimed, handicapped
mancomunar, v, associate
mancomunidad, n f, association
manda, n f, proposal
mandadero, n m, messenger
mandado, n m, mandate
mandamiento, n m, mandate, order,
command
mandar, v, command, order, send
mandatario, n m, attorney, agent
mandato, n m, mandate, order
mandíbula, n f, jaw

mando, n m, command
manear, v, hobble
manejable, adj, manageable
manejar, v, manage
manejo, n m, management
manera, n f, manner, method
manga, n f, sleeve
mango, n m, handle
manguera, n f, rose
manía, n f, mania, phobia
maniatar, v, handcuff
manicomio, n m, mental hospital
manida, n f, resort
manifestación, n f, manifestation
manifestar, v, manifest
manifiesto, adj, manifest, obvious
manifiesto, n m, manifest (shipping)
maniobra, n f, maneuver
maniobrar, v, maneuver
manipulación, n f, manipulation
manipular, v, manipulate
maniquí, n m, mannequin
manivela, n f, handle
manjar, n m, food
mano, n f, hand
manojo, n m, bundle
manosear, v, feel, touch
manotada, n f, slap
mansión, n f, mansion
manso, adj, meek
manteca, n f, butter
mantel, n m, tablecloth
mantener, v, cherish
mantequilla, n f, butter
manual, adj, manual
manual, n m, manual, instructions
manubrio, n m, handle
manufacturar, manufacture
manuscrito, n m, manuscript
manutención, n f, maintenance
manzana, n f, apple
manzano, n m, apple tree
mapa, n m, map
máquina, n f, machine
mar, n mf, sea
maranta, n f, arrowroot
maravilla, n f, wonder, marvel

maravilloso, adj, marvelous
marca, n f, mark
marcadamente, adv, markedly
marcar, v, mark
marcha, n f, march
marchante, n m, merchant
marchantear, v, trade
marchar, v, go, march
marchitar, v, wither, fade
marchito, adj, withered
marco, n m, Mark (German currency)
marea, n f, tide
mareo, n m, seasickness
marfil, n m, ivory
margarita, n f, daisy
margen, n mf, margin, border
maridar, v, marry
marido, n m, husband
marimacho, n f, tomboy
marinero, n m, sailor
marino, adj, marine
mariposa, n f, butterfly
mariscal, n m, marshal
marisco, n m, shellfish
marmita, n f, kettle
mármol, n m, marble
marmóreo, adj, marbled
maroma, n f, rope
marra, n f, defect
marrano, n m, pig, hog
marras, adv, ancient
martes, n m, Tuesday
martillar, v, hammer
martillo, n m, hammer
marzo, n m, March
más, adv, more
mas, conj, but, yet
masa, n f, mass
mascabado, adj, inferior
mascar, v, chew
máscara, n f, mask
masculino, adj, masculine
mástil, n m, trunk
mata, n f, bush, shrub
matador, n m, murderer
matafuego, n m, fire extinguisher

matanza, n f, slaughter
matar, v, kill, slaughter, slay
mate, adj, matte, flat, dull
matemática, mathematics
matemático, adj, mathematical
matemático, mathematician
materia, n f, subject, matter
material, adj, material
material, n m, material
materno, adj, maternal
matiz, n m, shade, color
matizar, v, color ò
matorral, n m, underbrush
matraca, n f, joke
matrimonio, n m, marriage,
  matrimony
matriz, n f, matrix, mold
matute, n m, smuggling, contraband
matutear, v, smuggle
matutero, n m, smuggler
maula, n f, trash
mausoleo, n m, mausoleum
máxima, adv, primarily
máxima, n f, maxim
máximo, adj, maximum, primary
máximo, n m, maximum
mayúscula, n f, capital
mayo, n m, May
mayor, adj, older, greater, senior
mayoral, n m, leader
mayoría, n f, majority
mayormente, adv, principally
maza, n f, mace, club
mazo, n m, mallet
mazorca, n f, corn cob
me, pro, me
mecánico, adj, mechanical
mecánico, n m, mechanic
mecanismo, n m, mechanism
mecer, v, stir, shake
mecha, n f, match
mechar, v, force
mechero, n f, socket
medalla, n f, medal
medallón, n m, medallion
media, n f, stocking
mediación, n f, mediation
mediador, n m, mediator

medianía, n f, moderation
mediano, adj, moderate
mediar, v, mediate
medicina, n f, medicine
medicinal, adj, medicinal
medición, n f, measurement
médico, n m, doctor, physician
medida, n f, measure
medidamente, adv, moderately
medio, adj, half
medio, n m, middle
mediocre, adj, mediocre
mediocridad, n f, mediocrity
mediodía, n m, noon, midday
medir, v, measure
meditación, n f, meditation
meditar, v, meditate, cogitate, think
mediterráneo, adj, Mediterranean
medra, n f, progress
medrar, v, progress, prosper
medroso, adj, fearful
médula, n f, marrow
mejilla, n f, cheek
mejor, adj, nicer, better
mejorar, v, improve
melancolía, n f, melancholy
melancólico, adj, melancholy
melaza, n f, molasses
melcocha, n f, jelly
melena, n f, mane
melindroso, adj, fastidious
mella, n f, notch
melocotón, n m, peach
melodía, n f, melody
melón, n m, melon
membrana, n f, membrane
membrete, n m, note
membrudo, adj, robust
memorable, adj, memorable
memoria, n f, memory
memorial, n m, memorial
memorioso, adj, mindful
menaje, n m, furniture
mención, n f, mention
mencionar, v, mention
menear, v, direct, manage
menester, n m, necessity
menesteroso, adj, needy

mengua, n f, decay
menguar, v, decay
menor, adj, minor, smaller
menor, n m, minor
menoría, n f, minority
menos, adj, less, minus
menoscabar, v, deteriorate
menoscabo, n m, deterioration
menospreciar, v, deride
menosprecio, n m, derision
mensual, adj, monthly
mensualmente, adv, monthly
menta, n f, mint, peppermint
mental, adj, mental
mentar, v, mention
mente, n f, mind
mentecato, adj, foolish
mentecato, n m, fool
mentir, v, lie
mentira, n f, lie
mentiroso, adj, lying
mentiroso, n m, liar
mentitoso, adj, false
mentor, n m, mentor
menudamente, adv, minutely
menudear, v, repeat
menudeo, n m, retail store
menudo, adj, minute, small
meollar, n m, yarn
meollo, n m, marrow
meramente, adv, merely
merca, n f, purchase
mercadear, v, market
mercader, n m, marketer
mercadería, n f, merchandise
mercado, n m, market
mercancía, n f, merchandise
mercante, adj, mercantile
merced, n f, gift
mercenario, n m, mercenary
merecer, v, deserve, merit
merecido, n m, merit
merecimiento, n m, merit
merendar, v, lunch
merengue, n m, meringue
meridiano, n m, meridian
merienda, n f, lunch

mérito, n m, merit, value
merla, n f, blackbird
merma, n f, waste
mermar, v, waste
mermelada, n f, marmalade
mero, adj, mere
merodear, v, maraud
mes, n m, month
mesa, n f, table, desk
mesada, n f, wages
mesìn, n m, inn
mesita, n f, stand
mesonero, n m, innkeeper
mestizo, adj, mongrel
mesura, n f, measure
mesurado, adj, measured
meta, n f, boundary, border
metal, n m, metal
metálico, adj, metallic
meter, v, put, place
metìdico, adj, methodical
metido, adj, put, placed
metido, n m, insertion
método, n m, method
métrico, adj, metric
metrìpoli, n f, metropolis
metro, n m, meter
metropolitano, adj, metropolitan
México, n f, Mexico
mezcla, n f, mixture
mezclar, v, mix
mezclar, v, shuffle
mezquindad, n f, meanness, avarice
mezquino, adj, mean, petty
mezquita, n f, mosque
mi, adj, my
mí, pro, me
mía, adj, mine
miaja, n f, crumb
microscopio, n m, microscope
mìdulo, n m, modulation
miedo, n m, fear
miedoso, adj, fearful
miel, n f, honey
miembro, n m, limb
mientes, n fpl, thoughts
mientras, adv, while, when

miércoles, n m, Wednesday
mies, n f, harvest
miga, n f, crumb
migaja, n f, scrap, bit
migración, n f, migration
migratorio, adj, migratory
mil, adj, thousand
milagro, n m, miracle
milagroso, adj, miraculous
milenario, n m, millennium
milia, n f, mile
milicia, n f, militia
militante, adj, militant
militar, adj, military
militar, n m, military
millar, n m, thousand
millìn, n m, million
millonario, n f, millionaire
mimado, adj, spoiled
mimar, v, coax, spoil
mina, n f, mine
minador, n m, miner
minar, v, mine
mineral, n m, mineral
miniatura, n f, miniature
mínimo, adj, minimum, least
mínimum, n m, minimum
ministerio, n m, ministry
ministrar, v, minister
ministro, n m, minister
minuta, n f, minute, small
minuto, n m, minute (time)
mío, adj, mine
mira, n f, aim
mirada, n f, glance, gaze
mirado, adj, considerate
miraje, n m, mirage
miramiento, n f, consideration
mirar, v, consider, behold
mirasol, n m, sunflower
mirìn, n m, spectator
mirlo, n m, blackbird
misa, n f, mass
miserable, adj, miserable
miseria, n f, misery
misiìn, n f, mission
misionero, n f, missionary
Misisipi, n, Mississippi

mismo, adj, same, similar
mismo, n mf, self
misterio, n m, mystery
misterioso, adj, secretive
místico, adj, mystical
mitad, n f, half
mitigar, v, mitigate
mitin, n m, meeting
mitìn, n m, mitten
mixto, adj, mixed
mixtura, n f, mixture
mixturar, v, mix
moca, n f, mocha
mocasín, n m, moccasin
mocedad, n f, youth
mochila, n f, backpack
mociìn, n f, motion
moda, n f, style, fashion
modaraciìn, n f, moderation
modelar, v, model
modelo, n m, standard, model
moderado, adj, moderate
moderar, v, moderate, regulate
moderno, adj, modern, new
modestia, n f, modesty
modesto, adj, modest
modificaciìn, n f, modification
modificar, v, modify
modismo, n m, idiom
modo, n m, mode, method
modulaciìn, n f, modulation
modular, v, modulate
mofa, n f, mockery
mofar, mock, scoff
mofeta, n f, skunk
mofletudo, adj, chubby
mogollìn, n m, parasite
mohino, adj, fretful
moho, n m, moss, mold, mildew
mohoso, adj, moldy, mossy
mojar, v, moisten, wet
mojigato, n m, hypocrite
molde, n m, mold, pattern
moldear, v, mold
mole, adj, soft, mild
moledor, n m, grinder, crusher
moler, v, grind, crush
molestar, v, disturb, trouble

molicie, n f, tenderness
molido, adj, crushed, ground
molino, n m, mill
momentáneo, adj, momentous
momento, n m, moment
momia, n f, mummy
monarca, n m, monarch
monasterio, n m, monastery
mondadientes, n m, toothpick
mondar, v, clean, pick
mondo, adj, clean
moneda, n f, money, coin, currency
monedaje, n m, coinage
monja, n f, nun
monje, n m, monk
mono, adj, neat, pretty
monopolio, n m, monopoly
monstruo, n m, monster
monstruoso, adj, monstrous
monta, n f, amount, sum
montaña, n f, mountain
montañés, adj, mountainous
montar, v, mount, ride
monte, n m, mountain, forest
montìn, n m, heap, pile
monto, n m, amount, sum
monumento, n m, monument
morada, n f, home, abode
morado, adj, violet, purple
moral, adj, moral
moral, n f, morals, morality
moralidad, n f, morality
morar, v, inhabit, reside
morir, v, die
moro, n m, Moor
mortal, adj, mortal, fatal
mortalidad, n f, mortality
mortalmente, adv, mortally
mortero, n m, mortar
mortificaciìn, n f, mortification
mortificar, v, mortify
mortuorio, n m, burial, funeral
mosaico, adj, mosaic
mosca, n f, fly
mosquito, n m, mosquito, gnat
mostaza, n f, mustard
mostrar, v, show

mote, n m, motto, nickname
motejar, v, censure
motín, n m, mutiny
motivar, v, motivate
motivo, n m, motive, reason
motociclo, n m, motorcycle
motor, n m, motor
movedizo, adj, unsteady
mover, v, move
movible, adj, movable
móvil, adj, mobile
movilidad, n f, mobility
mozo, n m, waiter, porter
muchacha, n f, girl
muchacho, n m, boy
muchísimo, adj, very much
mucho, adj, much
mucho, n m, much, very much
mudanza, n f, change
mudar, v, shift
mudo, adj, speechless
muerte, n f, death
muerto, adj, dead, killed
muesca, n f, score
muesca, n f, slot
muestra, n f, sample
mujer sucia, n f, slut
mujer, n f, woman, wife
mula, n f, mule
mundo, n m, world, human race
muselina, n f, muslin
museo, n m, museum
muy, adv, very

N

nabo, n m, turnip
nacer, v, be born, rise
naciente, adj, growing
nacimiento, n m, birth, origin
nación, n f, nation
nacional, adj, national
nacionalidad, n f, nationality
nada, n f, nothing
nadador, n mf, swimmer
nadar, v, swim
nadie, pro, no one

nado, n f, swimming
nalga, n f, buttock, hip
naranja, n f, orange
naranjado, adj, orange
naranjal, n m, orange grove
naranjo, n m, orange tree
narcótico, adj, narcotic
nariz, n f, nose, nostril
narración, n f, narration
narrar, v, narrate, tell
nata, n f, cream
natal, adj, native
natal, n m, birthday
nativo, adj, native
natural, adj, natural
natural, n m, native
naturaleza, n f, nature, quality
naturalmente, adv, naturally
náufrago, n m, shipwreck
nave, n f, ship
navegar, v, sail
Navidad, n f, Christmas Day
navigar, v, sail
navío, n m, ship
neblina, n f, mist
nebuloso, adj, misty
necesario, adj, necessary
necesidad, n f, necessity
necesitar, v, need, require
necio, adj, stupid, foolish
nefando, adj, base, heinous
nefario, adj, nefarious, wicked
negación, n f, negation, refusal
negar, v, deny, refuse
negativa, n f, negative
negativo, adj, negative
negligencia, n f, negligence, neglect
negligente, adj, negligent
negociable, adj, negotiable
negociación, n f, negotiation
negociador, n m, negotiator
negociar, v, negotiate, trade
negocio, n m, business, occupation
negro, adj, black
nervio, n m, nerve, vigor
nervioso, adj, nervous
nervioso, adj, vigorous
neto, adj, neat, clean

neutral, adj, neutral
neutro, adj, neuter
nevada, n f, snowfall
nevar, v, snow
nevasca, n f, snowstorm
ni, conj, neither, nor
nicho, n m, niche, recess
nicotina, n f, nicotine
nido, n m, nest
niebla, n f, fog, mist, haze
nieto, n m, grandson
nieve, n f, snow
nina, n f, girl, child
ninguno, adj, none, neither, not one
niñito, n m, little child, little boy
niño, n m, boy, child
níquel, n m, nickel
nitrógeno, n m, nitrogen
nivel, n m, level, plane
nivelar, v, level, balance
no, adv, no, not
noble, adj, noble
noche, n f, night
Nochebuena, n f, Christmas Eve
noción, n f, notion, idea
nocivo, adj, noxious, poisonous, harmful
nocturno, adj, nocturnal
nodriza, n f, nurse
nogal, n m, walnut tree
nombradia, n f, reputation, fame
nombrado, adj, nominated, appointed
nombramiento, n m, nomination
nombrar, v, name, nominate
nombre, n m, name, noun
nominal, adj, nominal
nómino, n m, nominee
non, adj, odd, uneven
nonada, n f, trifle
norte, n m, north
norteamericano, adj, North American
nos, pro, us, to us, ourselves
nosotros, adj, we, us
notificar, v, summon
noviembre, n m, November
nube, n f, cloud
nuestro, adj, our, ours

nueve, n, nine
nuevo, adj, new
nuez, n f, nut
número, n m, number, size
numeroso, adj, numerous
nunca, adv, never

O

o, conj, or, either
obcecado, adj, blind
obcecar, v, blind
obedecer, v, obey, yield
obediencia, n f, obedience
obediente, adj, obedient
obeso, adj, obese, fat
óbicé, n m, obstacle
obispo, n m, bishop
obituario, n m, obituary
objeción, n f, objection
objetar, v, object
objetivo, adj, objective
objeto, n m, object
oblicuo, adj, oblique
obligación, n f, obligation
obligar, v, oblige
obligatorio, adj, obligatory
oblongo, adj, oblong
obra, n f, work
obrar, v, work, operate
obrero, n m, workman
obscuramente, adv, obscurely
obscurecer, v, obscure, darken
obscuridad, n f, obscurity, darkness
obscuro, adj, obscure, dark
obsequioso, adj, obsequious
observación, n f, observation
observante, adj, observant
observar, v, observe
observatorio, n m, observatory
obstante, adv, notwithstanding
obstar, v, obstruct, oppose
obstinado, adj, obstinate, stubborn
obstruir, v, obstruct
obtener, v, obtain
obtenible, adj, obtainable
obtuso, adj, obtuse

obvio, adj, obvious, evident
oca, n f, goose
ocasión, n f, occasion
ocasional, adj, occasional
océano, n m, ocean
ocho, n, eight
ocio, n m, leisure
ocioso, adj, idle, lazy
octava, n f, octave
octubre, n m, October
ocular, adj, ocular
ocular, n m, eyeglass
ocultamente, adv, secretly
ocultar, v, conceal
oculto, adj, hidden, secret
ocupación, n f, occupation, business
ocupado, adj, occupied
ocupar, v, occupy, employ
ocurrencia, n f, occurrence
ocurrir, v, occur, happen
odiar, v, hate
odio, n m, hatred
odioso, adj, hateful, odious
odómetro, n m, odometer
oeste, n m, west
ofender, v, offend
ofensa, n f, offense
ofensivo, adj, offensive
ofensor, n m, offender
oferta, n f, offer
oficial, n m, official
oficialmente, adv, officially
oficiar, v, officiate
oficina, n f, office
oficio, n m, business
oficioso, adj, official
ofrecer, v, offer
ofrecimiento, n m, offer
ofuscar, v, darken, obscure
oído, n m, ear, hearing
oír, v, hear, listen
ojeada, n f, glance
ojear, v, eye, glance
ojeriza, n f, spite, grudge
ojo, n m, eye
ola, n f, surf, wave
olar, n m, smell, odor

óleo, n m, oil
oleoso, adj, oily
oler, v, smell
olfato, n m, scent, smell
oliva, n f, olive
ollería, n f, pottery
olmo, n m, elm tree
oloroso, adj, perfumed, scented
olvidar, v, forget
olvido, n m, forgetfulness, oblivion
ominoso, adj, ominous
omisión, n f, omission, oversight
omiso, adj, neglectful
once, n, eleven
onda, n f, wave
ondear, v, undulate
oneroso, adj, onerous
onza, n f, ounce
opaco, adj, opaque
opción, n f, option
ópera, n f, opera
operable, adj, operable
operación, n f, operation
operar, v, operate
operario, n m, operator
opinar, v, argue, judge
opinión, n f, opinion
oponer, v, oppose
oportunidad, n f, opportunity
oportuno, adj, opportune
oposición, n f, opposition
opositor, n m, opponent
opresión, n f, oppression
opresivo, adj, oppressive
opresor, n m, oppressor
oprimir, v, oppress
optar, v, choose, select
óptica, n f, optics
óptico, adj, optical
optimismo, n m, optimism
optimista, n m, optimist
óptimo, adj, best, excellent
opuesto, adj, opposite
opulencia, n f, opulence
opulento, adj, opulent
ora, adv, present
ora, conj, whether, now
oración, n f, sentence

orador, n mf, speaker
oral, adj, oral
orar, v, pray
orden, n mf, command, order
ordenar, v, order, command
ordinariamente, adv, ordinarily
ordinario, adj, ordinary
ordinario, n m, ordinary
oreja, n f, ear
orfandad, n f, orphanage
orgánico, adj, organic
organización, n f, organization
organizar, v, organize
órgano, n m, organ
orgullo, n m, pride
orgulloso, adj, proud
oriar, v, border
oriental, adj, oriental, eastern
oriente, n m, Orient, East
orificio, n m, orifice, aperture
orín, n m, rust
orinal, n m, urinal
ornamentar, v, adorn
ornamento, n m, ornament
ornar, v, decorate
ornato, n m, decoration
oro, n m, gold
orquesta, n f, orchestra
oruga, n f, caterpillar
os, pro, you, yourself
osadía, n f, boldness, courage
osado, adj, daring, bold
osar, v, dare
oscilar, v, oscillate
oso, n m, bear
ostra, n f, oyster
otoñal, adj, autumnal
otoño, n m, autumn
otro, adj, another, other
oval, adj, oval
óvalo, n m, oval
oveja, n f, sheep
ovejero, n m, shepherd
ovejuno, edj, sheepish
ovillo, n m, clue
oxidación, n f, oxidation
oxidar, v,oxidize
oxígeno, n m, oxygen

oyente, n m, hearing

P

pabellón, n m, pavillion
pabilo, n m, wick
pábulo, n m, nourishment, food
paca, n f, pack, package
pacer, v, graze
paciencia, n f, patience
paciente, adj, patient
pacientemente, adv, patiently
pacificar, v, pacify
Pacífico, n f, Pacific
pactar, v, contract, arrange
pacto, n m, contract, agreement
padecer, v, suffer
padecimiento, n m, suffering
padrastro, n m, stepfather
padre, n m, father
padron, n m, poll
paga, n f, payment, fee
pagamento, n m, payment
pagar, v, pay
pagaré, n m, check
página, n f, page
país, n m, country
paisaje, n m, landscape
Países Bajos, n m, the Netherlands
paja, n f, straw
pájara, n f, bird
pajarillo, n m, little bird
pájaro, n m, bird
pajuela, n f, match (couple)
pala, n f, shovel, spade
palabra, n f, word
palacio, n m, palace
palanca, n f, lever
palenque, n m, passage, arcade, hall
palestra, n f, gymnasium
pálido, adj, pale, sallow
palma, n f, palm tree
palmo, n m, palm of the hand
palo, n m, stick, timber
paloma, n f, dove, pigeon
palpable, adj, palpable

palpar, v, feel, touch
palpitar, v, palpitate, beat, flutter
pan, n m, bread, wheat
panadero, n m, baker
panal, n m, honeycomb
Panamá, n m, Panama
pandilla, n f, union, political party
panecillo, n m, bread roll, small bread loaf
pánico, n m, panic
pañiete, n m, cloth
paño, n m, cloth
pantalla, n f, screen
pantalón, n m, pants, slacks
pantano, n m, swamp
pañuelo, n m, handkerchief
papá, n m, papa
papa, n m, Pope
papagayo, n m, parrot
papel, n m, paper
papelería, n f, stationery
paquete, n m, package
par, adj, equal, even
par, n m, pair, couple
para, prep, for, to, towards
parabién, n m, compliment
paracaídas, n m, parachute
parada, n f, parade
parado, adj, careless
paradoja, n f, t: paradox
parafina, n f, paraffin
paraguas, n m, umbrella
paraíso, n m, paradise
paraje, n m, place
paralelo, adj, parallel
paralelo, n m, parallel
paralizado, adj, paralyzed
paralizar, v, paralyze
parangón, n m, paragon, zenith
parar, v, stop
parasol, n m, parasol
parche, n m, parchment
parcial, adj, partial
parcialidad, n f, partiality
pardo, adj, drab
parear, v, match, pair
parecer, n m, opinion, advice

parecer, v, seem, appear
parecido, adj, similar
pared, n f, wall
pareja, n f, mate
parejo, adj, equal
paréntesis, n f, parenthesis
paridad, n f, parity, equality
parlamentar, v, talk
parlamento, n m, parliament
paro, n m, stoppage, gridlock
párpado, n m, eyelid
parque, n m, park
parra, n f, vine
párrafo, n m, paragraph
parte, n f, part, share
partición, n f, partition, division
participación, n f, participation
participar, v, participate
particular, adj, particular
particularmente, adv, particularly
partida, n f, departure
partido, n m, party (political)
partir, v, split, leave
partrocinio, n m, patronage
parvo, adj, little, small
pasa, n f, raisin
pasada, n f, passage
pasadero, adj, passable
pasado, adj, past, last
pasador, n m, deadbolt
pasaje, n m, passage
pasajero, n m, passenger
pasaporte, n m, passport
pasar, v, pass, go, come
pasatiempo, n m, pastime
Pascua, n f, Easter
pase, n m, pass
pasear, v, walk
paseo, n m, stroll
paseo, n m, walk, drive
pasión, n f, passion
pasivo, adj, passive
pasmar, v, marvel, wonder
pasmo, n m, wonder
pasmoso, adj, wonderful, marvelous
paso, n m, step, pace
pasta, n f, paste
pastel, n m, pie, pastry

pastilla, n f, cake
pasto, n m, pasture
pastor, n m, shepherd
pata, n f, foot
patada, n f, kick
patata, n f, potato
patear, v, kick
patentado, adj, patented
patentar, v, patent
patente, adj, patent, evident
paterno, adj, paternal
patético, adj, pathetic
patín, n m, skate
patinación, n f, skating
patinar, v, skate
patio, n m, yard
pato, n m, goose
patraña, n f, falsehood
patria, n f, native country
patriota, n m, patriot
patriótico, adj, patriotic
patriotismo, n m, patriotism
patrocinar, v, patronize
patrón, n m, employer
patrón, n m, patron
patrulla, n f, patrol
patrullar, v, patrol
paulatinamente, adv, gently, slowly
paulatino, adj, gentle, slow
pausa, n f, pause
pausadamente, adv, slowly, deliberately
pausado, adj, slow, deliberate
pausar, v, pause
pavimento, n m, pavement
pavo, n m, turkey
pavor, n m, fear, terror
pavoroso, fearful, awful, terrible
paz, n f, peace
peaje, n m, toll
peca, n f, speck, spot
pecado, n m, sin
pecador, n m, sinner
pecar, v, sin
pecho, n m, breast, chest
peculiar, adj, peculiar
pedal, n m, pedal
pedazo, n m, piece

pedestal, n m, pedestal
pedido, n m, order, request
pedimento, n m, petition
pedir, v, ask
pega, n f, varnish
pegajoso, adj, sticky, viscous
pegar, v, join, unite
peinar, v, comb one's hair
peine, n m, comb
pelar, v, pluck, skin
peldaño, n m, stairstep
pelea, n f, battle, fight
pelear, v, fight
película, n f, film
peligrar, v, risk, danger
peligro, n m, peril, danger, risk
peligroso, adj, perilous, dangerous
pelo, n m, hair
peloso, adj, hairy
peña, n f, rock
pena, n m, pain, sorrow
penalidad, n f, penalty
penar, v, grieve, mourn
peñascoso, adj, rocky
pendencia, n f, quarrel, dispute
pender, v, depend
pendiente, adj, pendant
péndola, n f, pendulum
penetrable, adj, penetrable
penetración, n f, penetration
penetrante, adj, penetrating
penetrar, v, penetrate
península, n f, peninsula
penique, n m, penny
penitencia, n f, penitence
penoso, adj, painful, grievous
pensamiento, n m, thought
pensar, v, think
pensativo, adj, pensive, thoughtful
pensión, n f, pension
peonza, n f, top (toy)
peor, adj, worse
pepinillos, n mpl, pickles
pepino, n m, cucumber
pepita, n f, core
pequeñito, adj, very little
pequeño, adj, little, small

pera, n f, pear
peral, n m, pear tree
percepción, n f, perception
perceptible, adj, perceptible
percha, n f, perch
percibir, v, receive, perceive
perdedor, n m, loser
perder, v, lose
pérdida, n f, loss
perdón, n m, pardon
perdonar, v, pardon, condone, excuse
perdurable, adj, perpetual
perdurar, v, endure, last
perecedero, edj, perishable
perecer, v, perish
perejil, n m, parsley
perenne, adj, perennial
pereza, n f, laziness
perezoso, edj, lazy
perfección, n f, perfection
perfeccionar, v, perfect
perfectamente, adv, perfectly
perfecto, adj, perfect
perforación, n f, perforation
perfumar, v, scent
perfume, n m, scent
pericia, n f, skill, knowledge
periferia, n f, periphery
perillán, n m, rascal
periódicamente, adv, periodically
periódico, adj, periodical
periódico, n m, newspaper
periodismo, n m, journalism
periodista, n m, journalist
período, n m, period of time
peritaje, n m, survey
perito, adj, skillful, experienced
perito, n m, expert
perjuicio, n m, prejudice, injury
perjurar, v, perjure
perla, n f, pearl
permanecer, v, remain, endure
permanencia, n f, permanence
permanente, adj, permanent
permisible, adj, permissible
permisión, n f, permission

permiso, n m, permission
permitir, v, permit
permuta, n f, exchange, barter
permutar, v, exchange, barter
perno, n m, pin, spike
pero, conj, but, except
perpendicular, adj, perpendicular
perpetrar, v, perpetrate
perpetuar, v, perpetuate
perpetuo, adj, perpetual
perplejo, adj, perplexed, puzzled
perro, n m, dog
persecución, n f, persecution
perseguidor, n m, persecutor
perseguir, v, sue, pursue
perseverancia, n f, perseverance
perseverante, adj, persistent
perseverar, v, persevere
persistencia, n f, persistence
persistente, edj, persistent
persistir, v, persist
persona, n f, person
personal, adj, personal, private
personalidad, n f, personality
personalmente, adv, personally
perspectiva, n f, perspective
persuadir, v, persuade
persuasión, n f, persuation
persuasivo, adj, persuasive
pertenecer, v, belong, pertain
perteneciente, adj, pertinent
pertenencia, n f, pertinence
pértiga, n f, pole, rod
pertinente, adj, pertinent
perturbar, v, perturb
Perú, n m, Peru
perversidad, n f, perversity
perversión, n f, perversion
perverso, adj, perverse
pervertir, v, pervert
pesa, n f, weight
pesadamente, adv, heavily, slowly
pesadez, n f, heaviness, slowness
pesadilla, n f, nightmare
pesado, adj, heavy, tedious
pesadumbre, n f, chagrin, grief
pesar, n m, sorrow, grief
pesar, v, weigh, grieve

pesaroso, adj, sorrowful
pesca, n f, fishing
pescado, n m, fish
pescante, n m, crane
pescar, v, fish
pescuezo, n m, neck
pesebre, n m, crib, manger
peseta, n f, peseta (Spanish currency)
peso, n m, weight, heft
pesquisa, n f, inquiry
pestaña, n f, eyelash
peste, n f, pest
petardo, n m, cheat, fraud
petición, n f, petition, demand, request
petróleo, n m, petroleum, oil
pez, n f, tar
pi rata, n m, pirate
piadoso, adj, pious
piano, n m, piano
picada, n f, puncture
picante, adj, sharp, pungent
picar, v, pick
pícaro, n m, scoundrel
pichel, n m, mug
pichón, n m, pigeon
pico, n m, beak, bill
pie, n m, foot, leg
piedad, n f, pity
piedra, n f, stone
piel, n f, peel, skin
pierna, n f, leg
pieza, n f, piece
pigmento, n m, pigment
pignorar, v, pledge
pila, n f, stack
pilar, n m, pillar, column
pilón, n m, pile, heap
piloto, n m, pilot
pimienta, n f, pepper
piña, n f, pineapple
pináculo, n m, pinnacle
pincel, n m, pencil
pinchar, v, sting
pingüe, adj, plentiful, abundant
pino, n m, pine
pinta, n f, spot, blemish

pintado, adj, colored, variegated
pintar, v, paint
pinto, adj, colored, variegated
pintor, n m, painter
pintoresco, adj, picturesque
pintura, n f, painting, picture
pinzas, n f, tpl, pincers, forceps
pío, adj, pious
pipa, n f, pipe
piqueta, n f, pitcher
piratería, n f, piracy
pisada, n f, footstep, footprint
pisapapeles, n m, paperweight
pisar, v, tread, trample
piso, n m, floor
pisotear, v, trample
pista, n f, track, print, clue
pistola, n f, pistol
pistón, n m, piston
pitillo, n m, cigarette
pito, n m, pipe, whistle
pivote, n m, pivot
pizarra, n f, blackboard, slate
placa, n f, plate
placentero, adj, pleasant
placer, n m, pleasure, consent
placer, v, please
plácido, adj, placid
plaga, n f, plague
plagar, v, plague
plan, n m, plan, design
planada, n f, plain
plancha, n f, plate
planchado, n m, ironing, laundry
planchar, v, iron (clothes)
planchear, v, plate, cover
planeta, n f, planet
plañir, v, lament
plano, adj, plain, flat, level
plano, n m, plan, draft
planta, n f, plant
plantación, n f, plantation
plantador, n m, planter
plantar, v, plant
plantear, v, plan
plantilla, n f, model, copy
plata, n f, silver

plataforma, n f, platform
plateado, adj, silver plated
plateadura, n f, silver plating
platear, v, silver
plática, n f, conversation
platicar, v, converse, talk
platillo, n m, saucer
platino, n m, platinum
plato, n m, dish, plate
plausible, adj, plausible
playa, n f, beach
plaza, n f, square
plazo, n m, term, time
plegable, adj, pliable, pliant
plegadura, n f, fold, crease
plegar, v, fold, crease
pleitear, v, plead, litigate
pleito, n m, litigation
plenamente, adv, fully, completely
plenario, adj, full, complete
pleno, adj, full
plétora, n l, plethora
pliego, n m, sheet
plomero, n m, plumber
plomo, n m, lead
pluma, n f, feather, pen
plumaje, n m, plumage
plural, adj, plural
pluralidad, n f, plurality
poblacho, n m, populace
población, n f, population
poblado, n m, town, village
poblar, v, populate
pobre, adj, poor
pobreza, n f, poverty
poción, n f, potion
poco, adj, little
poco, adv, little, not very
poco, n m, little
podar, v, prune
podenco, n m, hound
poder, n m, power
poder, v, be able, can, may
poderoso, adj, powerful
poema, n m, poem
poesía, n f, poetry
poeta, n m, poet

polar, adj, polar

polea, n f, pulley

policía, n f, police

política, n f, politics

político, adj, political

póliza, n f, policy

pollo, n m, chicken

polo negativo, n m, cathode

polo, n m, pole

poltrón, adj, idle, lazy

polvo, n m, dust, powder

polvorizar, v, pulverize

polvoroso, adj, dusty

pomo, n m, apple

pomposo, adj, pompous

ponche, n m, punch (drink)

ponderar, v, ponder, weigh

poner, v, put, set

popular, adj, popular

popularidad, n f, popularity

popularizar, v, popularize

populoso, adj, populous

por, prep, for, by, as

porcelana, n f, china, porcelain

porcentaje, n m, percentage

porción, n f, portion, part

porfiado, adj, obstinate, stubborn

porfiar, v, dispute, contend

pormenor, n m, detail, particular

poroso, adj, porous

porqué, adv, why

porque, conj, because

porquería, n f, nastiness, filth

porra, n f, stick

portal, n m, porch, gate, portal

portamonedas, n m, purse

portar, v, carry

portátil, adj, portable

porte, n m, postage

portillo, n m, opening, passage, gate

portugués, adj, Portuguese

portugués, n, Portuguese

porvenir, n m, future

posar, v, house, lodge

posdata, n f, postscript

poseedor, n m, possessor, owner

poseer, v, possess, hold

posesión, n f, possession

posibilidad, n f, possibility

posible, adj, possible

posiblemente, adv, possibly

posición, n f, position

positivo, adj, positive, certain

posponer, v, postpone

posta, n f, post office

postal, adj, postal

poste de señales, n m, signpost

poste, n m, post, pillar

posteridad, n f, posterity

postizo, adj, artificial, false

postre, adj, last

postrero, adj, last

postres, n mpl, dessert

postular, v, postulate

póstumo, adj, posthumous

postura, n f, posture, position

potasio, n m, potassium

pote, n m, pot, jar

potencia, n f, power, potential

potencial, adj, potential

potente, adj, potent, powerful

pozal, n m, bucket, pail

pozo, n m, well

práctica, n f, practice

practicable, adj, feasible

prácticamente, adv, practically

practicar, v, practice

práctico, adj, practical, skilled

pradera, n f, meadow

prado, n m, lawn, field, meadow

preámbulo, n m, preamble, preface

precario, adj, precarious

precaver, v, prevent

precedente, adj, preceding

preceder, v, precede

preciar, v, value, appraise

precio, n m, cost, price

precioso, adj, precious

precipitación, n f, precipitation

precipitar, v, precipitate

precisamente, adv, precisely

precisar, v, compel

precisión, n f, precision

preciso, adj, precise

precursor, n m, precursor

predecesor, n f, predecessor

predicción, v, predict, foretell
predicción, n f, prediction
predominante, adj, predominant
predominar, predominate
prefacio, n m, preface
preferencia, n f, choice
preferible, adj, preferable
preferir, v, prefer
prefijo, n m, prefix
pregunta, n f, question
preguntar, v, ask
prejuicio, n m, prejudice, bias
prejuzgar, v, prejudge
prelación, n f, preference
preliminar, adj, preliminary
preludio, n m, prelude
prematuro, adj, premature
premiar, v, reward
premio, n m, prize, reward
premisa, n f, premise
premura, n f, pressure
prenda, n f, pledge
prender, v, seize, grasp
prendero, n m, broker
prensa, n f, press
prensado, n m, luster, gloss
prensadura, n f, pressure
prensar, v, press
preocupación, n f, preoccupation
preocupar, v, preoccupy
preparación, n f, preparation
preparar, v, prepare
presa, n f, seizure, capture
prescribir, v, prescribe
prescripción, n f, prescription
prescripto, adj, prescribed
presencia, n f, presence
presentación, n f, presentation
presentar, v, present
presente, adj, present
presente, n m, present, gift
presentemente, adv, presently
preservación, n f, preservation
preservar, v, preserve
preservar, v, spare
presidente, n m, president
presidir, v, preside

presilla, n f, loop
presión, n f, pressure
preso, n m, prisoner
préstamo, n m, loan
prestar, v, lend, pay
presteza, n f, quickness, speed
prestigio, n m, prestige
prestigioso, adj, prestigious
presto, adj, quick, prompt
presto, adv, soon, quickly
presumir, v, presume
presunto, adj, presumed
presupuestar, v, estimate
presuroso, adj, hasty, prompt, quick
pretender, v, pretend, imitate
pretendiente, n m, pretender
pretensión, n f, pretense
pretexto, n m, pretext
prevención, n f, prevention
prevenido, adj, prepared
preventivo, adj, preventive
prever, v, anticipate, foresee
previamente, adv, previously
previo, adj, previous, prior
prieto, adj, dark
prima, n f, cousin (female only)
prima, n f, premium
primacía, n f, primacy, priority
primario, adj, principal, primary
primavera, n f, spring
primero, adj, first
primitivo, adj, primitive
primo, n m, cousin (male only)
primor, n m, beauty, excellence
primoroso, adj, excellent, graceful
princesa, n f, princess
principal, adj, chief
principalmente, adv, principally
príncipe, n m, prince
principiar, v, begin
principio, n m, beginning, origin
prior, adj, prior, preceding
prioridad, n f, priority
prisa, n f, hurry, speed
prisión, n f, prison
prisionero, n m, prisoner
privación, n f, privation

privado, adj, private
privar, v, deprive
privilegio, n m, privilege
pro, n m, profit, benefit
probabilidad, n f, probability
probable, adj, probable
probablemente, adv, probably
probación, n f, probation
probar, v, prove
procurar, v, try
prodigioso, adj, stupendous
producto, n m, product
profesión, n f, calling
profesor, n m, teacher
profesora, n f, teacher
profeta, n m, seer
profundo, adj, deep
programa, n m, program
promesa, n f, promise
prometer, v, promise
pronto, adj, speedy
pronto, adv, soon
pronunciar, v, pronounce
proseguir, v, prosecute
próspero, adj, successful
prosunción, n f, presumption
proteger, v, protect
provenir, v, prepare, foresee
provisión, n f, supply
próximo, adj, next
proyecto, n m, scheme
prudencia, n f, caution
publicar, v, publish
pueblo, n m, village, people
pueril, adj, childish
puerta, n f, door
puerto de mar, n m, seaport
Puerto Rico, n m, Puerto Rico
puerto, n m, seaport
pues, adv, then, well
puesta del sol, n f, sunset
puesto que, adv, since
pulido, adj, sleek
puñado, n m, handful
puñal, n m, dagger
puño, n m, fist
punto y coma, n f, semicolon
punto, n m, point

puntuación, n f, punctuation
puntual, adj, punctual
puntualidad, n f, punctuality
puntualmante, adv, punctually
puntuar, v, punctuate
puntura, n f, puncture
punzar, v, punch
punzó, adj, red
pupila, n f, pupil (eye)
pupilo, n m, pupil (school)
pupitre, n m, schooldesk
puramente, adv, purely
pureza, n f, purity
purgar, v, purge
puridad, n f, purity
purificar, v, purify
puro, adj, pure
púrpura, n f, purple
pútrido, adj, putrid

Q

qué, pro, what, which
que, pro, who, that, because
quebradizo, adj, brittle, fragile
quebrado, adj, broken
quebrado, n m, bankruptcy
quebrantador, n m, breaker
quebrantamiento, n m, fracture, rupture, violation
quebrantar, v, break, crash, weaken
quebranto, n m, weakness, damage, loss
quebrar, v, break, fail, bankrupt
quedar, v, stay, remain, continue
quedo, adj, quiet, still, easy
quehacer, n m, occupation, business
queja, n f, complaint, grumbling
quejarse, v, complain
quejido, n m, complaint
quejoso, adj, querulous
quejumbroso, adj, complaining, plaintive
quemador, n incendiary, burner
quemadura, n f, burn
quemar, v, burn, kindle, scorch
quemazón, n f, combustion, burn, conflagration

querella, n f, complaint, petition
querellante, n m, murmuring, complaining
querellarse, v, lament, complain
querer, v, wish, desire, love
querido, adj, beloved
quesero, n m, cheesemaker
queso, n m, cheese
quevedos, n mpl, eyeglasses
quicial, n m, sidepost jamb
quicio, n m, hinge
quiebra, n f, fracture, loss, damage
quien, pro, who, he who
quién, pro, who, whom
quietamente, adv, quietly, calmly
quieto, adj, quiet, still
quietud, n f, quietness, rest, repose
quijada, n f, jaw, jawbone
quijo, n m, ore
quilatar, v, assay (minerals)
quilate, n m, carat (gemology)
quilla, n f, keel
química, n f, chemistry
quémico, adj, chemical
quémico, n m, chemist
quimón, n m, fine cotton, print
quincalla, n f, hardware
quincallería, n f, metal working
quincallero, n m, metal worker
quince, n, fifteen
quincena, n f, two weeks
quinina, n f, quinine
quinque, n m, lamp
quinquillería, n f, hardware
quinquillero, n m, hardware
quinta, n f, country house
quintería, n f, farm
quintero, n m, farmer
quinto, n m, fifth (fraction)
quíntuplo, adj, quintuple, fivefold
quirúrgico, adj, surgical
quisicosa, n f, riddle, enigma
quisquilla, n f, nicety
quitamanchas, n m, launderer
quitanza, n f, receipt, discharge
quitar, v, quit, remove, free
quitarse, v, take off

quitasol, n m, parasol, sunshade
quite, n m, obstacle
quizás, adv, perhaps

R

rábano, n m, radish
rabia, n f, rage, fury
rabiar, v, rage
rabioso, adj, rabid, mad
rabo, n m, tail
raciocinar, v, reason, argue
raciocinio, n m, reasoning
ración, n f, ration
racional, adj, rational
racionalidad, n f, rationality
rada, n f, road
radiante, adj, radiant
radical, adj, radical
radio, n m, radius
radlación, n f, radiation
raedura, n f, scrape
raer, v, scrape, erase
raído, adj, scraped worn
raíz, n f, root, base
raja, n f, splinter, crack
rajar, v, split
ralea, n f, race, species
rálfaga, n f, gust
rama, n f, branch
ramificación, n f, ramification
ramo, n m, branch
rana, n f, frog
ranchero, n m, rancher
rancho, n m, ranch
rancio, adj, rancid
randa, n f, trimming
rango, n m, rank, quality
ranura, n f, groove
rapacidad, n f, robbery
rapar, v, shave, peel
rape, n m, shaving
rápidamente, adv, rapidly, fast
rapidez, n f, rapidity
rápido, adj, swift
rápido, n m, express
raposo, n m, fox

raqueta, n f, racket
raramente, adv, seldom
rareza, n f, rareness
raridad, n f, rarity
raro, adj, rare, unusual, queer
ras, n m, level
rasar, v, strike
rascador, n m, scraper
rascadura, n f, scratch
rascar, v, scratch, scrape
rasgar, v, tear, cut
rasgo, n m, stroke
rasguñar, v, scratch
rasguño, n m, scratch
raso, adj, clear, flat
raso, n m, satin
raspa, n f, rasp
raspador, n m, eraser
raspar, v, rasp
rastitución, n f, restitution
rastrear, v, trace
rastro, n m, trace, sign
rasura, n f, shaving
rasurar, v, shave
rata, n f, rat
ratear, v, distribute, divide
rateo, n m, distribution
ratería, n f, larceny
ratificación, n f, ratification
ratificar, v, ratify, approve
rato, n m, short space of time
ratón, n m, mouse
ratonera, n f, mousetrap
raudal, n m, torrent
raya, n f, streak, stripe
rayado, adj, striped
rayano, adj, neighboring
rayar, v, streak
rayo, n m, ray
raza, n f, race
razón, n f, reason
razonable, adj, reasonable
razonar, v, reason
reabrir, v, reopen
reacción, n f, reaction
real, adj, real, royal
realeza, n f, royalty
realidad, n f, reality

realizar, v, realize
realmente, adv, really
realzar, v, raise, elevate
reanudar, v, renew, resume
reaparecer, v, reappear
reaparición, n f, reappearance
reapertura, n f, reopening
reasegurar, v, reassure
reaseguro, n m, reassurance
reasumir, v, resume
reatar, v, retie
rebaja, n f, discount
rebajar, v, reduce, discount
rebanada, n f, slice
rebanar, v, slice
rebaño, n m, flock
rebasar, v, exceed
rebato, n m, surprise, alarm
rebelar, v, rebel, revolt
rebelde, adj, rebellious
rebelde, n m, rebel
rebelión, n f, rebellion
reblandecer, v, tenderize
rebusca, n f, research
rebuscar, v, search
recado, n m, message
recaer, v, relapse
recaída, n f, relapse
recalar, v, soak
recalcar, v, squeeze
recalmón, n m, lull
recambio, n m, reward
recapacitar, v, recollect
recargar, v, reload, recharge
recatado, adj, prudent, modest
recatar, v, try again
recato, n m, caution, modesty
recelar, v, suspect, distrust
recelo, n m, misgiving, distrust
receloso, adj, apprehensive,
  suspicious
recepción, n f, reception
receptáculo, n m, receptacle
receptor, n m, recipient
receta, n f, prescription
recetar, v, prescribe
rechazar, v, repel, reject
rechazo, n m, rejection

rechinar, v, creak
reciamente, adv, strongly
recibí, n m, receipt
recibidor, n m, receiver
recibir, v, receive, accept
recién, adv, recently, lately
reciente, adj, recent, new
recientemente, adv, recently, lately
recio, adj, strong, stout
recio, adv, strongly
recipiente, n m, container
reciprocar, v, reciprocate
recíproco, adj, reciprocal
recitar, v, recite
reclamar, v, reclaim, demand
reclinar, v, recline
recluta, n m, recruit
reclutar, v, recruit
recobrar, v, recover
recobro, n m, recovery
recodo, n m, angle, corner
recoger, v, pick, pick up, reap
recogido, adj, secluded
recogimiento, n m, retreat, shelter
recolección, n f, recollection
recomendable, adj, recommendable
recomendación, n f,
  recommendation
recomendar, v, recommend
reconciliación, n f, reconciliation
reconciliar, v, reconcile
reconocer, v, recognize
reconocido, adj, recognized
reconocimiento, n m, recognition
recontar, v, recount
reconvención, n f, charge
reconvenir, v, charge
recordar, v, remind, remember
recorrer, v, examine, survey
recorrida, n f, repairs
recorrido, n m, journey
recortar, v, shorten
recorte, n m, outline
recostar, v, recline
recreación, n f, recreation
recrear, v, amuse, recreate
recreo, n m, recess

rectamente, adv, rightly
rectificación, n f, rectification,
  correction
rectificar, v, rectify, correct
rectitud, n f, rectitude, veracity
recto, adj, straight, honest
recuento, n m, inventory
recuerdo, n m, souvenir, memory
recuperación, n f, recovery
recuperar, v, recover
recurrir, v, recur
recurso, n m, recourse
recusar, v, challenge
red, n f, net, snare
redacción, n f, publishing
redactar, v, write, edit
redactor, n m, editor
redención, n f, redemption
redimir, v, redeem
rédito, n m, revenue
redoblar, v, double
redonda, n f, neighborhood
redondo, adj, round
redondo, n m, globe
reducción, n f, reduction
reducido, adj, reduced
reducir, v, reduce
redundante, adj, redundant
redundar, v, overflow
reelección, n f, re-election
reelegir, v, re-elect
reembolsar, v, reimburse
reemplazar, v, replace
reexaminar, v, re-examine
refacción, n f, refreshment
referencia, n f, reference
referir, v, refer
refinado, adj, refined
refinar, v, refine
reflectar, v, reflect
reflejar, v, reflect
reflejo, n m, reflex
reflexión, n f, reflection
reflexionar, v, reflect
reflexivo, adj, reflective
refluir, v, ebb
reflujo, n m, ebb

reforma, n f, reform
reformar, v, reform
reforzar, v, strengthen, fortify
refrán, n m, proverb
refrenar, v, coerce
refrescar, v, refresh, cool
refresco, n f, refreshment
refrigerador, n m, refrigerator
refrigerio, n m, refreshment
refuerzo, n m, reinforcement
refugiar, v, shelter, refuge
refugio, n m, refuge, shelter
refutar, v, refute
regadura, n f, irrigation
regalar, v, give
regalo, n m, present, gift
regañar, v, growl, grumble
regañón, adj, grumbling
regañona, n f, shrew
regar, v, water, irrigate
regatear, v, bargain, haggle
regateo, n m, bargaining, haggling
regazo, lap,
regia, n f, rule, order
regido, n m, governor
régimen, n m, regimen
regimiento, n m, regiment
regio, adj, regal
región, n f, region
regir, v, rule, govern
registrado, adj, registered
registrador, n m, registrar
registrar, v, register
registro, n m, register
reglamentado, adj, fixed
reglamento, n m, regulation, order
reglar, v, rule, regulate
regocijarse, v, rejoice
regocijo, n f, rejoicing, pleasure
regresar, v, return , regreso
regreso, n m, return
regulación, n f, regulation
regulado, adj, regulated, regular
regulador, n m, regulator
regular, edj, regular, moderate
regular, v, regulate
regularidad, n f, regularity
regularizar, standardize

regularmente, adv, regularly
rehabilitar, rehabilitate
rehacer, v, repair
rehuir, v, retire
rehusar, v, refuse
reina, n f, queen
reinado, n m, reign
reinante, adj, reigning
reinar, v, reign
reino, n m, kingdom, reign
reintegrar, v, reintegrate
reir, v, laugh, smile
reiterar, v, reiterate
reivindicar, v, recover, claim
rejilla, n f, cane
relación, n f, report, narration
relacionar, v, relate, report
relajar, v, relax
relatar, v, relate
relativamente, adv, relatively
relativo, adj, relative
relato, n m, relation
relator, n m, reporter
releer, v, revise
relegar, v, relegate
relevación, n f, relief
relevante, adj, relevant, important
relevar, v, relieve
relicario, n m, shrine
relieve, n m, relief
religión, n f, religion
religiosamente, adv, religiously
religioso, adj, religious
reloj, n m, clock, watch
relojero, n m, clockmaker
reluciente, adj, light, clear
relucir, v, shine, glow
relumbrar, v, sparkle, glitter
relumbrón, n m, lustre
remachar, v, clench
remanente, n m, remnant, remainder
remar, v, row
rematar, v, close, terminate
remate, n m, conclusion, end
remedar, v, copy, imitate
remediar, v, remedy, cure
remedio, n m, remedy

remendar, v, mend, patch
remiendo, n m, patch
remisión, n f, remission
remiso, adj, remiss
remitir, v, remit send
remo, n m, oar
remojar, v, soak
remolcar, v, tow
remolino, n m, whirlwind, whirlpool
remolón, adj, soft, hazy
remontar, v, remount
remordimiento, n m, remorse
remotamente, adv, remotely
remoto, adj, remote
remover, v, remove
remplazo, n m, substitution
remunerar, v, reward
rencilla, n f, grudge
rencor, n m, rancor
rencoroso, adj, rancorous
rendición, n f, rendition
rendido, adj, overdone
rendija, n f, crevice, crack
rendir, v, surrender, yield
renegar, v, deny
renglón, n m, line
rengue, n m, gauze
reñir, v, quarrel, dispute
reñir, v, scold
reno, r m, reindeer
renombrado, adj, renowned
renombre, n m, renown, fame
renovación, n f, renovation
renovar, v, renovate
renta, n f, rent, profit
rentar, v, rent
rentero, n m, renter
renuevo, n m, sapling, sprout
renuncia, n f, renunciation
renunciar, v, renounce
reo, n m, criminal, offender
reorganizar, v, reorganize
repagar, v, repay
reparable, adj, objectionable
reparar, v, repair, mend
reparo, n m, repair
repartir, v, distribute, pass

reparto, n m, distribution
repasar, v, review
repaso, n m, revision
repeler, v, repel
repentinamente, adv, suddenly
repentino, adj, sudden, abrupt
repetición, n f, repetition
repetidamente, adv, repeatedly
repetido, adj, repeated
repetir, v, repeat
repicar, v, chime
repintar, v, repaint
repique, n m, chime
repisa, n f, pedestal
replegar, v, redouble
repleto, adj, replete
réplica, n f, reply, answer
replicar, v, reply, answer
reponer, v, replace
reportar, v, obtain, get
reposar, v, rest, settle
reposo, n m, repose, rest
representación, n f, representation
representar, v, represent
representativo, n m, representative
represión, n f, repression
reprimenda, n f, reprimand
reprobar, v, reprove, reject
reprochar, v, reproach
reproche, n m, reproach
reproducción, n f, reproduction
reproducir, v, reproduce
república, n f, republic
republicano, adj, republican
repudiar, v, repudiate
repuesto, adj, replaced
repugnante, adj, repugnant
repulsar, v, reject, decline
reputación, n f, reputation
reputar, v, repute
requerimiento, n m, request, summons
requerir, v, request, require
requisición, n f, requisition
resaltar, v, rebound
resarcir, v, compensate
resbaladero, n m, slide

resbaladizo, adj, slippery
resbalar, v, slide, slip
rescatar, v, ransom
rescate, n m, ransom
rescindir, v, rescind
reseña, n f, review, description
reseñar, v, review, describe
resentido, adj, resentful
resentimiento, n m, resentment
resentirse, v, resent
reserva, n f, reserve, reservation
reservado, adj, reserved
reservar, v, reserve, preserve
resfriado, n m, cold, chill
resfriar, v, cool, chill
resguardar, v, preserve, defend
resguardo, n m, guard, defense
residencia, n f, residence
residente, adj, resident
residir, v, reside, live
residuo, n m, residue
resignación, n f, resignation
resignar, v, resign
resina, n f, resin
resistencia, n f, resistance
resistente, adj, resistant
resistir, v, resist
resolución, n f, resolution
resoluto, adj, resolute
resolver, v, solve, resolve
resoplar, v, snort
respaldar, v, endorse
respectivamente, adv, respectively
respectivo, adj, respective
respecto, n m, respect
respetable, adj, respectable
respetar, v, respect
respeto, n m, respect, regard
respetuoso, adj, respectful
respiración, n m, respiration, breathing
respirar, v, breathe
resplandor, n m, splendor, brilliance
responder, v, respond, answer
responsabilidad, n f, responsibility
responsable, adj, responsible
respuesta, n f, response, reply
restablecer, v, reestablish

restante, n m, remainder
restar, v, subtract
restauración, n f, restoration
restaurant, n m, restaurant
restaurar, v, restore
restituir, v, restore
resto, n m, rest
restricción, n f, restriction
restringir, v, restrain
resuelto, adj, resolute
resulta, n f, result, effect
resultado, n m, result, consequence
resultar, v, result
resumir, v, resume
retar, v, challenge
retardar, v, retard, delay
retardo, n m, delay
retazo, n m, scrap
retén, n m, stock, reserve
retener, v, retain
retirada, n f, retreat, withdrawl
retirado, adj, retired, withdrawn
retirar, v, retire, withdraw
retiro, n m, retreat, hideaway
reto, n m, challenge, threat
retocar, v, finish, retouch
retoño, n m, seedling
retorcer, v, retort
retornar, v, return
retorno, n m, return
retorta, n f, retort
retracción, n f, retraction
retractar, v, retract
retraer, v, retrieve
retranca, n f, brake
retrasar, v, defer, delay
retraso, n m, delay
retrato, n m, portrait
retrete, n m, closet
retribución, n f, retribution
reunión, n f, reunion
reunir, v, reunite
revelar, v, reveal
revender, v, retail
reversible, adj, reversible
reverso, n m, reverse
revisar, v, examine
revisar, v, supervise, revise

revisión, n f, revision
revista, n f, review, revision
revivir, v, revive
revocar, v, revoke
revolución, n f, revolution
revolver, n m, revolver, pistol
rey, n m, king
rezar, v, pray
rezo, n m, prayer
rico, adj, rich, good
rima, n f, rhyme
rio, n m, river
riqueza, n f, riches, wealth
risueño, adj, smiling
roca, n f, rock
rodear, v, surround
rogar, v, crave
rojo, adj, red
rollo, n m, scroll
romano, adj, Roman
romper, v, break, smash
roncar, v, snore
ronco, adj, hoarse
ronquido, n m, snore
ropa, n f, clothes, clothing
rosa, n f, rose
rosal, n m, rosebush
roto, adj, broken, torn
rubio, adj, blond, fair
ruido, n m, noise
ruido, v, splutter
ruina, n f, ruin
ruta, n f, route

S

sábado, n m, sabbath
sábado, n m, Saturday
sábana, n f, sheet
sabedor, adj, acquainted, informed
saber, n m, learning, knowing
saber, v, know, find out, be able
sabiduria, n f, learning, knowledge
sabiendas, adv, knowingly,
  consciously
sabio, adj, wise, sage, learned
sable, n m, sabre

saboneta, n f, hunter
sabor, n m, taste, relish
saborear, v, enjoy
sabroso, adj, savory, palatable
sabuoso, n m, bloodhound
saca, n f, bag, sack
sacacorchos, n m, corkscrew
sacamanchas, n m, cleaner,
  cleanser
sacar, v, take out, take
sacarina, n f, saccharine
sacarino, adj, saccharine
saciar, v, satiate
saco de arena, n m, sandbag
saco, n m, sack, bag
sacramento, n m, sacrament
sacrificar, v, sacrifice
sacrificio, n m, sacrifice
sacrilegio, n m, sacrilege
sacudida, n f, shock
sacudir, v, shake, jolt, throw
saeta, n f, arrow, dart
sagacidad, n f, sagacity
sagaz, adj, sagacious
sagrado, adj, sacred
sainete, n m, farce, play
sal blanca, n f, table salt
sal gema, n f, rock salt
sal marina, n m, sea salt
sal, n f, salt
sala, n f, hall, saloon, parlor
salado, adj, salty, salted
salado, adj, witty
salar, v, salt, cure
salariar, v, pay a salary or wage
salario, n m, salary
salazón, n f, seasoning, salting
salida del sol, n f, sunrise
salida, n f, start, departure, exit
saliente, adj, salient, prominent
salino, adj, saline
salir, v, go out, depart, leave
salmón, n m, salmon
salmuera, n f, brine
salón de patinar, n m, skating rink
salón, n m, hall, saloon
salpicadura, n f, splash

salpicar, v, splash, splatter, sprinkle

salsa, n f, sauce, dressing, gravy

salsera, n f, saucer

saltar, v, jump, leap, skip

salto, n mf, leap, spring, jump

salubre, adj, healthy, healthful

salubre, adj, salutary

salud, n f, health

saludable, adj, healthful, wholesome

saludar, v, salute, greet, hail

saludo, n m, salute, greeting

salutación, n f, salutation, salute, greeting

salvado, n m, bran

salvador, n m, Savior

salvaguardia, n m, safeguard, security

salvaje, adj, savage, uncivilized, wild

salvaje, n m, savage

salvamento, n m, salvage, salvation

salvar, v, save

salve, v, hail

salvia, n f, sail

salvilla, n f, tray

salvo, adj, safe

saña, n f, anger, passion

sanar, v, heal, cure

sanción, n f, sanction

sancionar, v, sanction

sandalia, n f, sandal

sandez, n f, folly, simplicity

sangrar, v, bleed, drain

sangre, n f, blood

sanguíneo, adj, sanguine

sanidad, n f, sanity, soundness, health

sanitario, adj, sanitary

sano, adj, sane, sound, healthy

sano, n mf, sound

santiamén, n m, moment

santo, adj, saintly, holy

santo, n mf, saint

saquear, v, sack, plunder, spoil

sarao, n m, ball, entertainment

sarcasmo, n m, sarcasm

sarcástico, adj, sarcastic

sardina, n f, sardine

sarga, n f, surge

sargento, n m, sergeant

sastre, n m, tailor

satán, n m, satan

satánico, adj, satanic

satélite, n m, satellite

satín, n m, satin

sátira, n f, satire

satírico, adj, satirical

satírico, n mf, satirist

satisfacción, n f, satisfaction

satisfacer, v, satisfy

satisfactorio, adj, satisfactory

satisfecho, adj, satisfied

saturar, v, saturate

sauce, n m, willow

savia, n f, sap

saya, n f, skirt

sazón, n f, season, taste

sazonado, adj, seasoned, mature

sazonar, v, season

se, pro, one, they

sea que, adv, whether

sealón, n mf, session, seance

sebo, n m, tallow, grease

secamente, adv, dryly

secar, v, dry

sección, n f, section

seccionar, v, section, separate

seco, adj, dry, bare

secretar, v, secrete

secretario, n m, secretary

secreto, adj, secret, hidden

secreto, n m, secrecy, caution

secta, n f, sect

secuela, n f, sequel

secuestro, n m, seizure

secular, adj, secular

secundario, adj, secondary

sed, n f, thirst

seda, n f, silk

sedativo, n mf, sedative

sediento, adj, thirsty

sedimento, n f, sediment

sedoso, adj, silky, silken

seducción, n f, seduction

seducir, v, seduce

seductivo, adj, seductive

segar, v, reap, mow

segmento, n m, segment
segregar, v, segregate
seguida, n f, sequence
seguir, v, follow, continue
según, prep, according to, as
segundo, adj, second
segundo, n m, second (time)
segur, n f, ax, sickle
seguramente, adv, surely
seguridad, n f, security
seguro, adj, sure, secure, certain
seguro, n m, safe
seis, n, six
selección, n f, selection
selecto, adj, select
sellar, v, seal, stamp
sello, n m, seal, stamp
selva, n f, forest
semana, n f, week
semanal, adj, weekly
semanario, n m, weekly publication
semblante, n m, look, aspect, face
sembrado, n m, cornfield
sembrar, v, sow, scatter, spread
semejante, adj, similar, like
semejanza, n f, resemblance, likeness, likelihood
semejar, v, resemble
semestre, n m, half-year, six months
semianual, adj, semi-annual, half-yearly
semicírculo, n m, semicircle
semilla, n f, seed
seminario, n m, seminary
sempiterno, adj, everlasting, eternal
seña, n f, sign
senado, n m, senate
senador, n m, senator
señalado, n m, signal
señalar, v, sign
sencillez, n f, simplicity, plainness, silliness
sencillo, adj, single, plain, simple
senda, n f, path, footpath
sendos, adj, either
senil, adj, senile
seno, n m, bosom, breast

seno, n m, sine
seno, n m, sinus
señor, n m, sir, mister, gentleman
señora, n f, lady, madam, wife
señorita, n f, young lady, girl, miss
sensación, n f, sensation, feeling
sensatez, n f, prudence, good sense
sensato, adj, sensible, prudent, wise
sensibilidad, n f, sensibility
sensible, adj, sensible, sensitive
sentado, adj, judicious, sedate, grave
sentar, v, sit, fit, become
sentencia, n f, sentence
sentido, n m, sense
sentimiento, n m, sentiment
sentina, n f, sink
sentir, v, regret, be sorry
separación, n f, separation
separar, v, separate, sever
séptico, adj, septic
septiembre, n m, September
sepulcro, n m, sepulchre
ser, n m, being, person
ser, v, to be
serenamente, adv, serenely, coolly
serenar, v, clear, settle
serenata, n f, serenade
serenidad, n f, serenity, coolness
sereno, adj, calm, serene
seriamente, adv, seriously
sérico, adj, silky
serie, n f, series
seriedad, n f, seriousness
serio, adj, sedate, serious, staid
sermón, n m, sermon
serpentino, adj, serpentine, winding
serpiente, n f, serpent
serrado, adj, toothed, serrated
serrar, v, saw
serrín, n m, sawdust
serrucho, n m, handsaw
servible, adj, serviceable
servicio, n m, service, favor
servilleta, n f, napkin
servir, v, serve
sesenta, n, sixty

sesgo, adj, slant
setenta, n, seventy
severo, adj, severe, stern
shinela, n f, slipper
sí, adv, yes
si, conj, if, whether
sí, pro, himself
sidra, n f, cider
siega, n f, harvest
siempre, adv, always, continually
sien, n f, temple
sierpe, n f, serpent
sierra, n f, saw
siesta, n f, afternoon nap
siete, n, seven
sigilar, v, seal, secret
sigilo, n m, seal, secret, secrecy
siglo, n m, century
significación, n f, significance
significado, n m, meaning
significante, adj, significant
significar, v, signify, mean
signo, n m, sign, mark, meaning
siguiente, adj, following, next
sílaba, n f, syllable
silbar, v, whistle
silbido, n m, whistle, whistiing
silencio, n m, silence, still
silencioso, adj, silent
silla, n f, chair, seat
sillón, n m, armchair
silueta, n f, silhouette
símbolo, n m, symbol
simétrico, adj, shapely
similar, adj, similar
simpatía, n f, sympathy, fellowship
simpático, adj, nice, attractive
simpatizar, v, sympathize
simple, adj, simple
simplemente, adv, simply
simplificar, v, simplify
simular, v, simulate
simultáneo, adj, simultaneous
sin, adv, without
sinagoga, n f, synagogue
sinceramente, adv, sincerely
sinceridad, n f, sincerity
sindicato, n m, syndicate, trust

singular, adj, singular, single, particular
singularidad, n f, singularity
siniestra, n f, left hand
siniestro, adj, sinister
sino, conj, but
sinónimo, adj, synonymous
sinónimo, n m, synonym
síntoma, n m, symptom
sirena, n f, siren
sistema, n f, system
sitio, n m, siege
sitio, n m, site
situado, v, situate
sobre, n m, envelope
sobre, prep, on, upon, over
sobrenatural, n f, supernatural
sobrepujar, v, surpass
sobrevivir, v, survive
sobrina, n f, niece
sobrino, n m, nephew
sobrio, adj, sober
socarrón, adj, sly
sociable, adj, sociable
social, adj, social
sociedad, n, society
soda, n f, soda
sofá, n f, sofa
sofocar, v, suffocate, choke
sol, n m, sun
solamente, adj, only
solamente, adv, singly
soldado, n m, soldier
soleado, adj, sunny
soledad, n f, solitude
solemne, adj, solemn
soler, v, be accustomed
solicitar, v, solicit
solidificar, v, solidify
sólido, adj, solid, staunch
solitario, adj, solitary
solo, adj, alone
sólo, adj, only
solomo de buey, n m, sirloin
soltar, v, throw down
solución, n mf, solution
sombra, n f, shade, shadow
sombrero, n m, hat

sombrilla, n f, parasol
sombrío, adj, shady
somero, adj, shallow
someter, v, subject
soñar, v, dream
sonar, v, sound
soneto, n m, sonnet
sonreir, v, smile
sonrisa, n f, smile
sopa, n f, soup
soportar, v, support
sorber, v, sip
sorbo, n m,sip
sórdido, adj, sordid
sorprendente, adj, surprising
sorprender, v, surprise
sorprendido, adj, surprised
sorpresa, n f, surprise
sospecha, n f, suspicion
sospechar, v, suspect
sospechoso, adj, suspicious
sostén, n m, support
sostener, v, sustain
sotechado, n m, shed
sportsman, n m, sportsman
su, adj, his, her, its
su, adj, your, their, one's
suave, adj, soft
suavemente, adv, softly
suavizar, v, soften , subdividir
subdividir, v, subdivide
subir, v, get in, go up to
sublime, adj, sublime
submarino, n m, submarine
subscribir, v, subscribe
subscripción, n f, subscription
subsiguiente, adj, subsequent
subsistir, v, subsist
substancia, n f, substance
subterráneo, adj, subterranean
suburbio, n m, suburb
subversion, n f, subversion
subversivo, n mf, subversive
subyugar, v, subdue
sucesor, n mf, successor
sucio, adj, dirty, soiled
sudar, v, sweat

sudor, n m, sweat
Suecia, n f, Sweden
Sueco, adj, Swedish
Sueco, n mf, Swede
suelo, n m, ground floor
sueño ligero, n m, slumber
sueño, n m, sleep, dream, snooze
suficiente, adj, sufficient
sufrir, v, suffer
sugerir, v, suggest
sugestión, n f, suggestion
suicidio, n m, suicide
sujeto, n m, subject
sulfúrico, adj, sulfuric
suma, n f, sum
sumar, v, sum
sumario, n m, summary, synopsis
sumergir, v, submerge
sumergirse, v, subside
superior, adj, superior
superstición, n f, superstition
supervivencia, n f, survival
suplantar, v, supplant
suplemento, n m, suppliment
suplir, v, supply
suponer, v, suppose
supresión, n f, suppression
suprimir, v, supress
sur, n m, south
suroeste, n m, southwest
surtido, n m, set
suspender, v, suspend
suspensión, n f, suspense
suspirar, v, sigh
suspiro, n m, sigh
sustancial, adj, substantial
sustituir, v, substitute
sustracción, n m, subtraction
sustraer, v, subtract
sutil, adj, subtle
suyo, adj, yours, theirs, one's

T

tabaco, n m, tobacco
taberna, n f, tavern
tabique, n m, partition

tabla 185 *taza*

tabla, n f, board, table, Index

tablado, n m, stage, scaffold, flooring

tablazón, n m, planks, lumber

tablero, n m, board, panel

tableta, n f, tablet, board

tablón, n m, plank, beam

taburete, n Mf, Stool, chair

tacaño, adJ, mean, stingy

tacha, n f, fault, defect, flaw

tachar, v, censure, tax, blot

tácitO, adJ, tacit, silent, implied

tacón, n m, heel

táctica, n f, tactics

tacto, n m, touch

tafetán, n m, taffeta

tahona, n f, bakery

tahonero, n m, baker

taimado, adj, sly, crafty

taja, n f, cut, incision

tajada, n f, slice, cut

tajadera, n f, carving knife (for meat)

tajadero, n m, carving block (for meat)

tajar, v, cut, chop, carve

tajo, n m, cut, incision

tal, adj, such, so, as

taladrar, v, bore, pierce

taladro, n m, bore, drill, auger

talante, n m, appearance, disposition

talaraña, n f, cobweb

talco, n m, talc, mica

talego, n mf, bag, sack

talento, n m, talent

talentoso, adj, talented, able

talla, n f, stature, size

tallador, n m, engraver, carver

tallar, v, cut, chop, carve

talle, n m, shape, size, form

taller, n m, workshop, office, laboratory

tallista, n m, engraver

tallo, n m, shoot, sprout, stem

tallonar, v, retaliate

talón, n m, heel

talonario, n m, checkbook

tamaño, adj, great (size)

tamaño, n m, size, shape

támblén, adj, also, too

tambor, n m, drum

tambor, n m, drummer

tamiz, n m, sieve

tamizar, v, sift

tampoco, adv, neither, not either

tan, adv, so, so much, as well

tanda, n f, turn, rotation

tangible, adj, tangible

tañido, n m, tune, sound

tanque, n m, tank, vat

tantear, v, measure, proportion

tanteo, n m, computation, calculation, average

tanto, adv, so much, as much, so

taoría, n f, theory

tapa, n f, lid, cover, cap

tapar, v, cover, cork, conceal

tapete, n m, rug, carpet, cover

tapia, n f, adobe

tapicería, n f, tapestry, upholstery

tapicero, n f, upholsterer

tapioca, n f, tapioca

tapiz, n m, tapestry, carpet

tapizar, v, upholster

tapón, n m, cork, stopper, tap

taquigrafía, n f, shorthand

taquilla, n f, ticket office

taravilla, n f, latch

tardanza, n f, slowness, delay, detention

tarde, adv, late

tarde, n f, afternoon, evening

tardío, adj, late, slow, tardy

tardo, adj, slow, dull, tardy

tarea, n f, task, toil, exercise

tarifa, n f, tariff

tarja, n f, tally, check

tarjar, v, tally, check

tarjeta, n f, card, sign

tarro, n m, jar

tasa, n f, rate, measure, rule

tasación, n appraisement, evaluation

tasador, n m, appraiser

tasajo, n m, scrap

tasar, v, appraise, estimate, assess

taxi, n m, taxi

taza, n f, cup

taza, v, cup

té, n m, tea
tea, n f, torch
teatro, n m, theater, stage
teca, n f, teak (wood)
techado, n m, roof
techar, v, roof
techo, n m, ceiling, roof
teclado, n m, keyboard
técnica, n f, technique
técnico, adj, technical
tedio, n m, disgust, dislike, tediousness
tedioso, adj, tedious, tiresome
teja, n f, tile, roofing tile
tejedor, n m, weaver
tejedura, n f, texture, weaving
tejer, v, weave
tejido, n m, texture, tissue, fabric
tejo, n m, ingot
tela, n f, cloth, fabric
telefonar, v, telephone, phone, call
telefonema, n m, telephone call, phone message
telefónico, adj, telephonic
teléfono, n m, telephone, phone
telegrafiar, v, send a telegraph
telégrafo, n m, telegraph
telegrama, n m, telegram
telescopio, n m, telescope
tema, n m, text, topic, theme
temblar, v, tremble, shake
temblor, n m, trembling
temer, v, fear, dread, be afraid
temerario, adj, rash, daring
temeridad, n f, temerity, rashness
temeroso, adj, timid, fearful
temible, adj, dreadful, terrible
temor, n m, fear, dread
temperamento, n m, temperament
temperar, v, temper, moderate
tempestad, n f, storm, tempest
tempestuoso, adj, stormy
templado, adj, temperate, moderate, tempered
templanza, n f, temperance
templar, v, temper, moderate, cool
temple, n m, temperature, temperament
temporal, adj, temporal
temporal, n m, season
temporario, adj, temporary
temprano, adj, early, soon
tenacidad, n f, tenacity
tenacillas, n fpl, pincers, small tongs
tenaz, adj, tenacious, firm
tenazas, n fpl, tongs, forceps
tendencia, n f, tendency
tender, v, stretch
tendero, n m, storekeeper
tenedor, n m, holder, keeper, fork
teneduría, n f, bookkeeping
tenencia, n f, posession, holding
tener éxito, v, succeed
tener, v, have, hold, possess tener
tenería, n f, tannery
teniente, n m, deputy, lieutenant
teñir, v, dye, tinge stain
tenor, n m, tenor
tensión, n f, tension
tenso, adj, tense, light extended
tentar, v, attempt, try, prove
tentativa, n f, attempt, trial
tentativo, adj, tentative
tenue, adj, thin, slender
teórico, adj, theoretical
tercamente, adv, obstinately
tercería, n f, mediation, arbitration
tercero, adj, third
tercero, n m, third person, mediator, umpire
tercio, adj, third
terciopelo, n m, velvet
terco, adj, obstinate
tergiversar, v, shuffle
terliz, n m, ticking
terminación, n f, termination, conclusion
terminal, adj, final, ultimate
terminante, adj, closing, terminating, conclusive
terminar, v, end, finish, terminate
término, n m, term, end, object
termómetro, n m, thermometer
ternera, n f, cow, heifer

ternero, n m, calf
terneza, n f, softness, tenderness
terno, n m, dress suit
ternura, n f, tenderness, feeling
terquedad, n f, stubbornness
terrado, n m, terrace, platform
terraza, n f, terrace
terremoto, n m, earthquake
terrenal, adj, terrestrial
terreno, n m, land, ground
terrestre, adj, terrestrial, land
terrible, adj, terrible
territorial, adj, territorial
territorio, n m, territory, district, ground
terrón, n m, lump, heap
terror, n m, terror, dread
terso, adj, smooth, polished, pure
tersura, n f, smoothness, purity, terseness
tertulia, n f, assembly party
tesauro, n m, dictionary, inde, thesaurus
tesis, n f, thesis
tesón, n m, tenacity, firmness
tesorería, n f, treasury
tesorero, n m, treasurer
testamento, n m, testament
testar, v, will, bequeath
testarudo, adj, obstinate, stubborn
testera, n f, forehead
testificar, v, testify, witness
testigo, n m, witness
testimonial, n m, testimonial
testimoniar, v, testify
testimonio, n m, testimony
tetera, n f, teapot
tétrico, adj, grave, gloomy
textil, adj, textile
texto, n m, text
textura, n f, texture
tez, n f, complexion, hue
tía, n f, aunt
tibia, n f, shin
tibio, adj, tepid, lukewarm
tiburón, n m, shark
tiempo, n m, time, weather, season
tienda, n f, store, shop

tiento, n m, touch, stroke
tierra, n f, soil, earth, land
tieso, adj, stiff, firm, strong
tiesto, n m, flowerpot
tiesura, n f, stiffness, rigidity
tifón, n m, typhoon
tijeras, n fpl, scissors
tildar, v, brand
tilde, n m, tilde
timar, v, swindle
timbrar, v, stamp, seal
timbre, n m, seal, stamp, postmark
timidez, n f, shyness, timidity
tímido, adj, shy, timid
timón, n m, steering
tiña, v, scald
tiniebla, n f, darkness obscurity
tino, n m, skill knack, judgement
tinta, n f, tint, ink
tinte, n m, paint, dye
tintero, n m, inkwell
tintura, n f , smattering, dyeing
tío, n m, uncle
tipo, n m, type, pattern, model
tipografía, n f, printing, typesetting, typography
tipográfico, adj, typographical
tipógrafo, n m, printer
tira, n f, shred, strip
tirada, n f, cast, throw
tiradera, n f, strap
tirador, n m, marksman
tiranía, n f, tyranny
tirano, adj, tyrannical
tirano, n m, tyrant
tirante, adj, tight, extended
tirantes, n mpl, suspenders
tirantez, n f, tightness
tirar, v, throw, cast
tiritar, v, shiver
tiro, v, cast
tisú, n m, tissue
titubeante, adj, shaky
titubear, v, hesitate, doubt
titular, v, title
título, n m, title, heading
tiza, n f, chalk
tiznar, v, stain, blot, tarnish

tiznón, n m, smut
toalla, n f, towel
toalleta, n f, napkin
toca, n f, hood
tocado, n m, ornament
tocador, n m, toilet, dressing room
tocar, v, touch, play, interest
tocayo, n m, namesake
tocino, n m, bacon
todavia, adv, yet, still
todo, adj, all, every, any
todo, pro, everything, anything
tolerable, adj, tolerable
tolerancia, n f, tolerance, toleration
tolerante, adj, tolerant
tolerar, v, tolerate
toma, n f, capture, seizure
toma, n f, portion, dose
tomador, n m, buyer, purchaser
tomar, v, take, catch, get
tomate, n m, tomato
tomillo, n m, thyme
tomo, n m, bulk, importance, value
tonel, n m, barrel
tonelada, n f, ton
tonelaje, n m, tonnage
tongada, n f, layer
tónico, n m, tonic
tono, n m, tone, tune
tontería, n f, foolishness, folly, nonsense
tonto, adj, silly, foolish, stupid
tonto, n m, fool
topacio, n m, topaz
tope, n m, top
tóplco, n m, topic
topo, n m, mole
toque, n m, touch
torbellino, n m, whirlwind
torcer, v, twist, turn
torcida, n f, wick
torcido, adj, twisted, crooked
tormento, n m, torment
torna, n f, restitution, return, recompense
tornar, v, return, restore
tornasol, n m, sunflower

tornillo, n m, screw
torno, n m, wheel, gyration
toro, n m, bull
torpe, adj, torpid, slow
torpedo, n m, torpedo
torre, n f, tower
torrente, n m, torrent
torta, n f, cake, pie
tortilla, n f, omelet
tortuga, n f, tortoise
tortuoso, adj, tortuous, winding
torzal, n m, cord, twist
tos, n f, cough
tosco, adj, rough, coarse, clumsy
toser, v, cough
tosquedad, n f, roughness, rudeness
tostadas, n fpl, toast
tostado, adj, toasted, brown
tostar, v, toast, roast
total, adj, total
total, n m, total, whole
totalidad, n f, totality, entirety
totalmente, adv, totally
toza, n f, frog
traba, n f, obstacle, impediment, hindrance
trabacuenta, n f, mistake
trabajador, adj, industrious
trabajar, v, work
trabajo, n m, work
trabajoso, adj, laborious
trabazón, n f, union, connection
tracción, n f, traction
traducción, n translation, interpretaticn
traducir, v, translate, interpret
traer, v, bring, carry, wear
tráfago, n m, traffic
traficante, n m, merchant, trader, dealer
traficar, v, trade, traffic
tráfico, n m, traffic
tragadero, n m, pit, gulf
tragaluz, n f, skylight
tragar, v, swallow, devour
tragedia, n f, tragedy
trágico, adj, tragic

trago, n m, draught
traiclón, n f, treason
traidor, adj, treacherous, false
traidor, n m, traitor
traje, n m, dress, costume, suit
trajinar, v, carry, transport
trajinero, n m, carrier
tramador, n m, weaver
tramar, v, weave
trámite, n m, path, procedure
tramo, n m, piece, morsel
tramoyista, n m, impostor, deceiver
trampa, n f, trap, snare, swindle
trampista, n m, cheat, swindler
tramposo, adj, deceitful
trancazo, n m, influenza
trance, n m, peril, danger
tranquilamente, adv, quietly, tranquilly
tranquilidad, n f, tranquility, rest
tranquilizar, v, calm, tranquilize
transacción, n f, transaction
transatlántico, adj, transatlantic
transcribir, v, transcribe
transcripción, n f, transcription
transcurrir, v, elapse
transeúnte, adj, tranSitory
transferencia, n f, transfer
transferible, adj, transferable
transferir, v, transfer, move, convey
transformación, n f, transformation
transformar, v, transform
transitar, v, travel, journey
tránsito, n m, passage transit
transmisión, n f, transmission
transmitir, v, transmit, broadcast
transparente, adj, transparent
transpirar, v, transpire
transponer, v, transpose, transport, remove
transportar, v, transport
transporte, n m, transport, conveyance
tranvía, n m, commuter train
trapo, n m, rag, cloth, tatter
tras, prep, after, behind, besides
trasero, adj, behind
traslación, n m, translation

traslado, n m, copy, imitation, likeness
traslúcido, adj, transparent, clear
trasplantar, v, transplant
trasquilar, v, shear, clip
trastornar, v, overturn, overthrow, coup
trastorno, n m, overthrow, coup
trastos, n mpl, furniture
tratar, v, try
trato, n m, treatment, behavior, conduct
traza, n f, tracing, outline, appearance
trazar, v, trace, sketch
trébol, n m, shamrock
trece, n, thirteen
treinta, n, thirty
tren, n m, train
trepar, v, climb
tres, n, three
triste, adj, sad
tristeza, n f, sadness
triturar, v, crush
troncho, n, spindle
tronco, n m, stem, stump, trunk
tropezar, v, stumble
trovador, n m, troubadour
trozo, n m, piece
trucha, n f, trout
tu, adj, thy, your
tú, pro, thou, you
turba, n f, crowd
turba, n f, sod
turno, n m, turn
tuyo, adj, thine, yours, of yours

U

ublcación, n f, situation, position
ufanarse, v, boast
ufanía, n f, pride, haughtiness
ufano, adj, proud, haughty
ulterior, adj, ulterior, further
últimamente, adv, lastly, finally, ultimately
ultimar, v, end, finish, settle
ultimatum, n m, ultimatum

último, adj, last, final, ultimate
ultrajar, v, outrage, offend
ultraje, n m, outrage
ultramar, adj, ultramarine, foreign
ultramarino, adj, ultramarine
umbral, n m, threshold, beginning
un, art, a, an, one
una, art, a, an, one
uña, n f, nail, claw
unánime, edj, unanimous
unanimidad, n f, unanimity
unción, n f, unction
uncir, v, yoke
ungüento, n m, unguent, ointment
unicamente, adv, only, simply, merely
único, adj, sole, only, unique
unidad, n f, unity, conformity
unidamente, adv, jointly
unido, adj, united
uniforme, adj, uniform
uniforme, n m, uniform
uniformidad, n f, uniformity
unión, n f, union, combination
unir, v, join, unite, mix
universal, adj, universal, general
universidad, n f, university
universo, n m, universe
uno, adj, one, a, an
uno, n m, one, a, an
untar, v, anoint, rub, grease
unto, n m, grease, ointment
urbanidad, n f, politeness
urbano, adj, urban, urbane, courteous
urdidura, n f, warping
urdimbre, n f, chain
urdir, v, warp
urgencia, n f, urgency
urgente, adj, urgent
urgir, v, urge, press
urna, n f, urn, glass case
usado, adj, used, worn out
usanza, n f, usage, custom
usar, v, use, wear
usa, n m, use, employment
usted, pro, you

usual, adj, usual, customary
usufructo, n m, profit, enjoyment
usura, n f, interest, payment, usury
usurero, n m, lender
usurpar, v, usurp
utensilio, n m, utensil, tool
útil, adj, useful
utilidad, n f, utility, profit
utilizar, v, utilize
uva, n f, grape
uva pasa, n fpl, raisins

V

vaca, n f, cow
vacación, n f, vacation
vacancia, n f, vacancy
vacar, v, cease, stop
vaciado, n m, cast
vaciar, v, empty, evacuate, grind
vacilación, n f, vacillation, hesitation
vacilar, v, vacillate, hesitate, waver
vacío, adj, void, empty, unoccupied
vacío, n m, void, space, vacuum
vacuno, adj, bovine
vadear, v, wade, ford, surmount
vademécum, n m, handbook
vado, n m, ford
vagar, v, wander, rove
vago, edj, vagrant, vague
vagón, n m, wagon, carriage, train car
vaguedad, n f, levity, vagueness
vaho, n m, steam, vapor
vaina, n f, scabbard, case, sheath
vainilla, n f, vanilla
valvén, n m, fluctuation, risk, danger
vajilla, n f, plates, dishes
vale, n m, farewell
valedero, adj, valid
valentía, n f, valor, courage, gallantry
valer, n m, value
valer, v, to be worth, employ, make
valeroso, adj, valiant, brave
valla, n f, value, appraisement
validar, v, validate
válido, adj, valid, binding

valiente, adj, courageous, strong, brave

valiente, n m, brave man

valija, n f, mail, mailbag

valimiento, n m, use, utility, benefit

valioso, adj, valuable

valiza, n f, beacon, buoy

valla, n f, barrier, barricade

vallar, v, fence

valle, n m, valley, dale, vale

valor, n f, worth, value, price

valor, n m, courage, bravery

valorado, adj, valued

valorar, v, appraise, value

vals, n m, waltz

valuación, n f, valuation, appraisement

valuar, v, value, appraise, rate

válvula, n f, valve

vanamente, adv, vainly, idly

vandaval, n m, strong, wind

vanguardia, n f, vanguard, van

vanidad, n f, vanity

vano, adj, vain, useless

vapor, n m, vapor, steam

vaquería, n f, dairy

vaquero, n m, herd (of cows)

vaqueta, n f, cowhide

vara, n f, rod, pole

varadero, n m, shipyard, slip

varar, v, launch

variable, edj, variable, changeable

variación, n f, variation, change

variar, v, vary, change

variedad, n f, variety

varilla, n f, spindle, small rod, rib

vario, adj, various, different, several

varón, n m, man, male

varonil, edj, manly, masculine, male

vasar, n m, plate rack

vasija, n f, vessel, pipe, cask

vaso, n m, vessel, vase, glass

vástago, n m, stem, bud, shoot

vasto, adj, vast, immense, huge

vaticinar, v, divine, foretell

vaticinio, n m, prediction

vatio, n m, watt (electrical unit)

vecindad, n f, vicinity, proximity, neighborhood

vecindario, n f, neighborhood, vicinity

vecino, adj, neighboring like, next

vecino, n mf, neighbor, citizen, inhabitant

vedar, v, prohibit, forbid, obstruct

vedija, n f, flake, tuft

veedor, n m, overseer, caterer

vega, n f, meadow, plain

vegetación, n f, vegetation

vegetal, adj, vegetable

vegetal, n m, vegetable, plant

vehemeneia, n f, vehemence

vehemente, adj, vehement

vehículo, n m, vehicle

veinte, n f, twenty

vejar, v, vex, molest, harass

vejez, n f, old age

vejiga, n f, bladder

vela, n f, candle

vela, n f, watch, vigil

velador, n m, watchman

velador, n m, candlestick

velaje, n m, sails

velamen, n m, sails (in a set)

velar, v, watch, be attentive

velero, adj, sailing

velero, n m, sailboat, sailmaker

vetete, n m, veil

vello, n m, down

vellón, n m, fleece, wool

velloso, adj, downy, hairy

velo, n m, veil, curtain, cover

velocidad, n f, velocity, speed, rate

velocípedo, n m, bicycle

velón, n m, oil lamp

vena, n f, vein, fiber

venado, n m, deer, venison

vencer, v, conquer, overcome, bend

vencido, adj, subdued, bent

vencimiento, n m, victory

vencimiento, n m, expiration, maturity (financial)

venda, n f, bandage

vendar, v, bandage

vendedor, n m, seller, vendor

vendeja, n f, public sale

vender, v, sell, vend
vendible, adj, sellable
vendimia, n f, vintage
venduta, n f, auction
vendutero, n m, auctioneer
veneno, n m, poison, venom
venerar, v, venerate, venganza
venganza, n f, revenge, vengeance
vengar, v, avenge, revenge
venia, n f, pardon, leave, permission
venida, n f, arrival, coming
venidero, adj, future, coming
venido, adj, arrived
venir, v, come, fit, agree
venta, n f, sale
ventaja, n f, advantage, gain, preference
ventajoso, adj, advantageous, profitable
ventana, n f, window
ventarrón, n m, gale
ventear, v, blow
ventilación, n f, ventilation
ventilador, n m, ventilator
ventilar, v, ventilate, fan
ventoso, adj, windy
ventura, n f, chance, fortune, luck
venturero, adj, casual, vagrant, adventurous
venturoso, adlucky, fortunate
ver, n m, seeing, sight, view
ver, v, see, look
veracidad, n f, veracity
veraniego, adj, summer
verano, n m, summer
veras, n fpl, reality, truth
veraz, adj, veracious
verbal, adj, verbal
verbalmente, adv, verbally, orally
verdad, n f, truth, reality
verdadero, adj, true, real, sincere
verde, adj, green (color), unripe
verdugo, n m, executioner
verdulera, n f, market woman
verdulero, n f, m, produce grocer
verdura, n f, greens, garden stuff
vardusco, adj, greenish

vereda, n f, path, footpath
veredicto, n m, verdict
verga, n f, shipyard
vergonzoso, adj, shameful
vergüenza, n f, shame
verídico, adj, truthful, veracious
verificación, n f, verification, inquiry
verificar, v, verify, confirm, examine
verja, n f, grate
verosímil, adj, likely, probable
verosimilitud, n f, likelihood, probability
verraco, n m, boar
versado, adj, versed, conversant
versar, v, turn
versátil, adj, versatile
versión, n f, version
verso, n m, verse
vertedero, n m, sewer, drain
verter, v, spill, empty
verter, v, translate
vertical, adj, vertical
vestíbulo, n m, vestibule, hall, lobby
vestido, n m, dress, suit, clothes
vestigio, n m, vestige, footstep, trace
vestimenta, n f, clothes, garments
vestir, v, clothe, dress, wear
veteado, adj, striped, veined, streaky
vetear, v, variegate, grain
veterano, adj, experienced
veterano, n m, veteran
veterinario, n m, veterinarian
veto, n m, veto
vetusto, adj, ancient
vez, n f, time, turn
via, n f, way, road, route
viaducto, n m, viaduct
viajante, adj, travelling
viajar, v, travel, journey
viaje, n m, journey, voyage, trip
viajero, n m, traveler, tourist
vianda, n f, food, meat
vibrar, v, vibrate
vicepresidente, n m, vice-president
viceversa, adv, vice versa
viciar, v, spoil, corrupt, forge
vicio, n m, vice, defect, flaw

icioso, adj, vicious
ictima, n f, victim
ictoria, n f, victory
ictorioso, adj, victorious
id, n f, vine
ida, n f, life, livelihood
idriado, n m, crockery
idriar, v, glaze, varnish
idriero, n m, glazier
idrio, n m, glass
idrioso, adj, brittle, glassy
iejo, adj, old, ancient
iento, n m, wind, air
ientre, n m, belly
igente, adj, enforced
igía, n m, lookout, watch
igilancia, n f, vigilance, watchfulness
igilante, adj, vigilant, careful, watchful
igilar, v, watch, guard
igilia, n f, vigil, watchfulness
igor, n m, vigor, strength, force
igorar, v, invigorate
igoroso, adj, vigorous, strong
il, adj, mean, vile, low
ileza, n f, meanness, vileness, baseness
ilipendiar, v, revile
ilipendio, n m, contempt, disdain
illa, n f, town
illaje, n m, village
illano, adj, rustic
illano, n m, villain
iña, n f, vineyard
inagre, n m, vinegar
inatero, n m, vintner
incular, v, bind, continue
inculo, n m, link, tie, chain
indicación, n f, vindication
indicar, v, vindicate
iñero, n m, vintager
iñeta, n f, vignette
iñeta, n f, ticket
ino, n m, wine
iolación, n f, violation, infringement, offense
iolado, adj, violet

violar, v, violate, infringe, offend
violencia, n f, stress
violeta, n f, violet
violín, n m, violin, fiddle
virtual, adj, virtual
virtud, n f, virtue, power, force
virtuoso, adj, virtuous
viruelas, n fpl, smallpox
viruta, n f, shaving, chip
visita, n f, visit
visitar, v, call upon
visitar, v, visit
viso, n m, aspect, appearance
víspera, n f, vesper
vista, n f, seeing
vista, n f, sight
vistazo, n m, glance, glimpse
visto, adj, seen, clear
vivir, v, live
vocablo, n m, word, term
vocabulario, n m, vocabulary
vocal, adj, vocal
vocal, n f, vowel
vocal, n m, voter
volar, v, fly
volver, v, come back
volver, v, return
vosotros, pro, you
voz, n f, voice
vuelta, n f, return
vuestro, adj, your, yours, of yours

W

walkman, n m, walkman

X

xerocopia, n f, Xerox
xerocopiar, v, Xerox
xilófono, n m, xylophone

Y

y, conj, and
ya, adv, already, now
yacente, adj, lying
yacer, v, lie

yacimiento, n m, deposit, bed
yarda, n f, yard (U.S. measurement)
yardaje, n m, yardage
yate, n m, yacht
yedra, n f, ivy
yegua, n f, mare
yelmo, n m, helmet
yema, n f, bud, egg yolk
yermar, v, devastate
yermo, adj, waste, desert, uninhabited
yermo, n m, desert, waste, country
yerno, n m, son-in-law
yerro, n m, error, mistake, fault
yerto, adj, stiff
yesca, n f, tinder
yeso, n m, chalk
yo, pro, I
yodina, n f, iodine
yodo, n m, Iodine
yugo, n m, yoke
yunta, n f, couple, pair

Z

zabordar, v, run aground, drive
zabullir, v, plunge, dive, sink
zafada, n f, flight, escape
zafar, v, escape, avoid
zafir, n m, sapphire
zafo, adj, free, empty, clear
zafra, n f, sugar crop
zaga, n f, back
zaguán, n m, porch, hall
zaherir, v, censure, blame, reproach
zahúrda, n f, pigsty
zamarro, n m, sheepskin
zampar, v, conceal, devour
zanahoria, n f, carrot
zanca, n f, shank
zancada, n f, long stride
zancajo, n m, heel
zanco, n m, flag staff
zángano, n m, drone, idler
zanja, n f, ditch, trench drain
zanjar, v, open, excavate
zapa, n f, spade

zapar, v, mine (minerals)
zapatería, n f, shoe shop
zapatero, n m, shoemaker
zapatilla, n f, slipper
zapatillas, n fpl, dress shoes
zapato, n m, shoe
zaquizamí, n m, loft
zaranda, n f, screen, sieve
zarandear, v, Sift, stir
zaraza, n f, print
zarcillo, n m, earring
zarpa, n f, claw
zarpar, v, sail
zarza, n f, bramble
zarzamora, n f, blackberry
zarzaparrilla, n f, satsaparilla
zigzag, n m, zigzag
zinc, n m, zinc
zona, n f, zone, space
zoología, n f, zoology
zoológico, adj, zoological
zopenco, n m, blockhead, dolt
zopo, adj, lame, maimed, clumsy
zoquete, n m, block, dolt
zorra, n f, fox
zorro, n m, fox
zozobra, n f, anguish, anxiety, unease
zozobrar, v, upset, capsize
zueco, n m, wooden shoe
zumaque, n m, sumac (tree)
zumbar, v, resound, buzz, hum
zumo, n m, sap, juice
zumoso, adj, juicy, succulent
zuncho, n m, band, hoop, collar
zupia, n f, refuse, rubbish
zurcido, n m, stitching
zurcir, v, sew, join
zurdo, adj, left, left-handed
zurrador, n f, m, tanner
zurrar, v, curry, flog
zurriaga, n f, thong
zurriar, v, buzz, mutter
zurrido, n m, humming
zurrón, n m, bag, pouch
zurrullo, n m, rolling pin
zutano, n m, so-and-so